# THE
# UNIVERSITY

*An Owner's Manual*

# THE
# UNIVERSITY

## *An Owner's Manual*

# HENRY ROSOVSKY

W · W · *Norton & Company* · *New York* · *London*

*18765*

Printed in the United States of America.
*The text of this book is composed in Baskerville, with display type set in Bauer*
*Bodoni. Composition and manufacturing by the Haddon Craftsmen, Inc.*
*Book design by Debra Morton Hoyt.*

FIRST EDITION

Library of Congress Cataloging-in-Publication Data
Rosovsky, Henry.
    The university: an owner's manual / Henry Rosovsky.—1st
ed.
        p. cm.
    "Published simultaneously in Canada by Penguin Books
Canada Ltd."—T.p. verso.
    Includes index.
    1. Universities and colleges—United States—Administration.
I. Title.
LB2341.R59 1990
378.73—dc20                                            89–9466

    ISBN 0-393-02782-1

W. W. Norton & Company, Inc.
500 Fifth Avenue, New York, N. Y. 10110
W. W. Norton & Company Inc.
37 Great Russell Street, London WC1B 3NU


1 2 3 4 5 6 7 8 9 0

My warmest thanks to David Bloom, Derek Bok, John Bok, William Bowen, Ken Galbraith, Phyllis Keller, David Landes, Nitza Rosovsky, Frederick Starr, Yana Van Der Meulen, and Dean Whitla for constructive criticisms, insightful comments, and valuable suggestions. None of these good people can be held even slightly responsible for remaining deficiencies of fact or interpretation.

I am grateful also for help so generously given by Edwin Barber and Donald Lamm of Norton—model editors and publishers.

Finally, I am deeply indebted to Bonnie Currier, Ellen DiPippo, and Kim Ayres, who word-processed many versions of this manuscript and never, *never* lost their sense of humor. Without them, I would surely have lost my own.

# Contents

*For Leah*
*Judy*
*Michael*
*and Benjamin '09*

# INTRODUCTION

# Preface
## The Concept

Books about universities, especially those written by professors and administrators, usually have inspirational titles. President Derek Bok of Harvard gave us *Beyond the Ivory Tower;* the late President A. B. Giamatti of Yale recently offered *A Free and Ordered Space;* well over a decade ago, President Clark Kerr of the University of California presented *The Uses of the University* to the reading public. The titles alone inspire a certain amount of awe: at the very least one would like to be seen leafing through the pages of these volumes.

My title, *The University: An Owner's Manual,* intends to introduce a rather different subject matter and message. I used to be an economist—the past tense has been employed because no one who has toiled as an administrator for eleven years can again lay claim to full membership in a demanding academic field. Sometimes former administrators are charitably or deservedly called educators; unfortunately, only provincial American newspapers use that term as a compliment. Of course, I do remember some economics, and found two concepts—comparative advantage and product differentiation—useful in shaping my own literary testament. In plain English: know your subject and attempt something different.

Whenever approaching an unfamiliar object—for example, a new refrigerator or a personal computer—I have found manuals useful and comforting. Sometimes lacking style and clarity, they have nevertheless become a major literary genre of our civilization. Perhaps because of my love for automobiles (I confess to being a devoted subscriber to *Road and Track* magazine and a member in good standing of the SAAB Club of America), I am especially familiar with texts pertaining to cars. Invariably they strike an optimistic and practical tone. Let me quote briefly from Datsun 1978. No doubt it would make more of an impression to cite Mercedes-Benz 1986 or Jaguar 1988, but these authors are not generally found in professorial glove compartments. "Thank you for choosing a Datsun. We are sure you will be happy you did." Two sentences that are spoken each fall—with suitable name changes—by some president, provost, or dean on nearly every campus in America. Next, consider a few headings from a representative table of contents: Economy Hints, Instruments and Controls, Comfort and Convenience Features, In Case of Emergency. . . .

Is there a resemblance between refrigerators, personal computers, automobiles, and universities? Only in the sense that we may be confronting the unfamiliar. Many students are the first in their families to try higher education. A larger proportion of faculty members are the first in their families to pursue academic careers.[1] Social mobility is a

---

1. "In 1900, only 238,000 students—a little over 2 percent of the 18 to 24 year-old population—went to college. At the end of World War II, the figure had climbed to 2,078,000, and by 1975, 9.7 million—over one-third of the 18 to 24 year-olds—enrolled in accredited institutions of higher education." Obviously many young people are the first in their families to go to college.

As to the the parents of academics, surveys taken in 1969 and 1975 indicate that only 4 percent of the fathers of professors were college or university teachers and administrators.

sure sign of American vigor, but as a result our system of higher education has to accomplish very special tasks. We can take little for granted by way of preparation or common background. In many older, developed countries the transition from secondary school to university is a relatively small step for a select few—smooth, well rehearsed, and comfortable. For Americans, it is likely to be a more jarring experience. A didactic manual showing which knob to pull or when to schedule preventive maintenance might be useful.

But why a manual for *owners?* After all, one cannot buy a university and acquire it as a personal possession. Given current levels of tuition fees in some private institutions, parents may feel that they are buying significant portions of universities on the installment plan, but that is not what I have in mind. I am thinking of ownership in a broader, more sophisticated sense. People say: this is *my country.* That is the notion of ownership I wish to suggest to my readers.

Many claimants can be identified from this enlarged perspective. Faculty members often assert that they are the university. Teaching and research, acknowledged to be the key missions of higher learning, are in their hands. Without professors, it is hard to conceive of a university. Academic administrators have been known to behave as if the university belonged to them. In the United States there are large numbers of chairmen, deans, provosts, chancellors, vice presidents, presidents, and so on in control of private fiefdoms. I am personally certain that the quality of a school is negatively correlated with the unrestrained power of administrators, but that is a matter for later discussion.

Students are another important group claiming proprietary rights. They frequently claim to be the *raison d'être* of a

---

On both points, see Seymour Martin Lipset and Everett C. Ladd, Jr., "The Changing Social Origins of American Academics" in Robert K. Merton, James S. Coleman, and Peter H. Rossi, eds., *Qualitative and Quantitative Social Research* (New York: The Free Press, 1979), pp. 319, 321.

university. A university is a school, and without students scholarship would eventually wither away. Every social organism needs the young to replace the old in order to survive. When students graduate, they assume other "ownership" roles by becoming teachers, alumni, donors, and trustees. Furthermore, undergraduate students spend an average of four precious years pursuing a degree, and many believe that this entitles them to some control over curriculum, faculty selection, university investment policies, parietal regulations, quality and kind of food served in dining halls, who can and cannot speak on campus, and the selection of presidents and deans. The list is endless, and some of these claims are more valid than others.

Faculty, administrators, and students are the primary focus of this manual. There are, however, other categories that appear indirectly and only make occasional appearances. I have already mentioned three overlapping groups: trustees, alumni, and donors. These are the bodies that formally ratify major policies, give money, and care deeply about the reputation of *their* schools. The range of concerns tends to be broad, and typically includes quality of teaching, prowess of the football team, politics of students and faculty, admission policies, the sexual preferences of the community, and much else.

There are still other part-owners. One such is the government (federal, state, and local): financier of research, banker to students and universities, regulator, judge and jury of many academic activities. In the case of public institutions, the influence of legislatures and taxpayers is, of course, overwhelmingly strong. But the point is that virtually no university in this country can function without federal support and in many cases without state support. That means being owned in some fashion by government.

A last group to consider is the general public and in particular the self-appointed voice of that constituency: the press. The right to know is deeply engrained in our national tradition, most particularly with respect to public figures and public entities. What happens in America's major universities is national news; events at smaller centers of learning matter locally. New scientific discoveries make headlines. Curriculum debates—especially if they can be described in simple slogans such as "Back to Basics"—receive extensive newspaper and magazine coverage. So do all manner of university opinion surveys, particularly those featuring anything related to alcohol and sex. Editorial writers regularly offer advice to universities. I regret to note that currently one finds more criticism than praise. However, that is not the issue. All we need to understand is that universities are viewed as public property and many of their inhabitants are treated as public figures. That is a limitation on freedom—a requirement of accountability to yet another proprietor.

Each chapter of this manual is intended to be helpful to all those claiming some form of ownership. Through its use I hope that students will have a better grasp of the professorial life, and vice versa; that both professors and students will attain more knowledge concerning administrators and administration; and that the general public and the press will view our activities and mores with greater understanding. My broadest purpose is to show how all can derive maximum benefit from the university, how it can be used (perhaps even improved) without being abused—the test of any owner's manual.

# 1

# A Letter of Introduction

Before turning to what readers will probably consider a set of opinionated chapters (I have the sense that every group will approve what is said about others), a bit of autobiographical information might be helpful. I am seeking to establish my credentials.[1]

In that part of the world in which so much of my early professional personality was formed, Japan, a formal letter of introduction is *de rigueur*. When seeking an interview or a hearing it is most important to arrive with or be preceded by such a document, whenever possible composed by someone possessing a lot of "face." The contents may vary. Sometimes much attention is devoted to lineage and family connections. At other times, the introducer vouches for the

---

1. Thus I take exception with my friend and former colleague Carlo M. Cipolla, distinguished Berkeley economic historian, who replied as follows to his publisher's request for biographical information: "Arthur Koestler once remarked that to wish to meet an author personally because you have admired his work is as unwise as to want to meet a goose because you like *pâté de foie gras.*" See Cipolla's *The Economic History of World Population* (Harmondsworth, Middlesex: Penguin Books, 1962), inside flap.

subject's professional accomplishments. Always the fundamental purpose is the same: to personalize an awkward and
stiff initial encounter.

I propose to follow this civilized Japanese custom, and
will present the required letter, unusual in only one particular—it will be a self-introduction. Perhaps I should have
tried to get a "big name" to write on my behalf, but after
considering a variety of possibilities I decided that the advantages are largely on my side. The relevant facts are
known to me as to no one else and frankly I prefer my own
interpretations. Autobiography tends to be self-serving,
but then I do not intend to make a fetish of objectivity here
at the beginning or in the balance of the volume. This is
unabashedly a book of opinions and of observations based
on my own individual experiences. Let us begin.

Dear Sir or Madam:

I have the pleasure of presenting Mr. Henry Rosovsky,
who is the Lewis P. and Linda L. Geyser University Professor at Harvard University. His title, quite a mouthful, is
intended to be impressive, but do remember that universities are institutions that love hierarchies and distinctions at
least as much as the military. He is also the former Dean of
Harvard's Faculty of Arts and Sciences, a post frequently
described somewhat arrogantly in Cambridge, Massachusetts—alas, rarely elsewhere—as "the best and most important academic job in America."[2] For the rest of his life and
beyond he will always carry the tag "former." In one's early
sixties that should not be an inordinate burden.

HR's university career has been varied and eventful. He
was an undergraduate at the College of William and Mary,

2. See David S. Landes, *Revolution in Time* (Cambridge: Harvard University Press,
1983), p. xi. In a recent newspaper interview, the distinguished linguist Noam
Chomsky described those who run our universities as "commissars of the mind."
Given Chomsky's political views, it is not immediately clear whether one should
take offense at this description. But the end of the sentence leaves no doubt: these
are "the intellectual bureaucrats who run the nation's universities, news media,
and publishing concerns 'narrowing true freedom of thought' in the interest of
complacent obedience to status quo." A more exaggerated notion of administrative power in universities would be difficult to imagine. See Richard Higgins, "A
Critic with Targets Galore," *Boston Globe,* September 4, 1988.

and a graduate student at Harvard. His first teaching post was at the University of California at Berkeley in 1958, where he studied and researched Japanese economic growth at a time when the subject was far less on the public mind than today. As an "area specialist," he always lived under a professional cloud: economists were generous in their praise of his knowledge of things Japanese, and orientalists were prepared to testify to his excellence as an economist. Since these two groups hardly ever met, HR led—for some time—the quiet, untroubled life of a scholar.

The late 1950s and early 1960s were wonderful years for public higher education in California. University expansion and taxpayer generosity created an air of optimism. Achieving tenure—a lifetime contract and the goal of every professor—required only reasonable brightness and moderate industry. Add the California climate; what else could one want?

This idyllic phase ended abruptly during the academic year 1964–65. Berkeley happened to be the birthplace of the American student revolution. Nearly twenty-five years after the event, the causes of this important social phenomenon are sometimes still disputed. Vietnam and the civil rights movement played major roles. A certain revulsion against the impersonality of large organizations was also important. Remember the revolutionary slogan: do not fold, spindle, or mutilate! Another contributing factor was the inexperience of universities in managing sudden student unrest that now took the form of attacks on institutions that considered themselves non-political and neutral. But for present purposes, the causes do not matter. The consequences were unambiguous from the very beginning: an entirely new and most unsettled atmosphere. Mass meetings, building occupations, police actions, non-negotiable demands that led to perpetual negotiations, interminable faculty meetings full of bombastic political rhetoric—certainly not a setting in which to pursue knowledge, at least the sort of knowledge traditionally associated with universities.

At this point, HR made a very poor forecast, an achievement frequently shared with many prominent members of
the economics profession. Being largely raised in the East,
and born in Europe, he had a natural skepticism about California: the sunshine was rather monotonous, the population rootless, and all things odd and trendy seemed to
flourish in this strange environment. Berkeley had ex-
ploded, but surely—he believed—these unfortunate events
would never be repeated in the more established institutions on the East Coast. In the Ivy League and similar
places, students and professors still wore jackets and ties,
older people sometimes were addressed as Sir. Civility pre-
vailed. Most of all, teaching and research remained undis-
turbed. I might add that he also sensed in himself a dangerous inability to remain disengaged from university affairs.
Despite his loudly announced dislike of negotiations, faculty rhetoric, and committees, when crisis came to Berkeley
he contributed more than his share to all of these social ills.
It could be said that in doing so HR behaved like so many
other professors: claiming to yearn for peace and quiet in
the library while never missing an opportunity to engage in
academic politics or games of power. Of course, he would
urge a different interpretation: one that stresses love of
institutions, citizenship, moral values.

At any rate, toward the end of the academic year
1964–65 HR resigned his professorship in economics and
history at the University of California and joined that small
group of West Coast refugees, largely social scientists,
searching for traditional tranquility. Given the prosperity
of the times, a number of attractive invitations arrived. He
chose his old graduate school, Harvard University.

Harvard had always exerted a major influence on HR. As
an undergraduate he had studied economics and history at
the College of William and Mary (class of 1949), a four-year
school that—in those days—emphasized good teaching
and a good time. Professors were approachable, conscien-
tious, sometimes even inspiring. Southern friendliness—
quite genuine—was a major asset. William and Mary was

founded in 1693, only fifty-seven years after Harvard initiated higher education in America. Our country's second oldest college, it attempted to make much of its heritage. But the appeal to tradition had a slightly hollow ring in the 1940s. Perhaps in the eighteenth century William and Mary and Harvard could be viewed as a pair. Few would agree with that after the Civil War, although in recent years William and Mary gained renewed respect as a "public ivy."

Harvard was special to a new graduate student in 1949 not because it now represents the good old days or the period of HR's youth. Its essential qualities have remained unchanged. First, a faculty that continually seeks to create new ideas and knowledge; the people who wrote the books stood at the lectern. Second, students from every state and many foreign countries selected by rigorous standards—a diverse, contentious, and marvelously stimulating cohort. Third, a disdain for orthodoxy and "school solutions" combined with a great admiration for excellence. And finally, a meaningful tradition: by today, over 350 years of virtually uninterrupted progress.

Groucho Marx once said that he would not wish to belong to any club that would have him as a member. Harvard's invitation forcibly brought this thought to mind. HR had an exaggerated esteem for members of the Harvard faculty—it would not last unabated for long—and he briefly wondered whether he really deserved a place in that august company.

Much of the material to follow is based on HR's experiences at Harvard since 1965. They have not been years of ivory tower solitude. A few lectures or tutorials in the morning, a quiet walk along the Charles River after a leisurely lunch at the Faculty Club, followed by an afternoon in Widener Library—that would be a misleading picture. A realistic account has to begin by observing that what had been born in Berkeley swept the country. Columbia, Cornell, Michigan, Wisconsin—all these campuses and many others were engulfed by intense and long-lasting student protest movements. Harvard was no exception, although many insiders believed that what they rather boastfully called "the flagship of American higher education" would be spared. Some knew better by 1967 and 1968, years that featured a series of incidents increasing in size and seriousness. The climax came on April 9, 1969, with the occupation of University Hall—the symbol of faculty authority— by student protesters, and the subsequent police "bust." For nearly a decade thereafter, Harvard joined the ranks of politicized universities. A great number of the country's schools fell into this group; no section of the country was spared.

A few observations are appropriate in connection with HR's early years as a professor. We have already noted his inability to stay in the library and classroom and out of the world of affairs. Why could he not sit at boring faculty meetings without yielding to the urge to make a speech? Why participate in debates concerning the relation between the invasion of Cambodia and the cancelation of final examinations? Of all things, why get involved with Afro-American studies? Hard questions.

You will recall the assassination of Martin Luther King, Jr., in 1968: deep sorrow and guilt among liberals, riots in large cities, and feelings of anger among thinking people everywhere. A direct consequence on campus was the demand by militant black students for greater recognition of their culture and background in the curriculum and in research. Some time before the tragic death of Dr. King, HR had written a letter to Franklin Ford, at that time Dean of the Faculty of Arts and Sciences, raising what seemed to him a few simple questions of equity. He noted that Harvard helped many foreign students from less developed countries with scholarships and special training. This policy had general support: Harvard frequently aided those who had compelling educational needs. But did we not have even greater obligations toward our own citizens, and especially those among us who had suffered slavery, discrimination, and the wounds inflicted by racial prejudice? Was Harvard doing enough for American blacks?

Dean Ford's answer arrived during the summer of 1968. In time-honored and entirely reasonable fashion, he appointed a committee to study the feasibility of Afro-American studies and related issues, and predictably and classically selected HR as chairman. (He asked for it!) Composed of faculty members and a few black students, the committee issued its report to considerable internal and external acclaim during the fateful winter of 1969. *The New York Times* devoted almost a whole page to excerpts and placed HR's picture on the front page. (A danger signal: professors' names belong in learned journals, not in national newspapers.) At a faculty meeting in February 1969 the "Rosovsky Committee's" recommendations were adopted enthusiastically with hardly a murmur of dissent.

The details of the report are ancient history and need not detain us. Recommendations included the creation of an interdisciplinary concentration in Afro-American Studies (*not* a department), new posts for social scientists who specialized in black studies, and the founding of an Afro-American cultural center along the lines of the familiar Hillel Houses for Jewish students.

A very brief moment of glory. In the spring of 1969, barely two months after a great display of enthusiasm, the Harvard faculty—in the midst of police actions, student strikes, and threats—abandoned what seemed to HR to be the carefully crafted recommendations of the Rosovsky Committee and in essence gave to black students and black student organizations powers hitherto reserved for tenured professors: votes concerning curriculum requirements, hiring, tenure, and so on. A truly unbelievable moment in Harvard's long history. HR called the episode an "academic Munich" and again wondered whether he should not have followed Groucho Marx's advice: was this club that had chosen him one he wanted to belong to? He severed all his connections with Afro-American Studies and withdrew—all too temporarily—from faculty affairs.

In the fall of 1969 HR became chairman of the Economics Department, a post he occupied until 1972. This is a significant item of information. The outside world might be impressed by this selection, but at Harvard—as at most top-notch schools—these posts are frequently avoided. They carry little real power, entail no financial rewards, and consume a considerable amount of energy. Some of the best scholars manage to evade these jobs; they are considered too valuable to waste their time with administration. On the other hand, some professors are not considered fit for chairmanships because of character deficiencies: laziness, abrasiveness, weak-kneed attitudes, and even lack of common sense. Let it be said that a small minority carefully cultivates a selection of disabling traits so as to avoid these chores. From an intellectual point of view, HR's chairmanship was, somewhat unfortunately, uneventful. The Economics Department remained relatively stable in a university that continued to be battered by assaults from many directions. Student activism was reaching a peak; radicalism was chic; the Vietnam War was going from bad to worse. Commencements all over the country were disrupted, including Harvard's, and the National Guard shot and killed four students at Kent State. HR was glad to complete his term during the summer of 1972, and to resume research trips to the calmer reaches of Asia.

One day in February of 1973, while breakfasting in Jakarta, Indonesia, and reading the local English-language paper, HR noted an item that proved to be of great personal consequence. John T. Dunlop, Dean of Harvard's Faculty of Arts and Sciences, had just been chosen by President Nixon to chair the new Cost of Living Council in Washington, the agency charged with wage and price controls. A few days later there came an anxious call from HR's wife with the news that the *Harvard Crimson* had begun its usual speculations concerning Dunlop's successor. She said that much to her regret, HR's name appeared to be among the leading contenders. HR told his wife that the *Crimson* was frequently wrong; that President Bok had far better choices; and that even if the offer was tendered, he was inclined to say no. At age forty-six it seemed time to focus exclusively on Japan and the emerging economies of East Asia, on being a mentor to graduate students and a good teacher to Harvard's undergraduates. All other university activities were a waste of time. That was what he believed or, more accurately, what he thought he sincerely believed. Forecasting is not HR's strong suit.

On his return to Cambridge in April, President Bok issued the invitation. HR asked just one question: "If I say no, whom will you choose?" Listening to the president's gracious reply, he asked for twenty-four hours to consider the matter; of course the answer was affirmative. For the next eleven years HR served as Dean of Arts and Sciences, responsible for about 8,500 students, some 6,000 employees, a budget of over $200 million, and nearly 1,000 teachers of all ranks.

Why *him?* Comparative youth and energy were not unusual qualities. The willingness to say yes may have counted for something, but many others were eager for authority. One could, of course, ask President Bok. However, his reputation for discretion is entirely deserved, and the answer will not be too enlightening. Perhaps a few suggestions from an insider are in order.

I have already alluded to the politicization of the Harvard faculty in the second half of the 1960s. There were two parties or caucuses. One called itself liberal and tended to support left-wing positions. The other was labeled conservative; to call them reactionary would not be entirely inappropriate. These two parties saw the selection of a new dean as an opportunity to gain control. Their minimum goal was to prevent—at all cost—the selection of a dean from the opposing caucus.

A typical centrist—pragmatic is one of his favorite adjectives—HR was disinclined to associate with either caucus. He attended some meetings of both warring factions. Indeed, at times both groups considered him one of their own. (Surely, some light is shed on his character by observing that he took no steps to dispel these ambiguities.) Thus he was one of the very few individuals, maybe the only one, acceptable to both camps; a choice that satisfied minimal though crucial criteria.

In addition, remember that HR is an economist and you will ask: what is so good about that? Have economists shown particular talent and sophistication in running institutions of any kind? Do they ever meet a payroll? Are their theories of any value in attempting to understand what we call "the real world"? I will not object too strenuously if these questions are all answered in the negative. And yet it is a fact that in the last few decades economists (and lawyers) have increasingly moved into top jobs in academic administration. The presidents of Princeton, Northwestern, and Michigan in recent years have all been practitioners of the "dismal science." HR's predecessor was an economist; so is his successor. Many other examples could be cited: are these just random events? That is hard to believe.

But what do economists understand better than many of their academic colleagues? First of all, they are comfortable with the notion of "trade-offs": choices involve a little more of this and a little less of that. Humanists often find this kind of reasoning repellent and scientists tend to believe it is immoral when applied to their choices. Secondly, economists are trained to consider "indirect effects." To comprehend the complete effect of any decision or policy, one must carefully work out all the obvious and hidden results. For example, to raise tuition will produce more income only if there are enough students who can pay the price and only if increased scholarship obligations do not exceed the added revenue. Thirdly, economists use marginal reasoning: they tend to think in incremental rather than in absolute terms. Lastly, anyone trained in economics knows that the value of money changes. As our society has experienced long-term inflation, this simple truth is now more apparent, but the money illusion has not disappeared. None of the above are fancy theories or high-falutin' techniques, but they may help to explain why economists may have some comparative advantages. Whatever the reasons for his selection, HR took the job with enthusiasm, and held office longer than any Arts and Sciences dean in the postwar era.

After eleven years as Dean of the Faculty of Arts and Sciences, HR did something rather unusual: he resigned from his administrative post—*voluntarily* giving up power—and returned to teaching and research. Eleven years is a very long time in anyone's life. It is about one third of a normal tenured career; most Ph.D.'s in English are awarded in less time! Is it possible, after such an interval, to resume the self-disciplined and inner-directed life of intellectual creativity? Time will tell, but HR strongly believed in what he called the John Quincy Adams Principle, named in honor of our sixth President, who served in the House of Representatives after completing his term as head of the government. Soon after announcing the decision to leave office, HR was immensely pleased to receive a letter from Edward B. Hinckley, Harvard class of 1924, welcoming him to the Retired Administrators' Teaching Society (RATS) whose motto is *ministrare sed non administrare* (to minister, but not to administer). According to its "Chief Cheese" (Mr. Hinckley):

> The purpose of this august group of sage philosophers is obvious: to band together in a loose, intellectual association those men [and women!] wise enough to forego the doubtful authority and certain, ineluctable responsibilities of administration in favor of the indubitable joys of intellectual and spiritual dissemination of eternal truths—the scholar's happy hunting ground of libraries and manuscripts, the sharp give and take, or cut and thrust, of academic investigation and discovery.

Perhaps Mr. Hinckley should have taken a cold shower before composing these lines, but they expressed HR's own feelings quite well. His life as dean had lacked neither "give and take" nor "cut and thrust"—far more of the latter than the former—but he had grown weary in office and realized that a return to the classroom and library, while difficult after eleven years, would soon be impossible. Staying on meant a life sentence in administration: HR chose parole. In 1985, he also chose to accept an invitation to join the Harvard Corporation—the university's senior governing board. He was the first Harvard professor in a century to receive this call, which he accepted with alacrity. At all ceremonial occasions, male members of the governing boards appear in morning coats, striped pants, and top hats. Aside from Harvard University, I have the impression that these strange garments are only used for Japanese weddings, funerals, and at the Imperial Court. That may have been one of the attractions, because he was most anxious to think more and more about Japan.

Dear Sir or madam: this letter of introduction is already too long, but my fascination with the subject made brevity difficult. I hope that enough background has been given to establish the author's credentials—at least in terms of experience. I know that he thinks of the chapters that follow as an act of penance. But do remember that *caveat lector* always is a sound idea.

Yours faithfully,

# 2

## Two Thirds of the Best

In much of the foregoing, readers may have sensed a certain pride taken by the author in his profession. I do not deny it. To me, some parts of American higher education are one of the country's greatest glories. In fact, I make bold to say to our critics—and they are many these days—that fully two thirds to three quarters of the best universities in the world are located in the United States. (That we also are home to a large share of the world's worst colleges and universities is not now my concern.) What sector of our economy and society can make a similar statement? One can think of baseball, football, and basketball teams, but that pretty much exhausts the list. No one has suggested that today America is home to two thirds of the best steel mills, automobile factories, chip manufacturers, banks, or government agencies. It has been suggested to me that we are home to a similar proportion of the world's leading hospitals. Since most of these are part of university medical schools, my point is only reinforced. Our position at the upper end of the quality scale in higher education is unusual, may be a special national asset, and needs to be explained.

By two thirds (perhaps three quarters) of the best, I mean that surveys of world universities rank a majority of American *public and private* institutions at the top. A recent exercise by Asian scholars (published in the *Asian Wall Street Journal*)[1] produced the following rankings: 1. Harvard; 2. Cambridge, Oxford; 3. Stanford; 4. University of California (Berkeley); 5. MIT; 6. Yale; 7. Tokyo; 8. Paris-Sorbonne; 9. Cornell; 10. Michigan, Princeton. I attach no real importance to rank order—though it naturally pleases me to find Harvard in first place. These are only crude measures, no better than rough orders of magnitude, but I do believe that if this list were expanded to twenty or thirty or even fifty institutions, the United States proportion would not decline. (Columbia, Chicago, UCLA, CalTech, Wisconsin, and many others would find little competition abroad.) Note also that the Asian scholars' list contains dubious entries: Tokyo and the Sorbonne are probably mentioned among the top ten as a consequence of excessive Oriental courtesy. Some may argue that the very notion of rankings or "the best" is invidious, crude, and meaningless. I do not share that view if we adopt a sufficiently broad interpretation of these terms. The universities we are considering lead the world in basic science research; provide a significant share of the most competitive graduate programs; are generally at the cutting edge—rather blunt these days—of the social sciences. Students from all over the world, at all levels, seek entry in large numbers.[2]

Why this happy result? One might begin by mentioning the devotion to all levels of education exhibited by our Founding Fathers, the near classlessness of our society, and the consequent—nearly unique—devotion to universal ed-

1. May 5, 1986.
2. "The United States is currently overwhelmingly the primary national destination for students going abroad; only African students went in substantial numbers to a host (France) other than the United States," see Elinor G. Barber, ed., *Foreign Student Flows*, IIE Research Report No. 7 (1984), p. 8.

ucation. Our national wealth, large population, government support especially of science, are currently significant explanatory factors. The influence of Hitler refugees undoubtedly was important in elevating standards of quality beginning in the 1930s. Many world-class scholars fled Europe, came to our universities, and raised intellectual levels to new and unanticipated heights. Both the natural and social sciences were positively transformed. The American habit of private philanthropy and its encouragement through tax policy also remains crucial. All are influential factors, but in my opinion there are also less obvious and perhaps equally important internal university considerations.

An unusual characteristic of American university life is its competitiveness. Institutions of the same class compete for faculty, research funds, students, public attention—and much else. That Harvard or Stanford, for example, actively recruit and compete for students—undergraduate, graduate, and professional—is quite incomprehensible to the establishments in Tokyo or Kyoto Universities where an entrance examination determines all. It is almost equally unusual in most parts of the world to hire professors away from one institution—by offering higher salaries and better working conditions—for the benefit of individual *and* institution. In Japan, and to a lesser extent elsewhere, one nearly always has to graduate from the university in which employment is obtained. Inbreeding is rampant—a sharp contrast with top American universities, where faculties are assembled largely on the basis of individual quality without the constraint of considering where they received their education.

Institutional competitiveness is associated with some negative consequences—particularly if your university loses too many encounters with the market. The dark side includes too much movement by professorial stars from one university to another in relentless pursuit of personal gain; a consequently lower level of institutional loyalty; invidious comparisons between fields giving excessive advantages to those subjects where "market power" is strong (as in computer sciences vs. English); and not least, the deleterious effects of a Wall Street mentality that focuses too much on short-term highly visible achievements at the expense of the long run and the unfashionable.

I have no doubt, however, about the generally beneficial effects of university competition. It has prevented complacency and spurred the drive for excellence and change. In 1980, it was still possible for a British journalist to write that "Oxford is not obliged to compete. There are no challengers perpetually ready to depose Oxford from its preeminent position. . . . Oxford . . . unlike its American counterparts, is not out to prove itself. . . . This lends self-composure and dignity."[3] These sentiments may still apply to Tokyo, Paris, Oxford and Cambridge, but they cannot describe *any* American university. We may lack self-composure and dignity; but we do achieve higher quality at the top.

American practices also differ in the selection of faculty for "permanent employment" or tenure. I know that this is a vexing subject despite widespread security of employment in our society. Critics complain that teaching ability is ignored and that deadwood is encouraged to remain in place for many years. Without discussing these criticism— and I do *not* agree with them—this much is clear: in our leading universities, the granting of tenure is taken with utmost seriousness. It is not merely a question of time. Tenure is awarded only after a long period of probationary service (usually eight years), and extensive inside and outside peer review; it is a highly competitive selection process. At Harvard we ask a traditional question: who is the most qualified person in the world to fill a particular vacancy, and then we try to convince that scholar to join our ranks. We may reach the wrong conclusion, and we may not succeed in attracting our first or even second choice, but our goal is elevated. Details may differ, but in essence the

3. Christopher Rathbone, "The Problems of Reaching the Top of the Ivy League . . . and Staying There," *The Times Higher Education Supplement,* August 1, 1980.

process of achieving tenure is the same in our leading institutions—those that are included in two thirds of the best. All of these schools correctly assume that the quality of the faculty is the most important factor in maintaining their reputation and position. The best faculty attracts the finest students, produces the highest-quality research, gains the most outside support.

Governance is another area in which American universities are unusual. The extensive role of private higher education must be a major factor, but that is clearly not the entire explanation. Public and private university governance in this country is quite similar, and differs in important respect from what might be called the "continental model."

The American system is unitary: ultimately one person—a president—is in charge. Typically, educational policy—curriculum, nature of degrees, selection of faculty, admissions, etc.—is initiated by or delegated to academics. But budgets, management of endowment, decisions on new programs, long-range plans, and similar matters are in the hands of a hierarchy headed by a president who is responsible to a board of trustees. Two points are noteworthy in this system. First, chairmen, deans, provosts, and similar levels of senior and middle management are appointed—not elected—and they can be dismissed. This is crucial because academic elections tend to result in weak leadership. What professors in their right minds would vote for a dean advocating cuts in *their* subjects? Secondly, relatively independent trustees serve both public and private schools, giving considerable protection from political interference even to state universities. We have a system of governance that permits non-consensual and unpopular decisions to be made when necessary. We have learned that not everything is improved by making it more democratic. We have also learned that university governance functions best when conflict of interest is minimized.

One cannot, of course, describe "the continental model"—it is too much of an abstraction. In overall terms, it is designed to have universities interact with a ministry of education or some form of national grants committee disbursing government funds. Professors tend to be civil servants subject to many bureaucratic regulations; logrolling all too easily replaces competition. An elected administration—another common feature—ensures that leadership is weak: those who are strong and espouse change are unlikely to be popular favorites. During the last twenty years, a form of democratization known as "parity" became common in parts of Europe: decisions concerning universities made by an equal representation of students, staff, and faculty. In Holland, for example, the consequence has been an assault on the very notion of excellence in higher education. Professor Isaac Silvera, who taught physics at Leiden for many years, recently wrote: "The primary function of a university is teaching and research, but what seemed paramount in the Dutch system was to create a democratically structured institute with organization and rules that would promote the social contentment of the employees and students; only then would attention be focused on education and research." And Nobel laureate Nicholaas Bloembergen added somewhat mordantly: "In a few years . . . the Dutch will even be unhappy if their soccer team wins the World Cup—that would imply excellence."[4]

We also differ—if we confine ourselves to two thirds of the best—in our emphasis on liberal education for undergraduates, and sometimes in the effort that attaches to undergraduate studies. Of course, outside the United States the situation varies from country to country, but the following statements are correct. In Japan, even in the most prestigious institutions, students in the humanities and social sciences can and often do treat college as a three-year vacation; tennis appears to be the favorite "major." It is often said that Japanese students need a long vacation to recuperate both from the rigors imposed by a very demanding

4. See *Harvard and Holland* (A collection of essays published on Harvard's 350th anniversary, 1986), p. 72.

secondary school system and the deep anxieties associated with university entrance examinations. But three years?

In Great Britain, West Germany, and France, the first degree is highly specialized; the concept of general education is unknown at the university level. Students are expected to matriculate with general education completed in secondary schools. Compared to the United States, it is a valid expectation.

In many countries, no serious attempt is made to provide students or professors with even minimal facilities: no offices, rudimentary libraries and laboratories, totally inadequate classrooms—all true in Italy—and lectures that might as well emanate from a tape recorder. I have, in fact, encountered that practice in Indonesia, where no academic can live on his salary. While the recorded lecture is being delivered, the unfortunate professor is undoubtedly scrounging for a bit of additional income.

In explaining why we are home to a disproportionate share of the world's finest universities, I would suggest one other factor: regional pride. It may exist elsewhere, but not nearly to the same degree. Many of our best institutions—public and private—are clear expressions of local patriotism; the Universities of California, North Carolina, Wisconsin, and Minnesota all fit this category. Many other examples could easily be cited. In our large and decentralized country, each region wants its share of the best, and sometimes these ambitions are fulfilled. The state of California is an ideal illustration: a growing population and tax base, great local ambition, new wealth, and a wonderful climate have created, in less than one hundred years, an astonishing number of universities with international reputations. And all are far removed from the traditional cultural centers of the Northeast. In America, the preemptive power of Paris, Tokyo, or prewar Berlin simply does not exist—thank God!

In higher education, "made in America" still is a fine label—in fact, the finest label if our focus remains at the top end of the quality distribution. Perhaps we should add another sticker: "handle with care." The schools included in this group are the ones that I primarily had in mind in writing this book. What and how many am I talking about? In the United States there are slightly over three thousand institutions of higher education. At one extreme, we find over one thousand two-year institutions enrolling 36 percent of all students.[5] At the other extreme are the top research universities, about fifty in number (57 percent public) and enrolling 10 percent of the total student population. Only some—perhaps rather little—of what I have to say is likely to be relevant for junior colleges. Everything that I have written applies, in varying degrees, to research universities. Bracketed by the thousand junior colleges and the fifty major research universities, our country has an enormous variety of colleges and universities. There are universities that do very little research but teach many students; some offer no higher than a master's degree. We are home to liberal arts colleges of considerable variation in terms of quality; this category contains some of our finest schools. We should also note the many "specialized institutions" such as schools of art, music, and design, or military academies. All of these number about two thousand and experienced readers will have to judge for themselves what is or is not valid from the perspective of their school.

I would like to add, however, that my emphasis on our finest research universities should not unduly decrease the value of my observations. These institutions are the cutting edge of our national life of the mind. They determine the intellectual agenda of higher education. They set the trends. It is true that Princeton, Michigan, and Cornell are "typical" of only one portion of American higher education, and that there are considerable differences between these schools. But they are all very important universities—important to us in the United States and to the world.

5. For these and related statistics, see Burton R. Clark, *The Academic Life* (Princeton: The Carnegie Foundation for the Advancement of Teaching, 1987), pp. 17–23.

# 3

## A Dean's Day[1]

**6:30 A.M.**

Barely awake, I stumble downstairs in search of *The New York Times,* the *Boston Globe,* and *The Wall Street Journal.* At one time, I would have lingered over front pages, concentrating on major domestic or international stories. Not now. I quickly glance through three papers to see whether they contain a story—all too frequently critical—concerning Harvard. This morning there is one item in *The Wall Street Journal* that does not especially disturb me:

> Which phone call would President Reagan take first if the callers were the editor of the Washington Post, IBM's Chairman, the top Episcopal bishop and Harvard's president? In a Gallup Survey, 41% said the Post editor. Next . . . was the IBM chief, Harvard's president was last.

1. For the sake of historical accuracy, I acknowledge that this is a composite day. All the events happened, but over a protracted period of time.

And so, on to a relaxing shower and shave.

**7:00 A.M.**

Leave home for breakfast appointment at the Faculty
Club. Turn on the car radio and somewhat to my surprise
hear a voice saying—with evident satisfaction—that Dean
Rosovsky of Harvard University has been reprimanded for
sexually harassing an undergraduate. My surprise is limited
because on the previous day it had been my sad duty to
reprimand one of our professors for bestowing a most unwelcome and totally inappropriate kiss on a woman student. That the story was seriously garbled by the media I
had learned to expect. Given the early hour of the day—few
students are likely to be witting and faculty members at this
hour are probably enviously watching their friends on the
Today Show—very few people who mattered to me heard
the report before a retraction and correction was broad-
cast. (One of my secretaries did hear it and immediately
called the station. Interestingly enough, at the time she said
nothing to me, intending to provide protection from upset-
ting news.) A promising start to another long day.

**7:30 A.M.**

I enter the genteel and shabby environs of Harvard's
Faculty Club, where the local version of the power breakfast is getting under way. I note the presence of certain
regulars who come every day: bachelors and perhaps those
whose spouses refuse to fry eggs or make hot cakes. A number of meetings are in progress: I recognize most of the
groups and can generally divine the topic that brings them
together. A member of the Harvard Corporation (the principal governing body), a few sleepy students and professors; no doubt divestiture and South Africa are on the
agenda. Our vice president for alumni relations and a few
"development" specialists are off in a corner, no doubt discussing the progress of the capital campaign: how to raise

$350 million. They appear to be animated and smile a lot. As the major beneficiary of their labors, I am pleased to note their good mood.

My own meeting is with the dean of Harvard College—elsewhere called Dean of Students—and a couple of his assistants. The subjects: selection of new House Masters, crowding in the Houses (very fancy dormitories), and tensions with Radcliffe College. All of these subjects share a common characteristic of academic administration: they never go away; they are rarely solved. Harvard undergraduates live in thirteen Houses—vaguely modeled on Oxbridge Colleges—these days each one graced by a pair of "co-masters," ordinarily a faculty member and spouse. These are desirable jobs with many perks, but to find the right pairings—a "balanced"[2] couple, pleasing to students while upholding adult standards—is extraordinarily difficult. Many times, those one most wants are likely to decline the invitation. And so the dean of Harvard College and I go over faculty rosters and attempt to identify possibilities.

The crowding problem has a simple explanation. Harvard Houses were built in the 1930s and reflect notions of student lifestyle that included maids, suites, waitresses, menu selection, and tablecloths. In the post–World War II era it has been our lot to squeeze perhaps 25 percent more inhabitants into the Houses—larger classes produce additional tuition income and the demand for admission by highly qualified candidates appears infinite—while trying to preserve some semblance of gracious living. And so we discuss the possibilities of new construction and renovation. There is much talk of "bottom lines," tax-exempt bonds, interest rates, and so on. At this early hour, a rather indigestible topic—but better than divestiture!

Harvard and Radcliffe are separate institutions. In 1974, I suggested that the two colleges be merged and proposed a new name for the united entity: Harcliffe. Very few were amused, least of all the ruling circles at Radcliffe. Instead,

2. "Balance" seems to mean a couple in which the female spouse is not a housewife.

we developed an *entente cordiale*—the degree of cordiality
was subject to distinct cyclical variations—that I construed
as mandating co-education and that Radcliffe interpreted
as allocating to itself the role of women's champion in the
Harvard community.

Radcliffe was founded slightly over one hundred years
ago to give females access to a Harvard education. From
the beginning, it was not a college in the ordinary sense of
that word: no Radcliffe faculty ever existed. Women students always took courses from Harvard professors—for
too many years separately, and since the 1950s in mixed
classes. For the last fifteen years women and men undergraduates have lived in the same Houses (co-residence),
attended the same classes, received the same degrees, and
are cared for by the same Harvard administration. Radcliffe
has redirected its energies toward a major library devoted
to the history of women and an institute for female scholars. Nevertheless, it retains an advocacy voice in the affairs
of the college, and this can create both substantive and
diplomatic problems. Some of those are our subject for this
morning: we are accused of running a men's club, of sexist
behavior, of not recognizing the special needs of women. Is
it true? What to do?

**8:45 A.M.**

Having solved no problem and eaten too much breakfast, I rush across the Yard to my office in University Hall.
All is still quiet—no students in sight; a few professors are
on their way to Widener Library. My first appointment is
with a furious colleague from my own Economics Department. He had just received one of my annual form letters
announcing his salary for the next academic year. After a
quick calculation, this quantitatively oriented economist
concluded that his raise was all of 1 percent: an insult and
an outrage. I had the malicious pleasure of correcting his
mistaken calculation. The raise was 6 percent: he did not

know his own salary and had used the wrong base. My colleague departs in some embarrassment. In the wake of this small, spiteful triumph, I am, for the moment, eager to engage the rest of the day.

## 9:00 A.M. to 11:00 A.M.

My personal office staff has arrived, an administrative assistant and four secretaries. All phone calls are screened and the perpetual game of "telephone tag" gets under way: "X called. Please call back." Eventually one of the secretaries calls back and leaves a similar request, ad infinitum. No doubt Ma Bell is pleased.

Two hours—four appointments. One soon acquires the skill of terminating them on time. A buzz from the administrative assistant, repeated glances at one's watch, getting up and walking toward the door—all work some of the time.

Appointment 1: a troubled chairman. His department is small, and three of his senior professors have suddenly announced their intention to take leaves and sabbaticals next year. These are colleagues and he has to live with them for many more years; saying no is unpleasant and could affect personal relationships in future years. Saying yes is easier; only the students will suffer. This man has more conscience than courage—in my experience, a common situation—and wants me to issue a decanal edict denying two of the leaves. I understand my responsibilities; being the bad guy is one of them. A stern letter will be put in the mail by evening.

There are ten minutes left in the appointment. I would love to go to the toilet[3] but an early unilateral termination

3. I could, with little difficulty, write a chapter about toilets. My special problem was a direct consequence of Harvard's venerable age. The dean's office is located in University Hall, a structure erected in the early nineteenth century, before the use of indoor plumbing. When finally installed, these conveniences were tucked in on a space-available basis. For me it required a two-and-a-half-minute run in each direction, and my frequent dashes provided needed exercise and great amusement for all who worked in the building.

might be viewed as a discourtesy. My friend uses the opportunity to air a few perpetual grievances: inadequate office
space, too few secretaries, not enough concern with his
subject. MEGO: mine eyes glaze over. It is nine-thirty and
the buzzer intrudes.

Appointment 2: my chief financial assistant. Two topics:
next year's tuition and faculty salaries. This is deadly serious stuff, among the main factors determining faculty income and costs. Both have to be considered competitively;
the decisions of Stanford, Berkeley, MIT, Yale, and others
are crucial. We share information quite freely. To be a
leader in faculty salaries and a follower in tuition is my
somewhat contradictory ambition. The assistant urges
maximal tuition increases, and she has sound reasons. But I
know that the president and the Corporation will cause
difficulties, and also think of the burdens imposed particularly on middle-class parents. The rich can afford it; the
bulk of scholarship assistance goes to lower-income
groups; those in the middle are very squeezed. The assistant says that the budget cannot be balanced with my faint-
hearted and unmanly attitudes. Immediate action is required. Once again, the buzzer intervenes and we agree to
postpone the evil day. I know that very few decisions have
to be made immediately, and it is best not to make them in a
macho frame of mind.

Appointment 3: a most painful episode, unusual, but not
without precedent. One of our professors, a senior and
most distinguished scholar whom I had known since student days, was a semi-permanent resident of the Faculty
Club, where he created periodic disturbances. He was di-

---

What some might consider a humiliation turned out to be a boon in my relation with laboratory scientists. Here we have a species of scholar that "melts in the
rain": they require, at great expense, instant access to their laboratories. A short
walk in the fresh air from one building to another is out of the question. To these
people I would innocently say: "Surely you are willing to walk as far as I have to go
to the bathroom." Many believed, I think, that next to my office there existed a
secret Roman bath, made of marble, complete with Jacuzzi and masseuse. Their
answer always was an unhesitating yes. It may have saved Harvard millions of
dollars.

vorced, lonely, and behaved in an increasingly bizarre fashion. Most recently he has refused to meet his classes. We
have no difficulty in tolerating eccentricity; even a certain
level of paranoia can be accommodated. But a refusal to
teach is intolerable.

The professor arrives on time. He is a small man, and
appears to me to twitch and scratch more than normal. He
does not deny the one-sided decision to cease teaching.
The students, he tells me, are "inauthentic." A more com-
prehensible or rational explanation is not forthcoming. I
gently suggest the need for medical evaluation; it is rejected. I point out that strong disciplinary action will have
to be taken—that refusal to teach is an offense that we can
under no circumstances ignore. The professor says that he
may have to take his case to a meeting of the whole faculty.
We part with entirely different convictions. I am certain
that my colleague is insane, and he thinks me an utter fool
for being unable to distinguish between authentic and
inauthentic students.

Appointment 4: by now it is 10:30 A.M., and much to my
surprise I notice that a small delegation of student politicians is on my calendar. As dean, it is hard to see students
or faculty at their best since nearly everyone wants something. Students are generally pleasant in classrooms or during extracurricular activities, or at the dinner table. Unfortunately, as politicians they grow up much too fast:
argumentative, verbose, self-righteous, self-important,
condescending, and deeply suspicious of institutions and
elders. There are exceptions, but the model student-pol
should recognize him/herself in this description. That they
wanted to see me was not surprising—there was never a
shortage of issues—but that they had requested an appointment in the forenoon was rare.

The delegation consisted of three Jewish students, two
of whom were Orthodox. (That could explain their willingness to meet at 10:30 A.M. Morning prayers were over long
ago.) I knew that the issue on their minds was difficult and

that I disagreed with their position. In June, our commencement (graduation) would fall on the second day of *shevuoth,* the Jewish holiday that celebrates Moses receiving the Law on Mount Sinai. For the sake of Orthodox students, for whom it would be more difficult to attend their own graduation (though certainly not impossible, according to my own rabbinical advisers), and as a symbolic recognition of general Jewish concerns, these earnest young men urged—indeed, demanded—that the date of commencement be changed. I tried to clarify my strong opposition to their suggestion.

Was it reasonable to upset long-standing arrangements for over 25,000 people so that perhaps 100 strict observers would not be inconvenienced? What about the demands of many other religious groups for similar treatment? Were we not a secular university? We had, in fact, made many entirely desirable accommodations to observant Jews—not so long ago it was difficult to avoid Saturday examinations or registration on Yom Kippur or to get Kosher food—but it seemed to me that this request was unreasonable and a damaging precedent.

This issue generated far more pressure than warranted. The students gave me a petition signed by "3,000 members of the Harvard community"[4] asking for a change of date. A letter and telephone campaign was in full swing. (One letter from an Orthodox rabbi compared President Bok to Pharaoh and urged him not to harden his heart against the people of Israel.) Being intimately acquainted with and a frequent participant in the politics of Jewish action, I was able to place these tactics in perspective. My non-Jewish associates were less fortunate and lived in fear of being accused of anti-Semitism.

As they say, the students and I had a "frank exchange of views." In their eyes I was not much better than a seventeenth-century Court Jew, enforcing the dictates of an alien

---

4. One has to understand that in our community thousands of signatures can be obtained in a few hours for nearly anything.

master. Their feelings did not upset me in the least. I was absolutely convinced that my views were correct and supportive of the interests of the larger Jewish community.

One day, my administrative assistant, who had served four deans over a period of over forty years, said: "Mr. Rosovksy, being dean is a very difficult job; being a Jewish dean is impossible."

## 11:00 A.M.

I cross the Yard from University Hall to Massachusetts Hall to meet with the president. The path between the two buildings is well worn. My crossings alone could be the reason.

As always, the president's greeting is hearty. He slaps my back, laughs merrily, as we settle into our accustomed chairs in his office. Mine is comfortably worn. Chair and path are similar, perhaps for the same reasons. We meet very frequently, at least three or four times a week, and these are pleasant occasions. I enjoy his company; one of the nicer moments of the day.

Two wildly different subjects are discussed. My enthusiasm for saving money has led to a momentous decision: a reduction in the frequency of classroom painting; peeling paint has never prevented anyone from studying. Unfortunately, there is a domino effect, and some of Harvard's union painters would face a layoff. The president tells me that because of the "last in, first out" principle, all those selected for discharge are black. We quickly agree that the Faculty of Arts and Sciences should continue to paint at the old rate.

The other subject is President Bok's desire to encourage long-range academic planning and its inexorable by-products, studies and statistics. Our respective attitudes—no surprise to either one of us—are odd, out of character. As a lawyer, one might expect him to focus on here and now, and to stress the practical. As an economist—more pretentiously, a social scientist—I should have been enthusiastic about numbers, information, statistical manipulation, and all sorts of educational research. That was not the case because our positions and responsibilities affected attitudes. A president views the university from an Olympian perspective, always prodding, seeking weakness, suggesting improvement. He stands on the shoulders of the deans peering into the distance, thinking of new challenges in spans of years, even five years, and on occasion decades. I saw myself as a field commander, ducking bullets from unexpected directions. All too often goals were measured in hours, at best in weeks. A decanal Mount Olympus has not been discovered! Perhaps mistakenly, I felt that most plans and studies yielded obvious results that were already in my head by way of intuition. Of course I had great respect for the president's wisdom and intelligence, and also understood that he bolstered my weaknesses. We agreed to do new five-year financial projections and to study the Department of Romance Languages in depth.

### 12:00 P.M.

I hustle back to University Hall along the same worn path to attend a sandwich lunch of the academic deans in my office. In attendance: the dean of the Graduate School of Arts and Sciences (a Russian historian), the dean of the Division of Applied Sciences (a statistical physicist), the associate dean for undergraduate education (a political scientist), the associate dean for biological sciences (a neurobiologist), a special assistant on tenure issues (a professor of logic), and my special assistant for academic planning (a historian and career administrator). It is not an elegant occasion. We sit around a coffee table, always in the same chairs, munching the identical sandwiches, perching coffee and Coke amidst piles of documentation. Our meetings occur weekly, last two hours, and some of us have been at it for about a decade. These are my most intimate advisers. Nothing is hidden from them. They have in their possession nearly all facts known to me,[5] and many that I do not yet know.

A "typical" meeting does not exist; we simply review whatever is of the moment. All tenure promotions initially come before this group; most major financial decisions are examined; staffing, educational policy, specific events, troubles—all regularly appear on the docket. We do not vote. In the last analysis, most of the decisions are mine, but I would be foolish to ignore the advice of these colleagues.

Aside from routine matters, today's meeting features only one shouting match—slightly below average—and that between two scientists. Truly the clash of two cultures. Our stern physicist believes most biologists to be self-indulgent creatures whose efforts on behalf of the common good—e.g., undergraduate teaching—are minimal. Reduce their resources unless they mend their ways. The biological dean begs to differ, and explains with growing impatience the "very special circumstances" prevailing in this, the most rapidly developing subject in the entire academic world. Our humanistically inclined historian pours salt on the open wounds by reminding us of the plight of young language teachers, compared to whom all natural scientists do virtually no teaching. And so it goes. I listen and learn and attempt to arrange my features in the manner of a Buddha.[6]

5. There is one major exception. At Harvard, the dean of the faculty is the only person who sets and knows the salaries of tenured professors in Arts and Sciences (non-tenure salaries are in accordance with a published scale). At nearly all other universities, chairmen and sometimes committees have a voice in determining faculty salaries, and at many public institutions they are published as part of state budgets. Our system works because we avoid star salaries, try to minimize differences between fields, and have given this authority to the dean for a long time. I would not recommend the practice everywhere, and believe that the time has come for us to change as well.

6. At least this Buddha was thinking of an old Jewish joke. A rabbi was requested to settle a dispute between two merchants. The first merchant explained his case in great detail. The rabbi stroked his beard and said: "Umm, you are right." The second merchant gave his version of events, a diametrically opposed story. The rabbi turned to him, again stroked his beard, and opined: "Umm, you are right." The rabbi's wife who was sitting in the back of the room intervened with a question: "You have heard two totally different accounts of the same events. Is it not impossible for both of them to be right?" The rabbi nodded, once more stroked his beard, and said to his wife: "You are also right."

**2:00 P.M.**

The deans have been ushered out, remnants of the lunch are gone. My next engagement is a wooing session: the groom is the Faculty of Arts and Sciences, represented by me, and the bride is a young philosopher teaching at a Midwestern university. My assignment is to convince him to accept a full professorship at Harvard University. It is an important assignment—nothing that I will do today matters more. Whenever an opportunity exists to raise average quality, a dean's heart beats faster, and all sorts of evidence indicates that this young man borders on genius. (The bride is very beautiful!) But that is not all. Our Philosophy Department is excellent, frequently ranked first in the country. The department is so good that it exhibits a classic pathology: the inability to find anyone worthy of joining its ranks. It is in imminent danger of becoming a club of old gentlemen, more exclusive with every retirement and death. In my imagination I picture the department with only one member: a patriarch holding a gigantic bag of black balls in his hand. And now, at last, a candidate!

For these reasons I determine to be as charming and persuasive as possible, and to make an extremely generous offer. With a smile on my face—attempting not to think of Pagliacci—I step into the reception area to greet my visitors, the young philosopher and his wife. These days her presence is not unusual. She is a computer programmer, and her views concerning Harvard and her own employment opportunities may determine the outcome of our courtship.

In my large and beautiful office I have done my best to create the right atmosphere. The fireplace is lit. Bottles of sherry and brandy are at hand (I am convinced that these amenities are less customary west of the Allegheny Mountains). Outside, it is raining and I note that the young philosopher has carelessly put his muddy shoes on the cushions of my new white couch. My administrative assistant will not be pleased.

We begin with the usual recruitment speech. Harvard is special, perhaps unique. It is a place where scholars can grow, offering the finest colleagues and students. I have never regretted moving to Harvard and neither will you. The Boston area is exciting, etc.[7] This is not, let me stress, a cynical speech. Most of it I deeply believe, although I realize that dozens of recruiters are saying similar things at other universities, with equal conviction. I can also tell— and this is no surprise—that my visitors are not unfamiliar with this genre of exhortation. In all fields there is intense competition for the services of the finest scholars. Another offer is a familiar event. (The groom is anxious.)

The next part of the interview is also depressingly famil- iar. I have to listen to a recitation of everything that is wrong with Harvard, Boston, Cambridge, our depart- ments, salaries, and so on. Housing is too expensive; public schooling is bad and private education too expensive; the spouse sees few job opportunities; the Philosophy Depart- ment is much too small; good graduate students are going to Princeton; there is little collegiality at Harvard; *und so weiter.* There is some truth in all of these assertions, and their detailed and loving presentation is part of the bar- gaining game. (The bride is careful not to show too much enthusiasm.)

Soon we are dealing in specifics. I offer a high salary, inwardly cringing at equity considerations; add a most gen- erous housing subsidy; throw in a small "slush fund"—sort of academic mad money; promise to help the spouse find a job and to get their one child into Cambridge's leading private school. Institutional generosity is greeted with ex- pressionless faces. No words of gratitude. Instead, a new series of questions concerning sabbaticals, leaves, and re- tirement.

The hour is up. Others are waiting outside. An official offer letter will now have to be drafted, putting all my com-

---

7. When the candidate comes from California, I spend much time on the intellec- tual stimulation provided by four seasons.

mitments on paper. I bid my visitors adieu and hand them over to the chairman of the Philosophy Department. For them a round of cocktail parties, dinners, a brief interview with President Bok, and time with real estate agents. For me, the *Harvard Crimson.*

## 3:00 P.M.

The *Harvard Crimson* is a daily newspaper published by undergraduates. Its influence is considerable because the national and international press frequently use the *Crimson* as a principal source of news about the university. In general, the quality of writing is superb and lively. The paper attracts bright students for whom it becomes their main activity in college, more time-consuming than classes or other diversions. Many have achieved distinguished careers in journalism.

During my twenty-plus years as a reader, the accuracy of reporting has been uneven. In the 1960s and early 1970s it tended to be partisan, an exercise in advocacy journalism favoring the forces of revolution. More recently, standards have improved. Reporters are more accurate and sometimes impartial—no better or worse than the national press. Editorials are another matter. Here the *Crimson* has been consistently and determinedly left of center for a very long time. More important is the paper's adversarial style especially *vis-à-vis* "the administration." If "All the News That's Fit to Print" is appropriate for *The New York Times,* the *Crimson*'s motto should be "When Did You Stop Beating Your Wife?" During eleven years as dean I rarely found favor in their columns. They opposed nearly all of my initiatives, and their reports on my activities often hinted at darker, unrevealed, manipulative motives—suitably illustrated with unflattering photos. For the quality of the pictures I, no doubt, bear a major though unavoidable responsibility.

Three reporters come into my office for a regular monthly session. I look at these young men and women dressed in T-shirts, sweaters, and jeans, and wonder which one I will first encounter in a three-piece suit or its female equivalent. Is one of them a future Franklin Roosevelt, Cap Weinberger, or Anthony Lewis? The fencing match begins.

A popular woman assistant professor has been denied tenure. It seems that all good teachers are "fired," especially women. How can I explain my unsavory actions in this matter? As they know, I never comment on confidential personnel issues, but am willing for the nth time to explain our complicated promotion procedures. In my view, they are fair. (Student reporters change all the time and explanations have to be repeated on a regular basis.) What must appear to be a paternalistic reply is greeted with a slight smirk. They will have no difficulty in getting quotes—almost always anonymous—that cast doubt on my assertions.

Educational reform is now a hotly debated question on campus. I am known to favor a new Core curriculum that will impose more structure on undergraduate education. Do I not understand that this will limit the freedom of students? Why can't students make their own decisions? Why are students not given the *power* to determine what they wish to study? These are serious and legitimate questions, and I try to answer in some detail. I talk about faculty responsibilities, liberal education, the need for all to study science, humanities, and much else. Tomorrow's paper has a headline that reads "Welcome Back to High School."

For the last five minutes I have been ostentatiously looking at my watch. Reporters always overstay their welcome, but I have to get ready for a faculty meeting. My guests depart just as President Bok and members of the docket committee arrive for a brief pre-faculty meeting.

**3:45 P.M.**

The monthly meeting of the Faculty of Arts and Sciences is a well-choreographed ballet. A stage is provided by the imposing Faculty Room next to my office. It is by general consent the most beautiful location in the university. The walls are covered with portraits of illustrious professors and presidents, and quite a few busts—professors in toga— are scattered about. Harvard's past can be a burden or an inspiration. Eliot, Lowell, Benjamin Franklin, Theodore William Richards (the first American to win a Nobel Prize in Chemistry), William James, Samuel Eliot Morison, and others gaze in silence at the foolishness of our times. All the faces are white and male—mostly WASP—and that is an accurate portrait of our past. I hope to live long enough to see other categories represented.

The Faculty Room can quite easily accommodate 250 people and that is just about appropriate. Our membership—all those with teaching appointments and over one hundred administrators—approaches one thousand, but many wise professors choose not to attend unless there is a crisis. I would always be nervous when we were forced to shift the meeting to larger quarters. It brought back unwelcome memories of crises in the 1960s and 1970s, and luckily it did not happen often in my time. At the moment—just before the official opening at 4:00 P.M.—a small crowd has gathered at one end of the room, consuming tea and cookies. This civilized interlude may be my best chance for claiming a footnote in Harvard's history. I had heard that long ago, in the good old days, and ipso facto before my arrival, tea drinking had been the custom. And then in the midst of one of our worst and most politicized debates in 1971—the subject could have been abolishing grades because of the evils of American imperialism—I sponsored a successful motion to reinstitute this practice.

Our meetings are formal. We follow Roberts Rules, use a parliamentarian, and the president, who chairs all sessions, sits on an elevated dais flanked by an assortment of deans and the president of Radcliffe. After the meeting is called to order and the disposal of parliamentary boilerplate, we normally hear two or three memorial minutes. Frequently these are exquisite, loving, and humorous accounts of the lives of scholars, colleagues who have died in recent years. I am especially fond of this half hour. Many of those eulogized were teachers, friends, or acquaintances. And some of our members are first-class necrologists. To contemplate what others have accomplished can also be an exercise in humility, at least for those of us still capable of that sentiment.[8]

Most of our business today is routine reports, with only one docket item of significance. The Biology Department— like the proverbial amoeba—is proposing to split into two parts: organismic biology and cellular biology. Since this is a question of educational policy, a formal faculty vote is required. The "debate" is smooth and highly orchestrated. Movers and seconders rise and give prepared speeches, and a few selected members make supporting statements. There is no opposition, and nearly the entire audience is bored. Why should they care how many biology departments exist in Arts and Sciences? They do not realize that harmony and lack of opposition are the result of countless hours of negotiation and have left much residual bitterness. Furthermore, the intellectual issues are not trivial, involving as they do the future conception of a major discipline. None of these feelings emerges, and the motion is unanimously approved by voice vote. I am relieved: the bargain has stuck and people have played their assigned roles. That does not always happen, and faculty meetings often produce conflict and unanticipated events. Deans prefer harmony and order.

Six o'clock is the adjournment hour. I have less than an hour to get to Logan Airport. On the way out of the meeting, a *Crimson* reporter stops me and asks about the hidden significance of today's motion concerning biology. I mumble something and grab my suitcase.

8. For many good reasons I once declined a most exalted and exciting administrative position at a major university. One of the less likely reasons had to do with memorial minutes. Our custom is to compose them only for professors who retire at Harvard and not for those who leave early through resignation. At the time I told my wife that sitting at faculty meetings, listening to these minutes, I had frequently composed my own obituary. Writing one's own obituary is probably a common ambition that is rarely granted. But I did not wish to give up the chance to have mine read to this audience.

**6:15 P.M.**

I am in a cab on the way to Logan Airport. Traffic in the Callahan Tunnel is moving at two miles per hour. The plane for San Francisco leaves in thirty minutes. Will I make it? Should I feel a bit guilty about extolling the virtues of the Boston area?

Tomorrow, there is a meeting of the "augmented seven" in Palo Alto. This is a group of private university provosts[9] that gets together twice a year for group therapy. Founded nearly thirty years ago by my predecessor McGeorge Bundy, the members initially were Cornell, Yale, Columbia, Stanford, Chicago, Pennsylvania, and Harvard. We have a strong sense of exclusivity. Considerations of neighborliness led me to champion membership for MIT. A decade passed before that initiative met with success— hence the name. We exist to compare notes about policies, problems, future worries, government relations, or whatever else is topical. Most of the time we simply hold each other's hands in the atmosphere of a friendly encounter group. Picture each institution as a wagon, part of a circle fending off internal and external foes. I know of no more appropriate forum in which to complain about ignorant presidents, uncooperative faculty, pesky students, or stingy alumni. Some years ago Harvard's general counsel suggested that our activities might be interpreted as in restraint of trade and hence violations of anti-trust laws. I could not agree with such a sinister interpretation of our gatherings.

I barely make the plane and settle in my coach seat amid tourists and a few crying babies. The comforts of first class are forbidden by university policy, and rightly so. Still, six uninterrupted hours seem pretty good after twelve hours of frantic activity. After two Scotches on the rocks I open my briefcase to check out accumulated correspondence.

9. Harvard does not have a provost. We believe that our deans are equal to any academic rank, and apparently the members of the augmented seven agreed.

Most of it is pretty dull stuff, and I scribble answers in the margins. Two items are more interesting. The first is a copy of a note addressed to the chairman of our Chemistry Department in connection with the search for a senior professor in inorganic chemistry. Composed by a British Nobel laureate, it reads in part:

> With the reputation you have got for treatment of the branch of chemistry that has most rapidly developed over the past thirty years,[10] quite frankly, I wouldn't recommend an old burt to take a job at Harvard. Any of the distinguished gentlemen on your short list would be as mad as the proverbial March hares to leave their cushy nests, particularly those who have been spurned by Harvard in the past;[11] I would say you were wasting your time.

The other missive is a copy of a personnel resignation form submitted by one of my daughters who had been employed by the university's experimental animal facilities. Under reason for resignation, she wrote: "dissatisfaction with the role of a worker in a capitalist society; travel opportunity." As Scarlett O'Hara said: "I'll think about that tomorrow," and pull out the latest John le Carré novel. We land at San Francisco Airport. It is 12:30 A.M., EST.

10. Read: *my* field of research.

11. At one time this distinguished gentleman was an assistant professor at Harvard who was not promoted. Clearly a major error on our part.

# STUDENTS

# 4

# The University College

*Selectivity and Admission*

Higher education in the United States presents students (and parents) with a bewildering series of choices. Prospective students can select public and private colleges; denominational or non-denominational schools; single-sex and co-educational colleges; large and small institutions; specialized technological institutes; highly selective and prestigious colleges and others that practice open admissions. We have created an entire industry to make these choices more efficient: guides the size of large city telephone directories rate colleges much in the manner of restaurants, awarding stars for quality of teaching, cleanliness of dormitories, climate, food, and general happiness of the student body. School advisers and private consultants (for a sizable fee) will meet with prospective students and parents to refine initial choices into realistic possibilities, suggesting perhaps one famous school where the chances are small but higher than zero; a couple of places where the candidate has a better than even chance; and finally a safety school—if all else fails. A typical applicant may file ten applications.

Most young Americans do have a variety of options. Of the over 3,000 colleges and universities in this country, only 175 are considered selective,[1] and that leaves a lot of "unselective choice." Gaining admission to a selective private college may require good grades, recommendations, and resources. Chances for the applicant are improved because the quality of private institutions is closely correlated with the availability of scholarship funds. For example, since the 1950s most of the Ivy League has adhered to a "need-blind" admission and scholarship policy. Prospective students are evaluated without considering the family's ability to pay, and if they are chosen for the entering class on the basis of academic or other qualifications, the school will arrange a financial aid package (grants, loans, jobs) that should come close to meeting any shortfall.[2] Many of the better colleges offer academic merit awards (though not the Ivy League), and athletic scholarships have routinely widened the range of possibilities for entering students. Furthermore, in American higher education there is no simple relation between price and quality. Some of best and some of the worst are represented among the expensive schools, and many of the finest colleges are state institutions charging relatively low tuition and fees, particularly to residents.[3] There can be no question about the ability of American college students to explore real alternatives.

1. The term is used to indicate a college's capacity to pick and choose among applicants. Many colleges in the United States have relatively few options in selecting their entering classes—if they wish to fill available classroom seats. What this does to quality is fairly obvious. In 1985, Stanford accepted 15% of all applicants. That is highly selective. In the same year, the University of Arkansas accepted 99% of all applicants. That is not selective. See Edward B. Fiske, *Selective Guide to Colleges* (New York: New York Times Books, 1985), p. xiii.

2. I recognize that this is an idealized description of a system that works less well in practice. To receive aid, a student has to submit detailed financial information, including copies of parental income tax forms. The actual award is based on a formula that is not overly generous. Middle-class families with perhaps two children in college at the same time and an annual income of, say, $75,000 will not get much help; they may receive the offer of a loan on fairly favorable terms. These families may have to consider costs carefully in selecting schools for their children.

3. For example, tuition and fees at Sarah Lawrence College exceed those at Harvard and the University of Chicago. Jersey City State College has higher tuition and fees than the University of Michigan. See *Chronicle of Higher Education*, August 10, 1988.

## Noah's Ark: How to Get a Ticket

How do I get into a highly selective university college?
or,
How do I get my daughter/son into a highly selective university college?

We can define "highly selective" as meaning too many qualified applicants. At the margin, good people have to be kept out. Admissions officers face that task of inventing reasons for rejecting candidates, and candidates try to present themselves in the most favorable light so as to gain entry.

Even if we consider the very top group within the selective category—perhaps some fifty schools—the degree of difficulty in being admitted shows great variation. For example, in the Ivy League, Harvard, Princeton, and Yale each had nearly 13,000 applicants in 1985; between 17 and 19 percent of that group were accepted. Stanford, as already mentioned, with 17,000 applicants, selected 15 percent.[4] CalTech and MIT, with much smaller applicant pools—1,270 and 6,000 respectively—accepted between 30 and 34 percent. I do not think that it is easier to get into top institutes of technology. To some degree, the smaller number of applicants and the higher proportion of acceptances reflects self-screening: those without high-level scientific aptitude do not bother to apply.

The odds appear to be more favorable in major public universities. Berkeley, Michigan, and Wisconsin (Madison), each had between 12,000 and 13,000 undergraduate applicants in 1985. Berkeley and Michigan admitted slightly over half of those who applied, and Wisconsin took in over 80 percent. It is easier for some students to gain entry to public institutions because preference is given to in-state

---

4. Just to cite the numbers for a less selective private school, at New York University there were 10,000 applicants and an acceptance rate of 48% in 1985. Selectivity in American universities is essentially a postwar phenomenon. Before World War II, Harvard accepted some 50% of all applicants. Of course, there was selectivity in the form of discrimination against certain groups: Jews, blacks, public school graduates, etc.

residents, and that reduces the level of competition.[5] Whatever the odds and their variation, a lot of rejection slips are prepared every year by admission departments of our selective universities.

Selectivity in university admission is not at all unusual. Two characteristics, however, are peculiar to the United States: first, the comparative lack of selectivity practiced by 95 percent of our institutions of higher education; and secondly, the type of selectivity practiced by our leading private universities and colleges. In many parts of the world, the choices are or could be made by computer: an entrance examination consisting entirely of academic subjects is used to rank applicants and the number of vacancies determines those admitted, from first to last. That is essentially how it is done by each university in Japan. It is an inexpensive and relatively easily administered selection procedure.[6] Some would claim that it is the fairest method of determining eligibility. Highly selective American institutions could also rank applicants by scholastic aptitude test (SAT) scores, and leave the rest to a simple computer program. It would save a lot of money, time, and effort.[7] Would anything be lost?

Selection procedures in elite American institutions are

5. State universities frequently select students in certain broad predetermined categories: for example, the nine campuses of the University of California are supposed to admit the top 12.5% of state high school graduates. The top one third of high school graduates are guaranteed admission to one of the nineteen campuses of the California State University system. Students who cannot meet these standards do not bother to apply, thereby raising the percentage of acceptances.

6. The methods of selection vary from country to country. Japan uses a university-administered entrance examination. French university entrance is based on obtaining the *baccalauréat*, although the *grandes écoles*—the most prestigious advanced professional and technical schools operating outside the university system—require special examinations. Dutch universities employ lotteries to restrict entry into oversubscribed subjects, such as medicine. Compared to the approach favored by leading private universities in the United States, selection elsewhere (except for Oxford and Cambridge) is almost entirely formulaic and not at all personalized.

7. The annual budget of the Admission, Financial Aid, and Student Employment Office at Harvard is about $2.5 million. It employs approximately 25 professionals.

very different.[8] While objective criteria such as test scores and grades play a major role, they tend to be supplemented by subjective, qualitative, non-quantifiable, and personal components. I would describe the procedures as an exercise in social engineering, involving high school grades, essays, interviews, recommendations from teachers, and above all a general vision concerning the composition of an ideal freshman class. That ideal is most easily defined as an optimum degree of diversity—hence my allusion to Noah's Ark—within a framework of academic excellence, thereby maximizing the opportunity of students to learn from each other. The desired degree and type of diversity will differ from place to place and time to time. I will attempt to describe the most important classes that are considered today in private universities. Most of these will apply without modification to selective independent colleges and some are also considered by public universities.

One group that—for all the right reasons—has the easiest time in opening university doors consists of the *academically highly talented.* I do not use this term lightly. At the Stanfords, Princetons, and Berkeleys, all undergraduate students can be said to have "some" academic talent or they would not be permitted on the premises. I mean something rather different. Every year there graduate from high schools a small group of students with truly outstanding academic qualifications: some with cumulative SAT scores approaching 1600, achievement scores of 800, and 5's on advanced placement examinations. Others may show precocious science talent, or perhaps overall grade records that achieve near perfection in schools whose standards of quality are widely recognized. My guess is that Harvard annually gets no more than 200 to 400 applications that fit this description (out of 13,000), and here is a group that can write its own ticket. Top schools will fight over these

8. My discussion is largely confined to universities, because that is for me more familiar territory. I have, however, been advised that admissions procedures are nearly identical in the leading independent liberal arts colleges.

academic superstars even if they behave strangely in the presence of alumni interviewers or threaten to attend class barefoot. Such candidates—so rich in brains—have the least difficulty in passing through the eye of the needle, but do keep in mind that the term "academic talent" is used at a most elevated level.[9]

Another group consists of *legacies* and their close relative, *faculty children.* Both are treated on an "all other things being equal" basis. At Harvard, legacies are the sons and daughters of the graduates of Harvard and Radcliffe Colleges. At Stanford, they are defined as the children of all alumni—i.e., including the graduate and professional schools. Definitions vary. Faculty children are applicants whose parents are professors in one of the university's schools. Some 16 to 20 percent of Harvard's freshman class probably belong to one of these two categories. By "all other things being equal," I mean that legacies and faculty children will be given preference provided that their other qualifications are as strong as those with whom they have to compete. In other words, if there are two candidates with identical qualifications—a most unrealistic supposition in practice—the legacy or faculty offspring will be given preference.

Can these preferences be justified? Only in terms of the cultivation of loyalty within groups that are vital for the future well-being of any institution. Private universities depend on alumni financial donations and other forms of support to ensure continued or rising levels of economic and intellectual prosperity. There is some relationship between a school's wealth and its quality, and the bulk of that wealth consists of gifts made by graduates. For these reasons, it is

9. I asked a leading Ivy League dean of admissions: are the academically talented ever rejected? He made two important points. First, the term is not defined exactly the same way in all schools. A borderline case at, say, Yale may qualify as academically talented at a less selective school. Secondly, admissions officers have to be alert for "personal fragility." Great academic talent has to be combined with a personality sufficiently robust to withstand four years of undergraduate life. And finally, even the most generous "need-blind" schools tend to behave somewhat less generously toward foreigners. This could apply even to academically outstanding applicants.

vital for a private university to strengthen its ties with individuals and families. That is done—across generations—by encouraging the presence of legacies in the student body. Similar reasoning applies to faculty children. Those who run the university know that faculty quality is the most important factor determining relative institutional standing. One way of attracting and retaining the best faculty is to make available a scarce good under preferential circumstances: places for their offspring in the entering class—other things being equal. I should add that a large majority of legacies and faculty children do not need preference of any kind. As a group, this is usually a very strong pool of applicants.

The relationship between universities and some secondary schools can also acquire a special character, but this is a far less weighty factor than in the past. A number of well-respected public and private high schools have for many years directed a stream of first-rate applicants to our leading universities. At Harvard, there come to mind names like Andover, Exeter, and Boston Latin. After a while, these relations assume a family-style character. We learn to know and trust the recommenders and the type of student produced by a particular school. In turn, the high school expects that a fairly steady number of its applicants will be admitted. A major downward deviation from the historical norm would raise questions and cause distress. It does not happen frequently. And yet these ties have weakened during the last generation and the cause has been the ever-widening search for students. A small group of feeder schools could no longer satisfy the appetite for a sufficiently diverse group of candidates.

A more recent purpose that will—negatively or positively—affect some applicants is the goal of *national* and to a lesser extent *international representation.* Harvard, and similar American colleges, wish to be national schools, certainly since World War II, and the only way that can be achieved is by recruiting students from all parts of the country. Much more recently, many schools have also wanted to become

more international, and that means students from different
parts of the world. These goals are justified on educational
grounds: students (and teachers) benefit from geographical and cultural diversity. That is the way of the real world,
and certainly the nature of our own society. Different regional, national, and international perspectives add challenge and interest to education at all levels. These principles, when put into practice, have clearly favorable
consequences for some applicants. More students apply to
Harvard from Massachusetts, New York, and California
than from other states. Other things being equal, the applicant from these states faces tougher competition.[10] To
apply from rural Oklahoma or from a small town in South
Carolina may be an advantage. Residence in New York City
or one of its middle-class suburbs can raise the hurdle. It is
simply easier to stand out in a smaller pool of applicants:
best in Oklahoma or Vermont is more attainable than best
in New York City and may bring sufficient visibility. The
attitude toward foreign applicants is rather more schizo-
phrenic. "Internationalizing the university" is a most popular slogan on all of our better campuses, but putting this
desire into practice is extremely expensive. We strongly
wish for the presence of undergraduates from foreign
countries, yet very few can afford the high cost of an American education without large scholarships.[11] In general,
higher education in the United States is remarkably "need-
blind" for its own citizens by supplying grants, loans, and
various low-cost alternatives. For foreigners, however, a

10. But other things are only very rarely equal. Students from Massachusetts, New
York, and California will, on average, come from superior public and private
schools, and are thus able to submit better SAT scores. The number of legacies in
these states is also large. The main thing to remember is that an advantage in one
area is likely to be counterbalanced by some other factor. In the end, the admission decision depends on a weighted average of all relevant factors.

11. There certainly are quite a few rich foreigners anxious to send their children
to college in the United States, and there are colleges that cater to their needs. For
us—the highly selective institutions—the problems are more difficult. We want to
attract the best foreign students, regardless of parental wealth. In most countries,
salaries of civil servants, teachers, employees, will place American education out
of reach. Sometimes, exchange controls are a complicating factor. In practical
terms, very few foreign students can get their degrees without significant financial
aid.

budget constraint tends to be applied, especially at the undergraduate level; funds for these students are strictly rationed. It may still be possible for an individual foreign applicant to stand out more easily in a small group, but the average foreigner will be at some disadvantage.

Yet another group that has become targeted during the last twenty-five years consists of *underrepresented ethnic minorities:* primarily blacks, Hispanics, native Americans, and to a lesser degree Asian Americans. The search for these students is the equivalent of affirmative action in employment. Top university colleges desire to be national not only in the geographical but also in the ethnic sense; they wish, if at all possible, to educate students from all segments of our heterogeneous population. We believe that students learn a lot from each other, and that greater diversity enriches these opportunities. We also believe that education, particularly in selective schools, is one path leading to upward social and economic mobility, and are anxious to make available these advantages to segments of the population that have been, and in many cases still are, victims of discrimination and exclusion.

At the present time, these groups require affirmative recruitment and positive encouragement. They have to be convinced of a genuinely welcoming attitude; that financial barriers can be overcome by scholarship aid; and that potential personal and group gains outweigh inevitable feelings of loneliness and strangeness, at least at the beginning. I am not suggesting that these feelings are entirely absent for other categories already considered as passengers for the annual departure of our Noah's Ark. Far from it: there is a great deal of overlap. Many applicants belong to more than one category, but I think few will dispute that blacks, Hispanics, and native Americans—and some Asians—need the most positive reinforcement.[12]

12. I keep separating Asians from other minorities. In fact, the description "Asian" is much too broad. Americans of Japanese, Chinese, and Korean descent are the most "overrepresented" groups in higher education: fewer than 2% of the national population and well over 10% of the student bodies in our most selective schools (14% at Harvard, 20% at MIT, 21% at CalTech, 25% at Berkeley in

The groups that require and can take advantage of positive reinforcement are both broader and narrower than underrepresented minorities. For example, Harvard makes special efforts to enroll graduates of Boston and Cambridge public schools as part of its responsibility in the local community. (In fact, these schools are heavily black and Hispanic, illustrating an earlier point concerning overlap.) And schools that project an excessively male image— and that applies, I think, to nearly *all* university colleges— need to encourage women applicants. We know from experience that parents tend to be concerned about excessive competition in university colleges, the dangers of urban life, and the high cost of tuition—all problems that unfortunately still become magnified when dealing with daughters.

Up to now, I have described the social engineering that takes place in university college admissions from the point of view of some specially favored groups. Many applicants do belong to one or more of these groups, and many will belong to none. Not all of us can be academically gifted black women from rural Oklahoma, with mothers who graduated from Radcliffe. How, then, are the applicants chosen?

To begin with, everyone has to achieve a satisfactory level of academic competence—to meet what I would describe as high average academic standards. Cumulative SAT scores will rarely fall below 1100 and are typically 1400 or better; high school grade records will generally average A- or better; class standing in the upper quarter

---

1987–88). I am not suggesting that proportional representation should be our standard—although there is no other way to understand the terms "under" or "over" representation—but these numbers do indicate that some Asians have little difficulty in finding the best schools. On the other hand, Vietnamese, Cambodians, Laotians, Filipinos, and Indians may need as much assistance as, say, blacks.

I should also note that some Asian groups—especially Japanese and Chinese Americans—are claiming a certain amount of "affirmative inaction" in the form of "quotas" or limits on their representation in undergraduate populations. This highly controversial grievance might be more plausible if our admissions procedures relied on only a few indicators: grades and/or test scores. In my opinion, the complaint loses its validity in light of the much broader and more complex system described in this chapter.

would be required and most students will be in the top 10 percent; and teacher recommendations should stress quality and love of study. Certainly, no one will be admitted who is believed incapable of completing a demanding course of study, no matter what other attributes the candidate may possess. These are the necessary conditions, but they are not sufficient. It is important to rise above the crowd; to show that beyond living up to a high average standard, one can do "something" very well. An American student body is a residential community, active around the clock. The community fields teams that play athletic sports—intramural and varsity.[13] It is home to theaters and orchestras playing all types of music. Students write for and publish newspapers and engage in many forms of social action. The community needs poets, singers, basketball players, and political leaders. Academic departments also need students who will major or concentrate in all subjects that are offered. Not all undergraduate concentrations achieve a level of popularity that keeps professors sufficiently occupied, and contrary to certain unkind myths, that does not satisfy the departments offering less popular subjects. Even with gains in recent years, fewer women than men choose the hard sciences. Until recently, the physical sciences, in general, attracted a relatively small number of undergraduates. Departments of the classics can usually handle more students very easily. To indicate an intention to major in a subject that is searching for increased undergraduate enrollments may in a particular year boost one's chances for admission, although it is difficult to find out which departments are facing a shortage. Changes from year to year are considerable.

And so—gradually and annually—the entering class takes shape. Think of the dean of admissions as a sculptor turning clay into a beautiful work of art. Any special quality

13. Perhaps I should have described student athletes as a special class of applicant, analogous to legacies or minorities. In many schools that would, unfortunately, make sense. However, selectively is inversely correlated with athletic success *and* excess, and that is why I have included athletes as part of a much larger group.

or indication of excellence will improve the applicant's chances. A few desirable qualities are ascriptive: the applicant is or is not a member of a certain minority or a legacy. On his or her own, little can be done to become a member of a preferred group. Most qualities are based on achievement, and are affected by individual effort.

I have described the admissions procedures employed by our leading private universities.[14] There are individual variations, but the essential characteristics remain the same: a flexible, complex system that considers many variables, and that—at least implicitly—expresses a point of view concerning the social order. Is this system "fair"? Is a system that relies exclusively on an entrance examination or high school grades or diplomas fairer? Our system has many virtues. Applicants who receive some ascriptive preference are the beneficiaries of social or institutional priorities, and their number is not large enough to exclude too many able individuals without these advantages. My guess is that at most one third of the entering class at Harvard begins the admissions race with some handicap in their favor, but a significant proportion of that group would gain entrance without an initial advantage. For example, we can assume that legacies are just as smart as the average of other applicants, and they are more likely to have attended good preparatory schools. I also think that a consideration, in most cases, of the complete individual—beyond grades and examinations—makes sense and is in keeping with the American college's emphasis on liberal education. Undergraduates attend these schools not primarily to study a specific academic subject, but to grow and mature intellectually and socially. Our system also is forgiving, and tries to recognize the promise of a late bloomer. We are more concerned with the attainments of applicants at graduation than their standing at the point of entry, recognizing that

14. Selectivity, as already shown, is not confined to leading private universities. On the contrary, in the American system of higher education, selectivity is practiced in many public universities and in our better colleges. The greater the degree of choice, the closer their practices will resemble the description provided here.

not all begin the race with equal advantages. It is a most complex system, mixing consideration of social mobility, institutional loyalty and self-interest, academic ability, and consideration of other talents, ranging from being a fine place-kicker to playing the violin. I believe it to be as fair as other alternatives, and for three reasons.

First, ability to pay plays the smallest possible role in determining who gets in. True, admission is not the same thing as attending, and some lower- and middle-income families face financial obstacles, but by and large the need-blind system—as defined in the Ivy League and some other institutions—offers considerable support to all eligible applicants. Indeed, it is one of few social processes in our country in which the advantages of the rich are so consciously limited.[15]

Secondly, the system is not corrupt: pull, personal influence, bribery—buying your way into Yale or Duke—are inconsequential factors. In nearly all instances, the choices are made by admissions committees with strong faculty representation and reflect their best judgment, with minimal outside influence. Alumni, public figures, donors, and similar types try from time to time to exert extra influence on behalf of their children, relatives, and friends. Every fall, long-lost friends and casual acquaintances suddenly reappear, sometimes bearing little gifts, and express the strong desire to have me meet their children. They drag in awkward teenagers supposedly in search of avuncular advice: young people who would much prefer to be elsewhere. The true purpose of the visit is to request a letter of recommendation from me to the Harvard admissions office. In some cases, circumstances force me to acquiesce, but I always

15. I do not wish to appear naive. Having money is always advantageous, and rich is better than poor in claiming one's share of all that society has to offer. In admissions, ability to pay matters most as an indicator of previous circumstances: better education in primary and secondary school, a more supportive home atmosphere, greater respect for intellectual achievement. And yet, the advantages of wealth remain limited. In buying a house, the person with the most money can nearly always acquire the property. In hiring a first-class lawyer, wealth is a major advantage. In gaining admission to a university college, that power is far more attenuated.

inform the supplicants that a laudatory communication from a high school teacher is far more valuable. My letter, usually based on superficial knowledge, means little. It will not harm an applicant, and will at the very least assure an especially polite and personalized letter of rejection.[16] Americans know that I am telling the truth—I hope. Some years ago, Harvard rejected the granddaughter of one of its major donors and alumni leaders. It could not have been an easy decision, but the dean of admissions evidently had no other choice and called the grandfather to give him advance notice of the bad news. Much to the surprise of all concerned, the old gentleman expressed a certain sense of relief. A rather convenient result, he believed, because when friends bothered him for help in the future he could easily decline. After all, his word counted little—"they even rejected my granddaughter!"

Foreigners have a harder time believing that a scarce good can be rationed without the existence of a black market. I know a number of foreign parents who are falsely convinced that I am solely responsible for getting their offspring into Harvard. One especially interesting episode may be worth retelling in slightly disguised form. A gentleman from West Asia (GWA) of great wealth and achievement wanted to get his son into the college. We had a mutual acquaintance and this led to a number of telephone conversations on the subject. I assured GWA that all depended on the son's qualifications; nothing else was important. GWA did not appear convinced. The son was admitted without my lifting even an ineffective finger—he was an excellent student—and GWA called from very far away to express his great gratitude. Mrs. GWA, overcome by emotion, could be heard sobbing over the telephone. I disowned all attempts to give me the smallest amount of credit.

16. My good friend the president of Harvard sends out a well-disguised form letter in answer to all these requests. It says that "the statutes of the University" forbid his interfering in any way with admission procedures. I can sympathize with his reluctance to get involved. It is a "no-win" game.

A few months later, a young woman called from Boston's Ritz Carlton Hotel. In a slightly accented voice, she identified herself as GWA's confidential secretary carrying (what else?) a confidential message. I pleaded an overloaded schedule, but agreed to step out of my office whenever she arrived to shake her hand and accept the message. That is exactly what happened: in the late afternoon I ran out of an appointment, shook a charming hand, stuffed an envelope in my pocket, and returned to whatever unpleasant interview had just been interrupted.

At about 6:30 P.M., before going to a cocktail party, I opened GWA's message. The envelope contained a brief greeting and two first-class open airline tickets—one in my name, one in my wife's—round trip from Boston to GWA's home country. Now, open airline tickets are the equivalent of cash, but of course this was not a bribe, only perhaps an inappropriate expression of misplaced gratitude.[17] Still puzzled, I went to the cocktail party where I ran into the university president. The moment I began telling him of my strange encounter, he slapped his forehead in astonishment and explained that the young lady had also favored him with an envelope. It lay unopened at the office. We ran back and found—no surprise—two more tickets.

The next day I wrote a rather long letter to GWA; somewhat sanctimoniously I explained Western conceptions of merit, individual achievement, and appropriate donations. All four tickets were returned with my letter, together with what I still believe to be a high point of decanal prose: ". . . as a Harvard parent you will find many other ways to express your gratitude to the university." He had no difficulty in taking the hint: one of our faculties now has a GWA Chair!

Despite this story, I remain certain that many foreigners are not at all convinced by our proclamations in favor of

17. I say perhaps, because my wife was furious and felt degraded by what she saw as a crude attempt to give us cash. Somewhat paradoxically, she added that if the gift had been an art object of equivalent value—recognizing that we were people of taste—her attitude would have been friendlier.

merit. They still believe that pull and favoritism have to be involved—a conclusion that is most unfair to their very able children.

My third reason for claiming fairness is related to the misleading simplicity and deceptive justice produced by systems based exclusively on objective examinations. University entrance examinations in, say, Japan, or end of school examinations in France—or, for that matter, SATs in the United States—are achievement tests. They measure how well students have absorbed information and skills in primary and secondary school. This is not a neutral measure; much depends on the quality of pre-university schooling, supervision and intellectual stimulation at home, and time available for mental pursuits. And these factors are closely tied to socioeconomic status. Although it appears that, for example, the Japanese system treats all high school graduates absolutely impartially, we know that entrance to Kyoto or Tokyo University is easier for those belonging to middle and upper middle classes. The reason is that students from these families attend better public and private schools and are the beneficiaries of superior preparation and coaching from early childhood. That is no fairer than the American system of acting, in part, on the basis of much broader preferences. In both cases, preferences exist, but ours seems to me to encourage greater economic and social mobility.

# 5

## Making Choices

In the words of the German proverb, choice is torment *(die Wahl ist die Qual),* and I have long had the impression that we—parents, students, teachers, society in general—make far too much fuss concerning the selection of a school. Every April young people suffer heartbreak when receiving "thin" as opposed to "thick" envelopes from their top choices. Parents join in this sadness and imagine their offspring four years hence, unable to gain admission to a leading law or business school, and that could mean less interesting and less lucrative careers. Yet these fears are almost always misplaced. A career depends on far more than where one went to school, particularly in our large country with its distinct areas and strong regional pride. Those occupying leading positions in any field of endeavor—profession, business, government—will be graduates of a surprising number of undergraduate institutions, reflecting both the three thousand-plus colleges in the United States and the rewards that our society still bestows on individual achievement.[1] No American school can hope to have its alumni dominate the upper echelons of any field. Only the service academies are a possible exception, and even in this instance it is worth recalling that some of our most successful military leaders—General George C. Marshall being an outstanding example—never studied at West Point or Annapolis.

I have said that Americans have real choices in their academic life, that these real choices imply real differences, and that that is not sufficiently understood by those contemplating where to study. Every year, as dean of the Faculty of Arts and Sciences, it was my pleasant task to give a recruitment speech to those young men and women who had been granted early admission to Harvard College. This is an academically distinguished group of slightly over six hundred prospective students that we are especially eager to enroll in the freshman class. I understood my task well, having performed it many times, and this particular year gave one of my most patriotic—some would say chauvinistic—Harvard talks: this is *the* place, none is better, going elsewhere is a dreadful error; in so many words, a hard sell. The next morning when I reached my office at 7:30 A.M. the phone rang, and somewhat to my surprise the caller was a young man who had heard me speak yesterday. He declared himself confused, anxious, and desperately in need of an interview. Since business would not begin for another hour or so, I invited him to come over.

The young man who arrived a few minutes later was quite earnest, and appropriately self-centered—at the beginning of our interview. He acted as if the choice of school was, in long-term significance, on par with choosing a wife

1. In support of this proposition, I offer as an example the senior faculty of Harvard's Economics Department. Out of thirty full professors, all of them recognized authorities in their subject, four graduated from Harvard College, three from UC-Berkeley, two from Oberlin. Other colleges represented by only a single graduate were Michigan, Dartmouth, Rochester, Reed, Bowling Green, CCNY, Northwestern, Brown, University of Washington, Cornell, William and Mary, MIT, Connecticut Wesleyan, Johns Hopkins, and Princeton. Foreign universities included Amsterdam, Budapest, Ontario Agricultural, and Barcelona.

or husband. Many young people, egged on by their parents, share this view. Would Harvard make him happy? Could he find the right kind of intellectual companionship? Was he more serious than most of our students—that was another of his worries. Any other problems, I asked? Yes, his father, an alumnus, was pressuring him to go to Harvard—a typical situation. The visit to Cambridge and our propaganda had not eliminated all doubts. He was interested in Brown and Haverford. Could I help? Some of what follows I said to the young man; the rest I should have said.

## The Advantages of a University College

Let us try to forget your father. His preferences are not too important. He wants what is best for you, and as an adult you have to make your own choices. Parents in general tend to view their alma mater with great nostalgia—a relatively unwholesome emotion. No one ever put that better or more tongue-in-cheek than John Buchan,[2] at a Harvard commencement in 1938:

> . . . on one thing we shall all be agreed. I am speaking to a gathering of alumni, of former students, and we must regretfully confess to each other that the great day of Harvard is over. The great day of every university on the globe is over. At some date about forty years ago a golden age dawned on the world. Its beginning coincided with the appearance in Cambridge of the older members here today. In that age, life was more interesting than it can ever have been before; men were bolder and more humorous; friendship was a richer and warmer thing; the world was a succulent oyster waiting to be opened. Let some new Gibbon explain how the decline began; the subject is too painful for those who have suffered from it. It is sufficient to say that brightness has fallen from the air

2. 1875–1940, first Baron Tweedsmuir. Diplomat and author of many wonderful adventure stories, including *The Thirty-Nine Steps* and *Prester John.* A favorite author in the second decade of my life. See *Harvard Alumni Bulletin,* vol. 40, July 1, 1938, pp. 1142–43.

and the twilight of the gods descended. The few good men who are left from that time are now like Falstaff, fat and growing old, but at any rate they keep some rags of decency about them and are determined to testify to unbelievers of the great era in which they once lived. I am sure there is no one here today, however pitiless his optimism, who will deny that since we ceased to be undergraduates civilization has most grievously declined.

Despite these feelings of decline since their undergraduate years—a decline contradicted by all known facts—these alumni wish to strengthen the bonds between parents and children through shared experiences at the same school.

Of course, there are nice aspects to attending your parents' school, to be considered a legacy. Feelings of tradition and continuity are noble emotions; they encourage us to live up to high standards. On the other hand, showing independence can also be virtuous: you may understand your own needs much better than anyone else. The time may have come to emerge from your father's shadow.

That you are torn between Harvard, Brown, and Haverford may indicate some confusion. Frankly, the differences between Harvard and Brown are relatively minor; but the differences between both of them and Haverford are more significant. You can get a superb education at any of the three schools, but before making a choice you should carefully consider each major type of college and what it has to offer. I cannot possibly discuss the advantages and disadvantages of all types; there are too many varieties, my experience is limited, and it would not be easy to surmount my own prejudices. I do not, for example, share the popular view that small is always beautiful. Students often complain about the impersonality of large classes. My question for them: is there anything worse than a badly taught small class? I do know the genus university college very well—Harvard and Brown both belong in that group—and will try to explain its main features. By implication you may also get a better understanding of other varieties.

There really is no rigorous definition of university college. At the most inclusive level, I intend merely to refer to that part of a university that offers undergraduate instruction and grants the bachelor's degree. Thus a university college is a part of a larger whole, a university, that includes graduate and professional schools. Harvard, for example, offers professional graduate education in business, law, medicine, dentistry, public health, divinity, public administration, architecture, and education. In addition, the graduate school of arts and sciences trains scholars in all the traditional academic subjects, from anthropology to zoology. Only about one third of our students are undergraduates, enrolled in the college—6,500 out of 17,000. Undergraduates draw more attention to themselves than all other students combined, and their leaders like to leave the impression that they speak for everyone. I suppose that this is understandable: they have more time for hijinks, politics, noisy demonstrations and the like, activities that appeal to the media and interest alumni. Furthermore, there is a strange American habit that discounts the ties formed by graduate education. A *true* son or daughter of Harvard is a former undergraduate. A graduate degree bestows at best the status of a cousin, except when fund drives are in progress. At that time we are all one happy family.

A proportion of one-third undergraduate students is typical of large private universities. (Public universities are likely to be associated with an even larger array of professional schools.) Small universities with fewer professional schools and a larger proportion of undergraduates also exist—Princeton, Dartmouth, and a few others come to mind. The general point is that graduate, professional, and undergraduate education coexist in universities, and ordinarily college students are a minority in a larger setting. This applies to Harvard, Brown, and the University of Alabama. It is not true at Haverford, where the principal educational mission of the faculty is to instruct candidates for the first higher degree.[3]

These differences are anything but trivial. Universities tend to be large, busy places, most frequently located in urban areas.[4] University students range widely in age, from eighteen-year-old freshmen to mature individuals returning for professional training after many years in "the real world." The faculty range is equally wide: clinicians, lawyers, architects mingle with scientists, economists, and philosophers. While there is no such thing as the average (non-university) college, the ideal American vision for this type of school is far removed from the hustle and bustle of urban life. We are apt to think of a well-tended garden inhabited by young men and women, all between the ages of eighteen and twenty-two, surrounded by a suitable number of kindly mentors. Of course, these are only stereotypes, no more, no less.

Ambience may make a lot of difference, but intellectual distinctions are more important. Most of the graduate programs in a university do not affect the undergraduates in any way. Professional education is self-contained and inward-looking. The presence or absence of a law, business, or medical school is hardly noticed by the university college student. What does matter greatly is the need or opportunity to coexist with a graduate school of arts and sciences, the training ground for future generations of scholars. This has profound consequences for all concerned.

Contrast the teacher or professor in both settings: in the university college and what I will call the independent college. (Distinctions will be drawn between ideal types.) The

3. As usual, one could cite a whole series of exceptions and complications. Some colleges offer limited graduate programs and could just as easily call themselves universities. That applies to my own alma mater, the College of William and Mary in Virginia. Some have changed their names in recent years to reflect a new emphasis. Pennsylvania State College is now a university, and the town in which it is located changed its name from State College to University Park. There are also universities without undergraduates. Rockefeller University is one of the rare examples.

4. One reason: it is difficult to operate a medical school without access to a large flow of patients, and that is nearly impossible outside of cities.

independent college teacher is chosen with greater emphasis on his or her pedagogical abilities. These institutions
are looking for first-class expositors who can instruct, inspire, and motivate undergraduates in their study of elementary and intermediate subjects.

Obviously the best independent liberal arts colleges are
looking for more than expositors. During the last few
decades research talent has come to play a greater role in
faculty selection at what Burton R. Clark has called "the top
fifty liberal arts colleges," a list that would include Haverford, Oberlin, Smith, Earlham, and Reed. This reflects
both the opportunities of a buyer's market for academics
that in recent years allowed colleges to hire new teachers
who could not find university jobs, and also a recognition
of positive elements introduced into the community by way
of research. Thus the distinction I am suggesting is blurred
at the margins, but as a matter of emphasis it surely remains
valid. According to Clark, at leading research universities,
33 percent of the faculty spend over twenty hours a week on
research. That number falls to 5 percent in the top colleges. In these same universities, 49 percent of the faculty
"lean towards research," as opposed to teaching; in the
colleges, 44 percent "lean towards teaching," as opposed
to research.[5]

In colleges, the setting in which instruction takes place is
likely to be intimate: small faculty, small classes, and small
student body. Consequently, concerns about personality
are magnified: is the teacher/professor caring? Available to
students? Are the lectures lively? Is she a good adviser?
These goals yield expected results: teaching faculties of
great competence, strongly motivated to help and support
the undergraduate. From the teacher's perspective, we
need to stress that there is relatively little opportunity for
instruction in the independent college to rise above the
elementary or intermediate level; very few undergraduates

5. It is curious that the hours spent on administration are very similar in both
classes of institutions. See Burton R. Clark, *The Academic Life*, Tables 8 (p. 78), 9
(p. 81), and 10 (p. 86).

can absorb more advanced material. As a result, the faculty feels less need to do research. Elementary and intermediate presentations of an academic subject change slowly, and the pressure to remain up to date and to understand the frontiers of a subject is weaker. There are no graduate students who have to be instructed in the latest and trendiest ideas. Furthermore, institutional recognition is not as closely tied to being a productive scholar. Of course, some college professors do research—distinguished research—and cultivate learning for its own sake.[6] In relative terms, however, undergraduate teaching takes precedence.

The university professor is a different breed of cat. He or she teaches undergraduates and graduates—a strong preference for graduate teaching is assumed by our critics—and status (standing among peers), advancement, salary, and other distinctions supposedly hinge more on research performance than anything else. How can this be defended when one of the principal missions of universities is to train undergraduates? Why would anyone be so masochistic as to opt for a university college when the comfort and care of independent four-year colleges—including "research colleges"!—are readily available at the same or perhaps even at lower prices?

For a moment, let us dream. You have decided to come to Harvard and are now a freshman strolling on the banks of the Charles River on a beautiful October afternoon. Your left hand is held by one of Harvard's Nobel laureates in Physics. She is explaining her most recent theories concerning the origin of the universe. Your right arm encircles the shoulder of one of our kindly English professors, win-

6. A recent study has identified forty-eight so-called research colleges, including Carleton, Franklin and Marshall, Mount Holyoke, Oberlin, Reed, Swarthmore, and Williams. At these colleges, a significant proportion of the faculty does research and presumably ability to do so is considered at time of initial appointment and promotion. These schools claim to be especially successful in training future scientists. One reason may be the absence of graduate students. College science researchers have to rely on undergraduates as assistants and partners, and that may inspire career choices. See Gene I. Maeroff, "Science Studies Thrive at Small Colleges," *The New York Times,* June 18, 1985. See also "The Future of Science at Liberal Arts Colleges," a conference held at Oberlin College, June 9 and 10, 1985.

ner of three Pulitzer Prizes. He has no theories to propound, but is asking whether you would prefer tea at Elmwood (the residence of President and Mrs. Derek C. Bok) or at the (John Kenneth) Galbraiths. Tea *chez* Galbraith is your desire because you have always wanted to meet Teddy Kennedy, Mrs. Thatcher, and Jerry Falwell. Wake up! This has never been a picture of reality—not along the Charles, the Cam, the Seine, or on the shores of San Francisco Bay. A university college has never consisted of five hundred Mr. Chipses surrounded by a few thousand adoring and adorable undergraduates.

A description of Oxford in the 1950s stresses another reality:

> Now, as in Gibbon's time, the life of the university proceeded at an even pace without in any way involving the undergraduates, who swarmed through the Colleges during term like an array of barbarian invaders, their drunken noise, brutish pleasures and sheer numbers briefly troubling the ordered calm of university life during the short periods of the occupation. The Fellows of the Colleges went on with their lives as best they could, dining magnificently in hall, pursuing their researches, splitting the atom, analyzing Mallarmé's *Un Coup de dés,* disputing the finer points of ecclesiastical history, but they represented the permanent and enduring role of Oxford as an institution of learning, and stood apart from the undergraduates as the older and more respectable Romans must have during the occupation of the Visigoths.
>
> It was certainly possible for an undergraduate to get an education at Oxford but it was not easy and it was not, in those days, at all necessary to try.[7]

Of course, this is also a caricature. The truth lies somewhere in the middle, but both descriptions contain large elements of truth: famous names present but not necessarily close to undergraduates; a more detached faculty preoccupied with its own affairs; certainly a more impersonal atmosphere. Another world can be found in the smaller

7. Michael Korda, *Charmed Lives* (New York: Random House, 1979), p. 371.

independent college, but only at a cost that includes greater paternalism, less diversity among faculty and students and a smaller coverage of the fields that encompass human knowledge. From the student's point of view, size and range of choice are closely related, and this applies to courses, friends, extracurricular activities, and certainly what we now call lifestyle. This is a pure value judgment, but I believe that university colleges are the most exciting of all alternatives for those students able to handle the challenge.

## Why Teaching and Research?

The exact number of university colleges in the United States is a matter of definition. There are hundreds; after all, most states have more than one public university. As mentioned in chapter 4, my use of the term is intended to be more restrictive. I have in mind at most fifty or so places: those colleges housed in our most research-oriented universities (examples include UC Berkeley, Cornell, Johns Hopkins, Michigan, Texas, and, of course, Harvard and Brown). These institutions differ in location, style, curriculum, selectivity, and principal sources of funds. But they share the strong and sometimes controversial belief that research and teaching are complementary activities; that university-level teaching is difficult without the new ideas and inspiration provided by research; and that an ideal intellectual balance for the professor includes undergraduate and graduate instruction.[8]

I will have to agree that the point concerning the ideal intellectual balance is not as strongly believed as the others. Some university teachers like to confine their instruction to graduate students, as if this was more elevated and interesting. More important, these individuals may believe

8. Some of the finest colleges also believe in the value of faculty research, even though the relative importance attached to this activity will be smaller. The opportunities to combine graduate *and* undergraduate teaching, however, are confined to universities.

that graduate teaching confers greater prestige. A few would prefer not to teach at all, and desire to spend all their time doing research. In general, the university social contract—almost always unwritten—is well understood: professors in universities are expected to spend half their time in teaching-related activities and half their time in research-related activities. Half of the teaching should be undergraduate instruction and half graduate instruction. These formulas cannot be applied rigorously or in a simplistic manner. For example, in the laboratory sciences, teaching and research are so intertwined as to be virtually indistinguishable. Nonetheless, what I have called a social contract does act as a useful and usually enforceable guideline.

The world looks different to students and professors. Students are apt to interpret an interest in research as a sign of little interest in undergraduate teaching. They are encouraged to believe that teaching and research are a zero-sum game[9] by representatives of schools where research is not emphasized. Similar sentiments are expressed in many guides to colleges. And sometimes, unfortunately, the behavior of a few university professors confirms the negative stereotypes: casually prepared lectures, office hours skipped, students snubbed, all in the name of some greater god called research. But this can happen without the excuse of research. Irresponsible behavior in teaching is not the monopoly of university colleges; it may, however, be more common there than elsewhere. Temptations in the form of leaves, consulting contracts, conference invitations, and similar activities are greater.

A combination of teaching and research is part of the university faculty identity. The university professor is not a teacher who is expected to confine him- or herself to the transmission of received knowledge to generations of students. He or she is assumed to be a producer of new knowl-

9. More of one means less of the other, or better research leads to worse teaching, and vice versa. A perfect example from a recent California report: "Excellence in undergraduate instruction is often sacrificed to the pursuit of excellence in research." See "California Colleges Are Said to Neglect Quality of Teaching," *The New York Times,* August 4, 1987.

edge, frequently with the assistance of apprentice graduate students, who transmits state-of-the-art knowledge to students at all levels. The interaction of undergraduate student with college teacher and undergraduate student with university scholar is intellectually different, not better or worse, but different; in fact, better for some and worse for others. And remember that we are discussing ideal types. One way of describing the difference is to suggest that it resembles the distinction between using primary and secondary sources; both are indispensable, but they do not perform the same function.

### Why Would an Undergraduate Want a Research-Oriented Teacher?

This question is rarely given serious consideration. Those who feel that a college student has nothing to gain from teacher-researchers tend to consider a "no-advantage" answer axiomatic, not requiring further explanation. That is the "zero-sum" attitude.[10] In contrast, individuals like me who believe that the axiom is invalid all too often treat the matter as a mystery—beyond the need for and incapable of rational explanation. I would like to make an attempt to eliminate some of the mystery.

To start with, what do we mean by research? Webster's Collegiate Dictionary (1936, my favorite edition) tells us that the activity consists of: "Studious inquiry; usually critical and exhaustive investigation or experimentation having for its aim the revision of accepted conclusions in the light of newly discovered facts." A few aspects of this excellent commonsense definition need to be highlighted. We can

---

10. See David S. Webster, "Does Research Productivity Enhance Teaching?" *Educational Record* (Fall 1985). There is an empirical literature that attempts to demonstrate the "no-enhancement" hypothesis. I find the results unconvincing. First of all, enhancement is largely measured in terms of student satisfaction as expressed in surveys (usually undergraduate students). That may be an important item of information, but it is only one very limited item. Secondly, research productivity is treated almost entirely in quantitative rather than qualitative terms. Most of all, I do not believe that the relation between research and teaching lends itself to simple—simplistic?—empirical analysis.

infer that reading and research are not the same thing. One can read merely for pleasure, or to keep up with a subject, or to learn a new skill; perhaps simply to acquire new information. None of these includes the aim of revising an accepted conclusion—of saying something "in the light of newly discovered facts." Of course, reading (and experimentation) are indispensable research activities, but it is a special kind of reading: purposeful, planned, and goal-oriented. Secondly, research and publishing, while not identical, are very closely related. For the "revision of an accepted conclusion" to be meaningful, it has to be announced, debated, and adopted or rejected, and that means some form of publication.

What draws us to this activity? The word "research" is now used so commonly, has been so vulgarized, that any answer must be carefully defined.[11] Most research is done for commercial purposes: to develop new products or improve the old with the aim of increasing profits and stockholders gains. In our country much of it is sponsored by the military, to increase offensive or defensive capabilities. I want to confine my speculations to academic research, where the commercial motive is weak.

Weak but rarely wholly absent. In many fields the fruits of academic research, through technology transfer, can have great commercial value. In recent years, a number of my acquaintances—among them molecular biologists and economists—have become multimillionaires. The trick is to commercialize some process invented in a laboratory or researched in a library, to acquire the backing of venture capitalists, and to go public. At that point, the originator of the idea—i.e., the professor—will have made a bundle. Whether or not the subsequent commercialization succeeds somehow becomes less important. Research can also bring recognition and even fame, either professional or with the general public. In our society, fame of almost any kind has cash value. Writing a best-seller, appearing on tel-

11. See Jacques Barzun, "Doing Research—Should the Sport Be Regulated?" *Columbia Magazine* (February 1987).

evision, or giving public lectures all can help to line the pockets of "underpaid" academics.

Still, in thinking about what draws faculty to research, two factors I take to be of uppermost importance. First comes love of learning. That may sound trite, sentimental, and self-serving, but nevertheless it is true. Career choices are affected by the requirements "of the trade." Those who opt for the military must have a certain predisposition toward uniforms, demanding physical challenges, and patriotism. Politicians have to feel some attraction toward people, power, and oral communication. And academics are students who never grow up—people who wish to remain students for the rest of their lives. Is this not one way to express a love of learning?[12]

That is only one side of the coin. On the other side are the demands imposed by professional advancement. Promotion, tenure, salary, esteem in universities are all closely associated with research and publication, and that tends to make the love of learning less pure. We write, study, and publish not only selflessly to share our ideas with the international community of scholars, but also to advance from assistant to associate professor or to get a 7 percent salary increase when the average raise is 6 percent. No doubt these pressures can lead to adverse consequences usually associated with the slogan "publish or perish." At worst, the outcome might be a "torrent of inflated books and papers [that] steadily increases the unlikelihood of any synthesis."[13] One would have to be very pessimistic, it seems to me, to assume that self-interested motives associated with personal advancement inevitably lead to inferior research. It may happen, but there is no reason to suppose that it is a typical result.

12. True, we all know of individuals who wish to remain on a campus forever—for the wrong reasons. I would describe this group as the Joe and Josephine Colleges who fear growing old. Their satisfaction stems not from the life of the mind but rather from a social atmosphere associated with the non-academic aspects of student life. As the years go by, they are less and less happy, rejected by youth and not respected by their colleagues.

13. Barzun, *op. cit.*, p. 21.

I am really trying to examine a different question alto-gether. Whether or not research benefits the individual so engaged—spiritually or financially—is also not the main issue. Nor is whether or not our universities encourage too much bad research *cum* publication, thereby spreading the intellectual disease of "specialism."[14] Why might an under-graduate student voluntarily and reasonably choose an in-stitution where the majority of professors see themselves as scholar-teachers? That is the question. The answer is not all that difficult.

Research is an expression of faith in the possibility of progress. The drive that leads scholars to study a topic has to include the belief that new things can be discovered, that newer can be better, and that greater depth of understand-ing is achievable. Research, especially academic research, is a form of optimism about the human condition. Concern-ing the previous question of student choices, I can now suggest the first part of an answer. Persons who have faith in progress and therefore possess an intellectually optimis-tic disposition—i.e., teacher-scholars—are probably more interesting and better professors. They are less likely to present their subjects in excessively cynical or reactionary terms.

Closely connected is the relation between research and the ever present danger of professorial burnout. In the next section, devoted to professors, I have pointed out some of the peculiarities of the academic calling, not the least of which is the expectation that as teachers we will carry out essentially the same duties for forty or more years. Once in possession of a professorial post—many of us become assistant professors in our twenties—there is

14. Excessive publication could perhaps be cured by a scheme proposed many years ago by an unknown genius. All initial academic appointments would be made to the rank of full professor. Every book published after the initial appoint-ment would bring an automatic cut in rank. Obviously people would only publish if they truly believed that they had to say something of enormous importance. Note an additional benefit. Undergraduates frequently complain that they lack contact with well-known senior professors, especially those made famous by their books. Now, the most active publishers would have to be junior faculty mem-bers—according to the critics, those traditionally relegated to undergraduate teaching.

almost no change in obligation until retirement at age seventy (or later if current folly prevails): primarily, to teach the subjects of one's expertise—and they may not alter very much during the course of a career. Theorists remain theorists; so do experimenters; and lecturers on Shakespeare do not in their declining years become professors of modern American literature. How to remain interested in one's professional duties is a major problem. It is hard to see how anyone can teach, say, introductory economics for over a quarter of a century without falling asleep at the very mention of the assignment. Of course, boredom as a consequence of long-term repetition is not uniquely an academic problem. Doctors looking at one more runny nose, lawyers writing another routine will, and every salesman who ever sold face these problems.

Each profession probably has its own ways to deal with burnout. In higher education, some find invigoration in the ever-changing generations of students. That is the Mr. Chips solution. He looked at the fresh young faces every fall and drew inspiration from his role as father to thousands of boys. Others do it by reading, becoming bookworms who amass learning year after year without giving much back in return. But by far the healthiest and most efficient method of fighting burnout is research. Unlike the somewhat grasping and passive bookworm, the researcher invests in him- or herself while interacting with an international world of critics and colleagues. These are not activities congenial to deadwood or burned-out cases: they cannot share in the stimulation of give and take. And so to the second part of my answer. A research-oriented faculty is less likely to be the home of intellectual deadwood. Active, lively, thoroughly current minds that enjoy debate and controversy make better teachers.[15]

The last part of my answer has to do with the difficulty of

15. In my many years at Harvard as a graduate student and as a teacher, I encountered my share of bad, most of all, unskilled teaching. But I never encountered a type familiar to me from college days: the older professor, reading from lecture notes yellowed by time. Occasionally one of these sheets of paper would fall to the floor and disintegrate into a fine powder.

evaluating the quality of teachers and teaching. How can we arrive at valid judgments? Ask the students; surely that is a most obvious way. Yet that is a method with some flaws. Students can tell us whether or not they like a teacher, whether or not the material in the course is interesting, whether or not the lectures are clear, stimulating, and perhaps amusing. To some degree, these are measures of popularity and may have little to do with the essence of teaching: to cause someone to understand a subject. Student opinion may be flawed by lack of experience and long-term perspective and by the pursuit of the pleasure principle. But there is no need to exaggerate. At Harvard, student evaluations show a significant positive correlation between rated quality of a course and workload. The pleasure principle need not be a synonym for sloth.

All of us who have reached advanced years can recall teachers whom we vigorously detested in high school or college, only to discover in more mature years the excellence of their instruction. As evidence, I can cite my own and nearly everyone else's high school Latin teacher. Most of us will also remember some much beloved "old doc so-and-so"—unfortunately a fixture on so many American campuses—who in our more mature memories reveals his true self to us as a pathetic windbag. I am certainly not suggesting that student evaluations are of little value. Research has shown otherwise. I am trying to say that they are guides to be used only with great caution. Other evidence is needed.[16]

How about peer evaluation of teaching? This method is also full of difficulties. A standard technique is to visit classes, especially of younger staff members who are being

16. "Major studies have been conducted over the past decade of the potential sources of bias and the reliability and validity of students as evaluators. By this time, these questions have been extensively studied, with the generally-accepted conclusion that, while, decisions regarding promotion and tenure should not be made on the basis of student evaluations alone, students are, as a group, responsible and reliable witnesses to the quality of instruction in their classroom." K. Patricia Cross, "Feedback in the Classroom: Making Assessment Matter," The AAHE Assessment Forum, Third National Conference on Assessment in Higher Education, June 8–11, 1988, Chicago, p. 6.

considered for advancement. That is likely to lead to a command performance that bears little relation to what happens in the classroom on a daily basis. (Unannounced visits, in many places, are viewed as breaches of etiquette.) In theory, one could have many visits—even daily visits—by groups of experienced teachers, but that is on the whole an impractical mode of operation.

I do not wish to be misunderstood. Much can be done to improve teaching.[17] Young teachers can and should be provided with a support structure that includes mentors, technical critiques, seminars, case studies, and so on. However, we are not going to transform college and university teaching into a science, and therefore we have to live with a lot of disagreement concerning individual merit. To put it slightly differently, the degree of professional consensus as to what is meant by outstanding teaching is not great.[18]

A far greater consensus exists regarding research capacity and achievement. In the sciences and to a lesser degree in other areas of scholarship, there is much agreement concerning the relative merit of individual scholars. Convincing reasons can be given to back-up opinions. Peer evaluation is the method of choice. It may, on occasion, be conservative, sometimes political and subject to conflict of interest, but in nine cases out of ten it produces clear answers that have a considerable degree of consistency and objectivity—at least when compared to evaluations of teaching.[19]

It may seem that I have strayed from the purpose of this chapter: to explain why one might, not *should,* prefer a re-

17. See *ibid.,* pp. 17ff.

18. "Many students of teaching would say, quite accurately, that after all is said, we don't know that final formula for effective teaching—we can't explain why some instructors have success while others have so may difficulties." C. Roland Christensen in Margaret M. Gulette, ed., *The Art and Craft of Teaching* (Cambridge: Harvard-Danforth Center for Training and Learning, 1982), p. xiv. This legendary Harvard Business School teacher also paraphrased Amy Lowell as follows: "Teaching is like dropping ideas into the letter box of the human subconscious. You know when they are posted but you never know when they will be received or in what form." Neither passage supplies testable propositions.

19. Tenure is granted after an exhaustive peer review. The discussion in chapter 11 on Tenure: A Model Case is quite relevant here.

search-oriented faculty as an undergraduate. I now return to that very point with a third and final argument. I believe that faculty selection based primarily on research perform- ance leads to fewer mistakes than choices based more on hard to define teaching ability. Both talents should be taken into account, but research ability is a better long-term indi- cator. Emphasis on more objective, even measurable, re- search standards should yield higher average quality in terms of recognized goals: lively, innovative, inquiring minds. With the power to sustain those qualities.

Professional teachers, as opposed to teacher-scholars, frequently attain a high degree of effectiveness in their pre- sentations. In this, they compare most favorably with their scholar colleagues. Many achieve great skill in using the Socratic method—skillful and creative guidance of class discussion. They tend to read the essays of their students with great attention and many are famous for the length and thoroughness of their comments. All this is wholly pos- itive for the student. Most of the time, the teachers will have to focus on other people's ideas; their principal role is to transmit those ideas in the classroom. Of course, no teacher-scholar could instruct without using the viewpoints and results of recognized authorities. All of us who teach act as transmission belts of knowledge developed in the past and by others. But there does remain a question of proportion, emphasis, and capacity. Lacking time or incli- nation for research, the typical college teacher can mainly hope to add critical commentary. And that will not be easy because in most colleges there are not enough colleagues working on the same or similar subjects against whom ideas can be tested. There is an absence of "critical mass."

Scholars in research universities tend to think of them- selves first as members of a particular discipline—econom- ics, English literature, physics—and only secondarily as teachers. Their students fall into two distinct groups: disci- plinary novices (graduate student apprentices), and under- graduates. The former require advanced instruction; the latter have to be initiated to subjects at elementary and intermediate levels.[20] Besides teaching, the university scholar does much else—writing articles and books, consulting, testifying, attending professional meetings, raising research money, and similar activities. Some of these activities may not be necessary; a few may be self-indulgent. The average university teacher is very busy, and undoubtedly less accessible than his or her colleague in a small college.

Is it better to study with someone who travels a lot, for whom you—the prospective undergraduate—represent only one small aspect of professional life, rather than with a professor possessing admirably pastoral virtues with you as a treasured member of the flock? It all depends. At their best, university colleges are among the most exciting places on earth. Their professors have written the books that people talk about; they have engaged in public controversies and have held vital public posts. (One of my teachers served as an ambassador; one of my departmental colleagues also held an ambassadorial post; another was a cabinet secretary; three served on the Council of Economic Advisers, one as chairman; many have advised presidents and foreign governments.) Of course, this kind of visibility can be dismissed as meaningless touches of glamour, but I would disagree. Intellectual excitement is enhanced by contact with people who have written books, done major experiments, and held policy positions in government. As teachers, they may give you a less balanced picture; perhaps they will be tempted to proselytize on behalf of their own ideas and discoveries (they can lay claim to both!). A few yield to temptation and become name-droppers. Still, the rewards generally outweigh the risks. If a great controversy agitates the public, someone at the university is likely to take part; different sides in the dispute are more often than not openly and vigorously represented.[21] When a

20. Reality may be less neat. One advantage of universities is that particularly talented undergraduates sometimes find it possible to study at the graduate level when they have reached junior or senior standing. Only their intellectual sophistication sets limits.

21. At Harvard, "Students can crowd into Prof. Gould's lectures on the History of Life and the Earth and hear his environmentally oriented approach to evolution.

major discovery occurs, someone will certainly be available to interpret its significance; frequently, one of the discoverers will be on campus. The universities, especially the top research universities, are home to every political point of view, lifestyle, and nearly all esoteric academic specialties. (At Harvard, for example, we offer instruction in over sixty languages.)

We say that opposites attract, but when it comes to students and teachers, I think that like attracts like. In our leading university colleges, student bodies are national and international. They are also contentious and accomplished, mirroring the faculty in the diversity of its interests and the range of political and social views.[22]

The accomplishments of some student stars can have a repressive influence on their peers. You like to write plays in your spare time? Well, somebody a few doors down the hall has had a one-act comedy performed Off Broadway. Your ambition is to publish a short story? The young woman in your creative writing course happens to be the author of a well-received first novel. The same type of pressure is true of athletic accomplishments—especially outside of the Ivy League[23]—and also for academic achievements. The kid sharing your lab bench may have won the

---

Then next period they can hear them rebutted by his archantagonist, Prof. Wilson, who, in his course on evolutionary biology, argues for the genetic basis of social patterns and human behavior." Fiske, *Selective Guide to Colleges*, p. 237. This experience cannot be duplicated in any independent college.

22. Some years ago I was reading *The New York Times* at breakfast. A front-page story reported an incident from Washington. President Reagan had invited national merit scholars to a reception at the White House. In the middle of the festivities, a young woman rose and gave the President a short, highly critical lecture concerning his policies in Central America. I turned to my wife and said with great confidence: "*She* is coming to Harvard." I was not wrong.

23. The Ivy League does not offer athletic scholarships and attempts rather successfully to cultivate amateur sports even at the varsity level. This is not a recent development. Some years ago, in China, I encountered a professor of economics at Peking University who had gotten a Ph.D. at Harvard in 1925. The old gentleman told me of his passion for American football and remembered that during his last year in Cambridge, Harvard lost every game. The *Boston Globe* ran a story with the headline "Harvard Destroyed." The story itself commented unfavorably on Harvard's athletic prowess, and went on to say that all the university had left was "academic distinction." I was able to tell our alumnus that—thank God—the improvement in athletics had been modest during the last sixty years. Our academic distinction, however, appeared to be more or less intact.

Westinghouse science prize. I am not suggesting that these are common occurrences, but these types do exist. Brooke Shields did attend Princeton; Yo Yo Ma was a Harvard undergraduate; and a Yale undergraduate woman designed the Vietnam War Memorial, one of the most powerful artistic statements of the last few decades. For some students, the presence of these stars becomes a barrier to participation; they tend to crawl into their own shell. If this kind of anxiety is a problem, you might wish to avoid the most competitive university colleges. I would go further. If you prize participation above all else—without special regard for natural or trained talent—choose a college that adopts a familial attitude (on the family softball team, all the members are *entitled* to play). Competition is never absent in university colleges. A position on the school paper, a part in a play, a place on an intramural team—all are the product of stiff face-offs, with winners and losers. Not everyone enjoys these battles. They may not fit your particular stage of development. You may not learn well under these circumstances. Others are stimulated to reach unexpected heights of achievement.

At Harvard, I have often heard it said that students learn more from each other than from their teachers. That could be taken as a disturbing comment. Should it be interpreted as a putdown of professors who allegedly prance behind the lectern but have only little direct contact with students? I think not. Rather, I see it as a compliment to a large, diverse, highly selected, and talented student body that—as a group—provides everyone who is a member with a unique opportunity for personal growth.

One last comment. A distinguishing feature of university life is the presence of graduate students; men and women, a few years older than undergraduates, working toward advanced professional degrees. For the most part they will ignore you, believing themselves to be above childish undergraduate concerns. But you will encounter graduate students as apprentice teachers, and that practice is a frequent source of criticism.

At the colleges that stand alone—that are not part of universities—there are no, or very few, graduate students, and teaching is done by "regular" professors. In extolling this type of school, you will hear a familiar refrain: big names and famous professors can be found at (for example) Rice, Minnesota, and the University of Washington, but these persons will not be your instructors. Your most common contact will be with graduate teaching assistants: callow and inexperienced youths, not infrequently foreigners who barely speak English. Would any intelligent person choose teachers like this? When I hear these accusations, I like to recall that as a teaching fellow at Harvard, three of my co-workers were named Henry Kissinger, Zbigniew Brzezinski, and James Schlesinger. Even though they were still graduate students in the early 1950s and two of them were afflicted with heavy accents, I am sure that their performance as teachers was at least adequate and not below the level achieved by good college teachers. In fact, I can see advantages in the use of graduate teaching assistants— beyond the opportunity to understand heavily accented English or to improve one's Chinese conversation.

These relatively inexperienced individuals are not in charge of courses; ordinarily, they are leaders of discussion groups or tutorials. As graduate students, they have to be thoroughly familiar with their subject. They are more likely to know the latest techniques and current controversies than their counterparts in the colleges. They will not bear the burdens of a generation gap, and most of them—as members of highly selective graduate programs—are extremely bright. True, lack of experience can cause occasional difficulties. And the absence of a generation gap can create social problems in class, especially for members of the opposite sex. You may also wish to have more opportunity for one-on-one discussions and disputations with the "great name." Perhaps. My only point is that graduate student teachers should not simply be seen as a disadvantage of university colleges. They may provide some of your most stimulating classroom experiences.[24]

Some of these things I said to my young friend who came to see me in University Hall at seven-thirty in the morning. Other things I did not have a chance to say—but given time, should have said. His choices were Brown, Harvard, and Haverford, and he did not know how to make up his mind. In the end, I had to agree that the choice was not easy. The differences were subtle. All three schools represented a high level of excellence. No choice was bad and all were extremely selective. The differences—though real— were a matter of degree. Later I heard that he had decided not to come to Harvard. I hoped that our discussion had enabled him to make an informed and right choice.

24. The system is far from perfect and much undergraduate criticism is justified. Teaching fellows or teaching assistants are selected too casually and too often have no training as teachers. They are hired even when flaws are known—at the expense of undergraduates—because of larger than expected enrollments requiring sections and also as a way of making available scholarship help to graduate students. All this is wrong and in need of rectification. Teaching fellows have to be trained, supervised, and hired only when they show sufficient aptitude for their assignments. See Gary D. Rowe, "Why Not the Best?" *Harvard Crimson,* November 23, 1987, and November 24, 1987.

# 6

## The Purposes of Liberal Education

For American students, there are many different reasons for going to college. A common purpose is to acquire the first professional credential, perhaps in engineering, nursing, accounting, or some other field. In other cases, however, the first degree is not intended to provide vocational training. That is especially true in university colleges attached to research universities and in so-called research colleges.[1] Students matriculating at these institutions frequently aspire to membership in the learned or liberal professions, for example, law, medicine, or university teaching. They face years of specialized postgraduate education. A majority of all students in these schools eventually pursue some form of graduate education. The purpose of college then becomes an education in the liberal arts—to study "a curriculum aimed at imparting general knowledge and developing general intellectual capacities in contrast to

---

1. Together, these institutions enroll approximately 15% of all U.S. undergraduates. See Burton R. Clark, *The Academic Life*, p. 18.

99

a professional, vocational or technical curriculum."[2] Indeed, the attraction and value of the liberal arts is not confined to those aiming for graduate school. This type of curriculum is a perfectly reasonable end in itself.

Liberal arts, liberal education, and sometimes general education, is one way to describe the four years of instruction in some colleges. Ordinarily, the four years are divided into three parts: a year of requirements focusing on breadth, frequently called distribution, general education (in the narrower sense), or a core curriculum. The equivalent of another year typically consists of electives: allowing students to pursue their own academic interests. Finally, two years—sometimes less—are devoted to a major or concentration in a special subject (English, sociology, mathematics, etc.). The totality of these studies, leading to a B.A. or B.S. degree, is education in the liberal arts.

There can be no scientific definition of liberal or general education because education is not a science. Widely accepted theories do not exist, and experimental or logical proof of the many historical and current visions is rarely possible. There is no single truth, but let me cite two views that I have found to be particularly congenial. First:

> General education means the whole development of an individual, apart from his occupational training. It includes the civilizing of his life purposes, the refining of his emotional reactions, and the maturing of his understanding about the nature of things according to the best knowledge of our time.

We owe this fine statement written in 1946 to Howard Lee Nostrand, sometime professor of Romance languages at the University of Washington.[3] Had he written more recently, the adjective "his" would have been coupled with

2. *Encyclopaedia Britannica*, 15th edn., vol. VI, p. 195.

3. Jose Ortega y Gasset, *Mission of the University*, (London: Kegan Paul, Trench, Trubner, 1946), p. 1. This slim volume was translated by Nostrand, who also supplied an introduction from which the quotation is taken. He also wrote: "If we could solve the problem of general education, we could confidently strike any Third World War off the calendar." An appealing thought, but I am less confident.

"her," but that is a minor matter. Instead, note the key phrases: "apart from . . . occupational training," meaning non-professional and discouraging pre-professional,[4], "the civilizing of . . . life purposes," implying an emphasis on culture and on life beyond earning one's daily bread; and "according to the best knowledge of our time," suggesting the possibility of periodic change.

A slightly different viewpoint comes from John Buchan, whose thoughts I cited in the previous chapter:

> We live in a distressed and chaotic world whose future no man can predict, a world where the foundations seem to be cracking and where that compromise which we have christened civilization is in grave peril. What must be the attitude of those like ourselves in this critical time, those who have behind them a liberal education? For if that education gives us no guidance in such a crisis it cannot be much of a thing at all.[5]

(What a depressing statement in view of the distressed and chaotic world in which we still live fifty years after these words were spoken!)

Buchan suggested that a liberal education should endow recipients with three qualities: humility, humanity, and humor. Humility, because "if we are educated men, with the treasures of the world's thought behind us, we shall not be inclined to overvalue ourselves or to claim too much for the work of our hands." For him, humility obviously presupposed knowledge. Humanity, because "We need a deepened respect for human nature. There can be no such respect in those who would obliterate the personality and make beings mere featureless details in the monstrous mechanism of the state." This was 1938. He was undoubt-

---

4. This phrase could be read as advocating the separation of the liberal arts from professional and pre-professional education. I much prefer to interpret it as suggesting that the whole development of an individual should not be confined to occupational training, narrowly defined. Under ideal circumstances, all types of education would contain general and special subjects. The current emphasis on developing programs in professional ethics is one example of the liberal arts— moral philosophy—taught in the professional context.

5. *Harvard Alumni Bulletin*, vol. 40, July 1, 1938, p. 1143.

edly thinking of Hitler and Stalin. Lastly, humor: "In a time like the present, when the ties of religion have been sadly relaxed, there is a tendency for popular leaders to exalt themselves in a kind of bogus deity and to think their shallow creeds a divine revelation. The answer to all that sort of folly is laughter."[6] I do not know what was on Buchan's mind, but in the 1980s these thoughts strike uncomfortably close to home.

Next, an obvious but essential point: we are living at the end of the twentieth century. The consequences of this trite observation need a bit of elaboration. In our age, knowledge grows in unprecedented quantities, frequently at exponential rates. Because new knowledge often is—or is believed to be—superior to old facts, methods, or theories, the life span of conventional wisdom in certain fields has appreciably shortened. Science provides the clearest examples. Publication of scientific journals began in about 1665. In 1800, there were about 100 journals; there were 1,000 by 1850, and some 10,000 by 1900. Currently, there are close to 100,000 journals, and since the seventeenth century their number has doubled every fifteen years. The rate of growth of scientists is similar, so that "some 80 to 90 percent of all scientists that have ever been, are alive now."[7] Another illustration can come from economics, where the classical consensus ruled for well over a century. Its successor, the Keynesian world view, became critically ill before reaching the age of fifty.

I do not wish to suggest the existence of simple quantitative relations, much less laws of intellectual progress. Fields and subfields differ; not everything grows at similar rates. While scholarship in the humanities undoubtedly is expanding more rapidly than in earlier times, it is much more difficult to be precise about changing generally accepted views. My point is much simpler: our period in his-

6. *Ibid.*, pp. 1143–1144.
7. Derek de Solla Price, *Science Since Babylon* (New Haven: Yale University Press, 1975). See chapter 8 (Diseases of Science) from which these figures are taken.

tory is characterized by an unusually rapid growth of knowledge, and it follows that the proportion of outdated facts and theories will also be unusually large. Classics of permanent value are confined almost exclusively to what today we refer to as the humanities. The Bible, Shakespeare, Plato, Confucius, and Tolstoi are as timely as when they were written. The basic issues of human moral choice—for example, justice, loyalty, personal responsibility, and others—have remained the same, and the quality of current thinking on these topics cannot easily demonstrate its superiority. This cannot be said even of the genius mathematician-scientist Isaac Newton, whose discoveries and methods have frequently been improved and sometimes supplanted by 250 years of scientific progress. Accomplishments in social sciences lie in between these extremes. For example, Adam Smith's great eighteenth-century vision of laissez-faire and David Ricardo's early nineteenth-century theory of comparative advantage have not lost their significance. Yet, the analysis of both conceptions has gone much beyond these early statements, and economists research and teach these theories with largely ceremonial references to the great figures of the past.

Rapid growth of learning means that "the nature of things according to the best knowledge of our time" is not static. It also means that curricular requirements have to strike a balance between enduring classics (reinterpreted for each generation) and the presentation of current best practice. The emphasis chosen will reflect the need of a particular subject, and a combination of the two approaches may be most appropriate. But there can be no doubt about the obligation to teach students to deal with an environment that produces ever more information and a continual flow of new theories and explanations. In many subjects, this may serve a better purpose than emphasizing a specific database or a currently popular theory.

For these reasons, Oxford in the fourteenth century, the University of Chicago in the 1930s, and Harvard University right after World War II are models of limited usefulness.[8] This is only rarely questioned when it comes to special education—i.e., competence in a recognized, well-defined subject—because we are more cognizant of intellectual progress in familiar categories. Many of us know that the physics of today is not what it was fifty years ago, or that the use of mathematics now is a common and necessary tool in the social sciences. Change is equally essential to maintain the goals of liberal or general education, and just as in special education the pace of change will depend on modifications of intellectual consensus. At present, it seems to me reasonable to expect major curricular changes every twenty-five years or so.

Another aspect of the present is a lengthened educational time horizon. A lifetime of learning applies to an ever larger share of the population. It is no longer adequate to prepare oneself just for the initial stages of a career. Now we face the opportunity or problem of adjusting to longer life and greater leisure. Middle age may bring career changes, and increases in life expectancy mean either employment at advanced ages or long periods of retirement.[9] The rapid pace of technical progress and changes in the industrial structure—for example, from manufacturing to services—will require many of us to learn new skills and to absorb new ideas at various points in life. All of us will have to adapt, and flexibility is particularly essential for women, because they are likely to wish or be forced to combine career and family. Very often that means reentering the labor force after a lengthy interval. Suppose that the absence lasts a decade. Many methods pertaining to work will

---

8. In medieval times, the seven liberal arts (trivium and quadrivium) consisted of geometry, astronomy, arithmetic, music, grammar, logic, and rhetoric. On the whole, still a good list, though seriously dated. Social science did not yet exist and literature was largely ignored. In much more recent times, the Harvard Red Book of the 1940s made no provision for the study of non-Western ideas. The same is true of the famous curriculum of the St. John's Colleges in Annapolis, Maryland, and Santa Fe, New Mexico. Their list of 130 classics is entirely confined to Western civilization.

9. It is a commonplace, though unsupported by hard data, that "these days" the "average person" has three careers and seven jobs.

have altered, many theories been discarded; new discoveries will have been made. An educated person should have a mind prepared for this environment.

At every commencement, the president of Harvard University welcomes new graduates of the college "to the fellowship of educated men and women." Similar greetings are voiced throughout the land by thousands of college presidents every June. What do they mean? What should they mean? A bachelor's degree may signify little more than the satisfactory completion of a fixed number of undergraduate courses. It is a matter of simple observation that not all college graduates are educated persons, nor are all educated persons necessarily college graduates. Clearly, we mean—in these ritual greetings—to imply that students have achieved a certain level of intellectual development. We do not expect them to be learned in the arts, sciences, or professions; indeed, we will have failed if the bachelor's degree signified the acme of their intellectual growth. Welcoming graduates to the company of educated men and women makes sense only if it expresses our belief that their mental skills and powers have met a reasonable standard.

Some years ago I attempted to formulate a standard for liberal education in our time.[10]

1. An educated person must be able to think and write clearly and effectively. By this I mean that students, when they receive their bachelor's degrees, must be able to communicate with precision, cogency, and force. To put it in yet another way: students should be trained to think critically.

2. An educated person should have a *critical appreciation* of the ways in which we gain knowledge and understanding of the universe, of society, and of ourselves. Thus, he or she should have an *informed acquaintance* with the mathematical and experimental methods of the physical and biological sciences; with the main forms of analysis and the historical

10. The next few pages rely on one of my annual reports as dean of the Faculty of Arts and Sciences. See Harvard University, Faculty of Arts and Sciences, *Dean's Report, 1975–76:* "Undergraduate Education: Defining the Issues."

and quantitative techniques needed for investigating the workings and development of modern society; with some of the important scholarly, literary, and artistic achievements of the past; and with the major religious and philosophical conceptions of mankind.

This ambitious definition may appear to be impractical. Most members of university faculties would have to confess their own difficulty in measuring up to such a standard. But that is a shortsighted view. First, to have a stated ideal is valuable in itself. Second, the general formulation that I have used does translate into standard areas, for example, physics, history, or English literature. I am not suggesting that each of these areas can be mastered by every educated person. But we are not in search of mastery; the goal is informed acquaintance and that can be adequately achieved—at any historical moment—by a set of requirements that has a sufficiently broad conception.

The leap from informed acquaintance to critical appreciation is more important and more difficult. To achieve that quality, we have to move beyond content to the general applicability of what is taught and how it is taught. The growth of knowledge is very rapid, and we should encourage our students to be lifetime learners. Time constraints are great and only certain subjects can be selected. We can expect a non-scientist to take science courses, but we cannot expect all of these students to study physics, biology, chemistry, geology, and mathematics. Therefore, the general utility of required subjects has to be especially great. Ideally, they should combine significant content with an emphasis on the larger methodology of a specific subject. For example, studying economics is all right from the point of view of liberal education, but considering that field in the general context of the social sciences is of much higher value.

3. An educated American, in the last quarter of this century, cannot be provincial in the sense of being ignorant of other cultures and other times. It is no longer possible to conduct our lives without reference to the wider world or to

the historical forces that have shaped the present and will shape the future. Perhaps few educated people will ever possess a sufficiently broad perspective. But it seems clear to me that a crucial difference between the educated and the uneducated is the extent to which one's life experience is viewed in wider contexts.

4. An educated person is expected to have some understanding of, and experience in thinking about, moral and ethical problems. While these issues change very little over the centuries, they acquire a new urgency for each generation when it is personally confronted with the dilemmas of choice. It may well be that the most significant quality in educated persons is the informed judgment that enables them to make discriminating moral choices.

5. Finally, an educated individual should have achieved depth in some field of knowledge. Here I have in mind something that lies between the levels of professional competence and informed acquaintance. In American college terminology, it is called a "major" or "concentration." The theory is straightforward: cumulative learning is an effective way to develop powers of reasoning and analysis because it requires the consideration of increasingly complex phenomena, techniques, and analytical constructs. It is expected that in every major, students will gain sufficient control of the data, theory, and methods to define the issues in a given problem, develop the evidence and arguments that may reasonably be advanced on the various sides of each issue, and reach conclusions based on a convincing evaluation of the evidence. (As such there is a close overlap with the first goal.)

The "reasonable standard" approach to undergraduate education is not without problems. Occasionally we encounter a student who fits the category of one-sided genius—the mathematical wizard, for example. Similarly, as Bertrand Russell has pointed out, someone with the gifts of a Mozart would gain little from a conservatory. But such occurrences are by definition extremely rare, and need not be central to a broad view of education. Our task can never

108 THE UNIVERSITY: *An Owner's Manual*

be the equivalent of custom tailoring, although we should always preserve sufficient flexibility to take care of very special cases.

There could also be political objections. The delineation of a set of standards requires a consensus—normally a faculty consensus—which in turn might be read as imposing conformity or, even more fallaciously, as socializing students on behalf of some ulterior purpose: say, this country's "ruling classes," or a particular religion, say, Christianity. I have never been able to accept this view. The standards I have suggested do not represent or preclude any political or doctrinal point of view; indeed, they favor the broadening of sensibilities and the displacement of conventional wisdom by critical thinking.

William Johnson Cory, a master at Eton, said it very well over a hundred years ago. Addressing a group of young men in 1861, he told them that

> you are not engaged so much in acquiring knowledge as in making mental efforts under criticism. A certain amount of knowledge you can indeed with average faculties acquire so as to retain; nor need you regret the hours that you have spent on much that is forgotten, for the shadow of lost knowledge at least protects you from many illusions.
>
> But you go to a great school, not for knowledge so much as for arts and habits; for the habit of attention, for the art of expression, for the art of assuming at a moment's notice a new intellectual posture, for the art of entering quickly into another person's thoughts, for the habit of submitting to censure and refutation, for the art of indicating assent or dissent in graduated terms, for the habit of regarding minute points of accuracy, for the habit of working out what is possible in a given time, for taste, for discrimination, for mental courage and mental soberness.
>
> Above all, you go to a great school for self-knowledge.[11]

In my view, these remarks describe some of the central principles for undergraduate education today. Students

11. *Eton Reform* (London: Longman, Green, Longman, & Roberts, 1861), pp. 6–7.

will forget many of the facts that they are taught, and new developments will make much of what is imparted today invalid in years hence. I think we might all agree that an understanding of the value and uses of intellect is essential for an educated person. But the question is: how are "arts and habits" inculcated in a most efficient and lasting manner? Certainly not by a one-sided or specialized curriculum and not by curriculum alone.

William Cory spoke of the goals of pre-college education, and some might argue that the standards and goals I have outlined more properly apply to secondary schooling, perhaps implying that American higher education should move toward a European model in which university training is more specialized. There are, however, good reasons why in the United States the four years of college are the time when most students acquire a liberal education. In our society, college represents the greatest opportunity for young citizens to enrich their lives this way. Any generalization about the American system of education is dangerous. Variations are great, but it is clear that the majority of Americans graduate from high schools that are not selective and that lack the resources—pedagogical, financial, and social—implied by the concept of liberal arts.

By way of contrast—and to supply perspective—note that the European and Japanese systems are both less democratic and, perhaps more important, less forgiving. A smaller proportion of the population attends college and universities. Formal and informal tracking begins very early. In Japan, getting into the right kindergarten (after interviews and examinations) will materially increase the chance for admission to the most elite Tokyo university. An elite kindergarten opens the door to a first-class primary school; that, in turn, helps the student gain admission to one of the fine secondary schools that is able to give the most effective preparation for the university entrance examination. In France, to gain entry to the right lycée is a major career determinant. And in Great Britain, an elitist philosophy combined with long-term financial stringency has effectively constricted entry for many segments of society. These systems can fairly be described as steep pyramids. Fewer can climb from the base to the top, and those who succeed have generally benefited from advantages associated with birth, class, and income.[12] Although not all these influences are absent in the United States,[13] differences are more significant than similarities. Tracking is less rigid, and early academic performance does not irrevocably determine the future. Second and third chances are real glories of the American system of education.

Steeper educational pyramids exercise an inevitable influence on the nature and standards of undergraduate education. Where they exist, university entrants are drawn from a smaller pool of applicants whose characteristics are more uniform. Those who are in charge of these matters in Tokyo, Oxford, or Paris know far better than we ever will what subjects their future students have studied, what books they have read, and what levels they have achieved. The smaller pool of applicants is the product of a more limited number of secondary schools, many of which attempt to give their graduates a liberal education, and some of them undoubtedly succeed.

A democratic society such as ours with the goal of having all its citizens graduate from high schools cannot avoid a somewhat depressed common denominator. At all levels the American system of education is decentralized. Local control is a prime aim and national standards are rare to the point of being practically nonexistent. The quality of schools of all types depend on a large variety of factors: the

12. Comparable statistics are difficult to obtain. One useful index is the percentage of the population over age twenty-five with post-secondary education. In 1984, the U.S. figure was 32.2%. In Japan, it was 14.3%; in Great Britain, 11% (in 1983). See *Britannica Book of the Year,* 1986, pp. 946–51. These are stock figures. The difference between Japan and the United States is getting smaller all the time.

13. "The United States once liked to believe it was founded on a tradition of common schools, where the local bank president's Harvard-bound daughter rubbed knees with the local drunk's disadvantaged son called Ronald Reagan. When suburbia was created by the growth in car ownership, this democratic ideal quickly proved hokum for inner cities and then for nearly everywhere else. Today you get your children into the best American public sector school by buying a small $250,000 house near it." Norman Macrae, "The Most Important Choice So Few Can Make," *The Economist,* September 30, 1986.

tax base of a community or state, the ethnic composition and age structure of a city, private endowments, the history of public-private school relations, and many others.

That is why, *on average,* we hope that our primary and secondary schools will at least prepare students in basic skills: reading, writing, mathematics, enriched as much as possible by some science, history, literature, and foreign languages. Obviously there are exceptions, superb public and private secondary schools in which liberal learning can achieve high levels. But they remain exceptions.

Our universities have to search for accomplishment, ability, promise, and talent, taking into account the peculiar diversities—geographical, ethnic, and economic—in our society (the process has been described in chapter 4). We are tolerant at entry, recognizing that not all candidates start the race equally advantaged. Our concern is how the race ends. Compared to most other countries, we can take very little for granted except various indicators of promise, and therefore the need for liberal education and basic intellectual training in college will remain, for us, undiminished.

The benefits of liberal education may also be enhanced by maturity, perspective, and experience. Its values are subtle, gain by repetition, and can sometimes even be wasted on those who are too young.[14] For most of us, college appears to be the ideal moment—at least for those students fortunate enough to attend schools that offer this type of curriculum.

It would certainly not be wise to postpone liberal education to the stage of graduate professional training. The proportion of Americans who go to graduate schools is much smaller than those who finish college. In 1983, only 8.9 percent of college graduates went to graduate school. Too many individuals would be deprived of this enriching

14. I can think of no better example than my own initial encounter with Leo Tolstoi's *Anna Karenina.* I first read the novel at the age of thirteen, and concluded that Alexey Karenin, Anna's husband, was the most sympathetic character in the book. With inadequate life experience, it was impossible for me to understand Tolstoi's intentions.

element in their lives. Second, postgraduate education has neither the time nor the inclination for what is seen—perhaps mistakenly—as a diversion from their primary mission: to produce highly trained professionals in a few years.[15] The amount of information that students need to digest is too large.

Most important, whenever it occurs, in college or later, liberal education is an indispensable prerequisite for professional practice at the highest level. We are entitled to expect superior technical expertise from professionals. A doctor should have superior knowledge of science and disease; a lawyer needs a deep understanding of major cases and legal procedures; a scholar must possess intimate familiarity with the state of the art in a particular subject. All of these attributes, however, while necessary, are far from sufficient. The ideal of a profession should not be a mere flow of competent technocrats. A more appropriate goal is professional authority combined with "humility, humanity, and humor." I want my lawyer and doctor to have a grasp of pain, love, laughter, death, religion, justice, and the limitations of science.[16] That may be far more important than knowing the most modern drug or the latest ruling of an appellate court. Up-to-date information can always be acquired without too much difficulty; human understanding cannot be reduced to asking the computer a few questions.

15. As previously noted, this attitude is undergoing desirable change at this time.

16. In 1930, Jose Ortega y Gasset said in a lecture: "The medical schools aspire to teach physiology and chemistry complete to the nth degree; but perhaps in no medical school the world over is there anyone seriously occupied with thinking what it really means to be a good physician, what the ideal type should be for our times," *Mission of the University*, p. 62. Is this still true? The New Pathway Program at the Harvard Medical School is an attempt to do just that. I believe that Ortega would have approved.

# 7

# One Version of Core

Liberal education is one way of describing college education in some schools. The term is also used in a narrower sense, referring to requirements outside of a major or concentration and designed to ensure breadth and balance, the whole development of an individual. What students are *required* to do is of the gravest importance—that is always true when interfering with the freedom of individuals. Some colleges require very little (e.g., Brown University), while others offer almost no choice (St. John's College). Most schools lie in between these extremes. Wherever an institution is on this spectrum, this much is clear: requirements have to make sense in terms of a coherent educational vision. The faculty should be able to explain to students why they are asked to study certain subjects; why it is necessary to impose constraints; or why they believe that the absence of constraints will produce a graduate with a better education.

Given the diverse character of American higher education, it is difficult to discuss the state of liberal education requirements in general. Instead, I intend very briefly to outline Harvard's Core Curriculum (Vintage, 1988), to discuss its philosophy, logic, and content, as one example of liberal education in our time. I do not claim that there exists a single perfect curriculum for American undergraduates, and even if we could agree on a standard of perfection, there is little reason to believe that any set of requirements is sufficient to endow students with all desirable "arts and habits." There are many different roads leading to the fellowship of educated men and women, and ideally we should travel on more than one. Choices will depend on the type of institution—its resources, faculty, student body, and perhaps other factors.

The Harvard Core represents one fourth of an undergraduate education, one year of required work for all students. It is not the work of the freshman year or any other specific year, but rather the equivalent of one academic year to be completed before graduation. Complemented by "learning in depth"[1] in the form of a major or concentration—the equivalent of two years of study—and enriched by a year of electives in which students have nearly absolute freedom of choice, the Core is intended to make the "fellowship of educated men and women" a more meaningful concept.

Harvard undergraduates have to fulfill three graduation requirements that are not, strictly speaking, part of the Core. They must take a course intended to develop students as writers of effective prose (an educated person must be able to . . . write clearly and effectively); show competence in a foreign language (one aspect of not being ignorant of other cultures); and demonstrate competence in quantitative reasoning defined as an introduction to the computer, numerical data, and some basic statistical techniques (another aspect of informed acquaintance with

1. Most of the phrases in quotes or parentheses in this chapter refer to the definition of an educated person given in chapter 6.

mathematical and quantitative techniques used in the natural and social sciences).

The Core proper consists of six specially designed groups of courses, in accordance with explicit guidelines formulated on an interdisciplinary (non-departmental) basis. In the words of the official description:

> The philosophy of the Core Curriculum rests on the conviction that every Harvard graduate should be broadly educated. . . . It assumes that students need some guidance in achieving this goal, and that the faculty has an obligation to direct them toward the knowledge, intellectual skills, and habits of thought that are the hallmarks of educated men and women.
>
> [The Core] does not define intellectual breadth as the mastery of a set of Great Books, or the digestion of a specific quantum of information, or the surveying of current knowledge in certain fields. Rather, the Core seeks to introduce students to the major *approaches to knowledge* in areas that the faculty considers indispensable to undergraduate education. It aims to show what kinds of knowledge and what forms of inquiry exist in these areas, how different means of analysis are acquired, how they are used, and what their value is. The courses within each area or subdivision of the program are equivalent in the sense that, while their subject matter may vary, their emphasis on a particular way of thinking is the same.[2]

## 1. Literature and Arts

Courses in this section of the Core concern reading, seeing, and hearing with an educated eye and ear. In this sentence, the crucial phrase is "an educated eye and ear." Reading, seeing, and hearing to most of us may appear natural and simple; no special training would seem necessary. And yet visual, aural, and other types of illiteracy abound if we conceive of literacy as including a full measure of appreciation, the capacity for critical judgment, and an understanding of quality. Literature and Arts presents

2. Harvard University, Faculty of Arts and Sciences, *Courses of Instruction, 1986–87* p. 1.

humanities courses that illustrate "how human beings give artistic expression to their experience of the world."[3] This means studying the possibilities and limitations of particular art forms—novels, poems, symphonies—and gaining an appreciation of the interplay between individual talent, artistic tradition, and a specific historical moment. To accomplish these goals, students are asked to work in each of three areas: a major genre of literature, for example, the study of "Great Nineteenth and Early Twentieth Century Novels," including such writers as Jane Austen, Dickens, Balzac, and James Joyce; a major genre of visual or musical expression, such as "Rembrandt and His Contemporaries" or "The Development of the String Quartet"; and lastly, a course that examines the relations among the arts in particular periods and the social and intellectual contexts of creativity as in "Renaissance Images of Man." In this way, students will acquire a closer acquaintance with some of the important scholarly, literary, and artistic achievements of the past and with some major religious and philosophical conceptions of man.

## 2. Science

That no one can be considered broadly educated in today's world without some understanding of science—its methods and principles—seems so obvious as to require little amplification; that it is a "major approach" to knowledge is self-evident. Ours is also a period of unusually rapid scientific advances: fresh discoveries, deeper penetration of fundamental physical and biological laws, and new technologies that constantly change our lives. Recent science gave us both atomic weapons and genetic engineering. The former may one day terminate life on earth; the latter may in the near future appreciably lengthen the span of normal life—and that would have complex social consequences. Surely an educated person should wish to have at least

3. *Ibid.*, p. 16.

some appreciation of the forces that play such a key role in our future. I consider it a necessary attribute of educated citizenship in a democracy where our votes may determine whether or not scientific advances can be turned into social progress or disaster.

There are those who believe that a meaningful level of scientific literacy lies beyond the capabilities of any general education program. Science is too complex, too deep, too cumulative, too specialized, and too mathematical. Today, even very few scientists are, in the broad sense, scientifically literate. Furthermore, some critics argue that the tie between scientific knowledge and responsible citizenship is vague and unconvincing. After all, professional scientists disagree too often about public policy issues, each citing reasons that can be equally plausible to laymen.

Professor Morris Shamos, a distinguished proponent of these doubts, provides a different justification for including science in a liberal arts curriculum. "Students have the most to gain . . . if they study science chiefly for the aesthetic and intellectual values it bestows."[4] This point of view was espoused by the nineteenth-century biologist Thomas Huxley and his contemporary, the mathematician Jules-Henri Poincaré. Shamos believes that it is an idea whose time may finally have come.

I agree that meaningful scientific literacy may be an unattainable goal; "critical appreciation" is a lesser, perhaps more attainable standard. I am less convinced about the uselessness of general education science when it comes to public policy questions—but there is no effective proof either way. I join wholeheartedly in urging the study of science for aesthetic and purely intellectual values. A better and more basic motive does not exist.

Science has been least well represented in most schemes that claim to educate students in the liberal arts. The reasons are evident. Even a non-professional, undergraduate understanding of science requires "an informed acquaint-

4. Morris Shamos, "The Lesson Every Child Need Not Learn," *The Sciences* (July–August 1988), p. 20.

ance with the mathematical and experimental methods of the physical and biological sciences." Many college students resist these studies for a variety of reasons: real or perceived lack of mathematical aptitude; poor instruction in high schools that alienate them from scientific topics; few science courses at most institutions specifically designed for non-concentrators—and that is a major educational problem.

I will always remember the reaction of one of my colleagues when the framework of our new Core program was under consideration. He was a world-famous art historian, and he started our conversation by asking me whether I considered his long career to have been of value to scholarship as well as a credit to his alma mater—he was one of our own most distinguished graduates. I gave the obvious and deeply desired affirmative answer to both questions. He then explained that some of our new requirements—especially in science and quantitative reasoning—would have made it impossible for him to graduate from Harvard. These were subjects that he could not master even at most elementary levels. Did I believe him to be unworthy of a degree? Had his professional achievements not proved otherwise? He begged me most sincerely to use my influence to prevent the adoption of these new requirements so that his type of person would not be retroactively or prospectively repudiated. I knew that this celebrated professor was speaking in earnest, and attempted to convince him that he underestimated his own abilities to handle these subjects *if* properly taught. He was not at all convinced.

There is, of course, a lack of parity between science and non-science students. Undergraduates majoring in science find it relatively easy to take courses in the humanities and social sciences. Literary and historical approaches, while perhaps not especially congenial to a budding biochemist, are only rarely daunting or frightening. For these students, attaining a liberal education, is—at least superficially—a smaller challenge. Not so for non-science undergraduates, and especially for those who believe themselves to be afflicted by science or mathematics phobias. These fears are greatly increased when students of different achievement and talent are taught in the same class. The issue is not teaching science condescendingly to "poets"; it is the recognition of special pedagogical needs of certain groups.

Faculty members are familiar with student feelings and offer their own forms of resistance. No teacher desires students who are forced into his or her classroom convinced that they will not be interested and cannot do well.[5] Science is also clearly marked by a progression of levels of difficulty—far more so than, let us say, history—and therefore the fear of being shallow is much greater. Does not the great danger lie in producing students who believe themselves to have learned some real science, when in reality they have succeeded only in absorbing some elementary concepts? None of these obstacles is without merit, but science is too important to leave out of any liberal arts curriculum. Difficulties have to be overcome for students and faculty by creating realistic expectations on both sides.[6]

Core science is designed for students who will not be scientists, and the common aim of the courses is "to convey a general understanding of science as a way of looking at man and the world."

5. Quite typically, college and university teachers of science exhibit a contradictory set of attitudes. On the one hand, they complain that their subject is slighted (at Harvard, for example, we require a year of Science and a year and a half of Literature and Arts). On the other hand, they show little enthusiasm for teaching undergraduates in the context of liberal education.

6. For a very stern, though not wholly realistic critique of core-type science, see F. H. Westheimer, "Are Our Universities Rotten at the 'Core'?" *Science*, June 5, 1987. He feels that our science requirements are too rudimentary; he recognizes that his colleagues are not interested in teaching the "unwashed"—i.e., non-concentrators; he deplores the signals that the level of non-concentration science sends to our high schools. His solution: admit a greater proportion of students eager to learn science. But that is not a solution at all; it would have little to do with liberal education. Of course, science requirements at CalTech or MIT can achieve a higher standard. There are no unwashed at those institutions—that is why these places are called institutes rather than universities. Universities will always face the special challenge of educating an intellectually more heterogeneous population. That is different, and progress is likely to be gradual.

Observations of the physical and biological world have led scientists to formulate principles that provide universal explanations of diverse phenomena.
These include the laws that govern classical dynamics, thermodynamics, radiation, and the microscopic structure of matter, and the basic principles that underlie chemistry, molecular and cellular biology, biological evolution and behavior. The Core courses in science treat such basic scientific concepts and findings in some depth. They consider not only what scientists believe to be true in some domain, but how they have developed and validated their laws and principles.[7]

Two separate areas of science are required fields of study. One set of courses "deal[s] primarily with the predictive and deductive analysis of natural phenomena through quantitative treatment of their simple elements" (largely physics, chemistry, some branches of biology), of which a typical example would be "Space, Time, and Motion." The other area analyzes scientific systems of greater complexity, whose explanation involves a more descriptive, historical, or evolutionary account of the natural world (for example, geology and organismic biology). "History of the Earth and of Life" is an excellent illustration.

## 3. Historical Study

History is perhaps more widely used than any other method of analysis in "gain[ing] knowledge and understanding of the universe, of society, and of ourselves." The historical approach is used not only by historians proper, but also by scientists when they study evolution, by humanists in analyzing the development of language or a particular art form, and by social scientists in, for example, economic history or political theory. At the risk of oversimplification, we can distinguish two types of method-

7. Harvard University, Faculty of Arts and Sciences, *Courses of Instruction, 1986–87*, p. 31.

ological emphases. In the work of particular historians these are usually combined and used simultaneously, but in principle they can be distinguished. The first is history as the study of trends or long-run changes. This approach tends to emphasize a macroscopic view, impersonal forces, and frequently the logic of socioeconomic developments or "historical necessity." There is, however, a very different—nearly opposite—side to historical analysis. It stresses a microscopic view, human beings, chance; the complexity of events rather than the necessary simplifications of trends.

Historical study in the Core familiarizes students with both approaches. One set of courses begins with a major aspect or issue of the modern world and explains its historical development and background.[8] For example, "Development and Underdevelopment: The Historical Origins of the Inequality of Nations" starts with the world as we know it today: perhaps fifteen or twenty countries that have experienced an industrial revolution and are wealthy, and well over one hundred nations classified as underdeveloped. The course proceeds to demonstrate that an understanding of the present requires identifying trends going back to the Middle Ages and the beginnings of European expansion, a valuable lesson especially for American undergraduates whose historical memories are apt to be short. The other set of courses is much more sharply focused on a moment of time: a major turning point or event removed from modern policy questions. Now the aim is to demonstrate the intricacies, complications, and uncertainties of historical explanation, paying particular attention to individual aspirations and decisions all too often lost in examining long-run change. An illustration would be "The Russian Revolution": was it an inevitable event? Why did it

8. It would be possible to study trends without taking a major issue of the modern world as a starting point. One could, for example, examine the decline and fall of Rome. Starting with a current issue, however, has the additional advantage of helping students achieve a better understanding of problems that they may have to deal with as citizens.

occur in 1917? Would the outcome have been different without Lenin? These are the types of questions that this course attempts to answer. An exposure to both kinds of courses should give students both important historical knowledge *and* a better understanding of historical methods.

## 4. Social Analysis

One of the major ways of understanding the societies in which we live is to be found in the relatively new methods of the social sciences. Starting with economics in the late eighteenth century, and currently including, among others, political science, sociology, and psychology, these intellectual approaches have as goals to enhance our understanding primarily of contemporary human behavior.[9] Any generalization will be subject to exceptions, but it is largely true that in explaining the behavior of people and institutions, social science has mainly proceeded by developing formal theories that are—insofar as possible—tested by empirical data. The group of courses in the Core called Social Analysis all share this character, and are intended to acquaint students with "some of the main forms of analysis and the historical and quantitative techniques needed for investigating the workings and development of modern society." An ideal type is "Principles of Economics": the theories are quite formal, professional consensus is strong, and empirical testing is highly developed. But similar insights can be achieved in learning about "Conceptions of Human Nature" rooted in psychology. The theories and philosophical presuppositions of Marx, Freud, B. F. Skinner, and E. O. Wilson, and their examination in terms of real data—ideology versus scientific theory—will also enable students to understand how social scientists attempt to explain human behavior.

9. Primarily, but not exclusively. Historians have employed the methods of the social sciences to explain events as far back as classical antiquity.

## 5. Foreign Cultures

In the years after World War II, the United States became one of the superpowers—one among a number of major nations. The Soviet Union is our chief rival in terms of ideology and military power. Japan is our principal economic competitor. Taken as a group, Western Europe can perhaps be considered as an economic and political superpower. China and India are population superpowers and exert considerable influence in international affairs. When it comes to oil, the Arab countries have exerted enormous leverage, and our future—financial and political—is certainly not unrelated to events in Latin American and Africa.

Until World War II, it was possible for Americans to ignore large parts of the world. As a continental nation protected by two oceans, we felt far removed from international vicissitudes. To the extent that we looked beyond our borders, with the exception of the pull of trade and empire, our sights were usually directed at Western Europe—primarily Great Britain—and at our roots in Western civilization. For a brief period after World War II, our heads swelled. We considered ourselves and our prosperity to be a model for the rest of the world: learn from us if you are able, we have little to learn from others.

Today, the conditions have altered in fundamental ways. The oceans afford little protection and international vicissitudes have an immediate effect on our daily life. Despite superpower status, we are becoming a smaller part of the world. Our share of world GNP, trade, and population are all in decline not because we are experiencing stagnation, but due to more rapid growth elsewhere. Even our traditional Western roots have altered as new waves of immigration change the ethnic base of the American population. It seems obvious that it is no longer possible to conduct our lives without references to the wider world. "An educated American, in the last quarter of this century, cannot be provincial in the sense of being ignorant of other cultures."

Readers with common sense will be surprised to learn

that education critic Alan Bloom has characterized this type of study as *demagogic.* In his words: "The point is to force students to recognize that there are other ways of thinking and that Western ways are not better." However, ". . . if students were really to learn something of the minds of any of these non-Western cultures . . . they would find that each and every one of these cultures is ethnocentric. All of them think their way is the best way, and all others are inferior. . . . Only in the Western nations, i.e., those influenced by Greek philosophy, is there some willingness to doubt the identification of the good with one's own way."[10] I am unable to judge the philosophical subtleties underlying these bizarre sentences. I find them mind-boggling. Surely ethnocentricity is not a non-Western monopoly. In comparing Japan and the United States, is it so obvious which country would rank higher on the "my way is best" index? Furthermore, even if non-Western thought is more ethnocentric (which I do not believe), there is absolutely no reason to preach that particular fallacy when studying the subject.

Mr. Bloom might be astonished by the following Japanese perspective. "The Western concepts embraced by the traditional liberal arts education made a tremendous contribution to intellectual history. Yet certainly their universality is compromised by ethnocentrism. It is only natural, for instance, that Western ideals should lead one to assume the cultural primacy of Europe over Asia, and such an assumption clearly lacks universal validity. In this sense the European liberal arts education possesses inherent limitations."[11] I would urge that a truce be declared in these ethnocentric wars!

The Foreign Cultures portion of the Core addresses these issues by requiring all students to take a course that "seeks to identify the distinctive patterns of thought and

10. See Alan Bloom, *The Closing of the American Mind* (New York: Simon and Schuster, 1987), p. 36.
11. Yasusuke Murakami, "The Debt Comes Due for Mass Higher Education," *Japan Echo* (Autumn 1988), p. 72.

action that account for the configuration or ethos"[12] of a particular area of the world. From the point of view of the student, the emphasis is selective. Studying foreign culture in generalized terms makes little sense, and the list of courses offers a variety of choices focusing on different regions of the world. Many courses are an introduction to major civilizations (India, East Asia, Russia, Islam, Africa, etc.). Some are much more narrow, such as "The Unification of Japan, 1560–1650," or "The Culture of Austria, 1890–1938" (requiring reading in the German language). All courses aim to expand the range of the student's cultural experience and to provide fresh perspectives on one's own cultural assumptions and traditions.

## 6. **Moral Reasoning**

As Americans, we do not share a unified religious or philosophical conception of man. Sometimes our politicians refer to the United States as a Christian nation, and that is clearly wrong. We may have more Christian citizens than Jews, Buddhists, or atheists, but a state religion does not exist and is constitutionally prohibited. It is even becoming more difficult to think of ourselves exclusively as representatives of Western civilization; too many of us have strong non-Western roots. The heterogeneity of our society in the twentieth century is, many believe, one source of our creativity and strength. At one time the American nation aspired to be a "melting pot." Today we recognize the values of maintaining diversity while insisting—not always successfully—on certain common rules of political and social behavior.

Instruction in moral reasoning in the Core Curriculum does not teach or preach a specific morality or philosophy. That would not be appropriate. Our aim is "to discuss significant and recurrent questions of choice and value that

12. *Courses of Instruction,* p. 2.

arise in human experience"[13]—moral issues that are shared by many religious and philosophical conceptions of mankind, and that cannot be resolved merely by appeal to emotion. "The courses are intended to show that it is possible to reflect reasonably [deeply and analytically] about such matters as justice, obligation, citizenship, loyalty, courage, and personal responsibility."[14] All of this instruction explores the nature of the virtuous life for individuals, groups, nations, and among nations. Here are two typical examples: "Justice" critically examines classical and contemporary theories (Aristotle, Locke, Kant, Mills, and moral philosopher John Rawls) and discusses present-day practical applications; "Jesus and the Moral Life" emphasizes violence and non-violence, wealth and poverty, and the relation of private morality to public morality.

These six groups of Core courses contain certain common features that deserve explicit recognition.

- All of the courses are designed according to guidelines on an interdepartmental basis for non-concentrators. Concentrators are exempted from the particular Core category that most closely approximates their special field. For example, an undergraduate majoring in physics does not have to take Core science courses.
- In each category, courses seek to introduce students to major approaches to knowledge. Choice is preserved because major approaches are presented in various forms: courses with differing content. In each case, however, content is chosen for its importance, and the goal is to achieve equal educational value for all courses in the same category.
- Aside from the emphasis on major approaches as opposed to more traditional surveys, the Core incorporates some other innovations. First, there is the inclusion of

13. *Ibid.*, p. 29.
14. *Ibid.*

the visual arts and music, frequently omitted in general education. Second, the explicit recognition of foreign cultures and moral reasoning is a departure from more usual practice. Third, a quantitative reasoning requirement emphasizing computation and data analysis is—at least for Harvard—an innovation.

A simple and accepted definition of a core curriculum is "an arrangement of a course of studies that combines under basic topics materials from subjects conventionally separated and aims to provide a common background to all students."[15] Does Harvard provide that common background? The answer is yes, though our way of doing so differs from other notions of core and common learning. The content of liberal education has been divided into six major approaches through which we gain "knowledge and understanding of the universe, of society, and ourselves." Common learning is defined as familiarity with these major approaches—historical studies, foreign cultures, etc.— rather than with specific content, such as, for example, the history of Western civilization or chemistry. Not all students study the same subjects, but all learn the ways of thinking or method of analysis associated with these comprehensive and significant modes of inquiry. Can one—as has been often asked—graduate from Harvard without reading Shakespeare? Yes, but one cannot get a degree without reading literary classics in a critical and analytical way under the guidance of a specialist. Can one graduate without studying economics? Yes, but not without a course dealing with the fundamentals of social analysis, of which economics is just one example.

A number of advantages are, I believe, associated with this conception of core curriculum. First, the emphasis on major approaches to knowledge should prepare a young person to live more effectively in an environment that produces ever more information and new theories. The carry-

15. *Webster's Ninth New Collegiate Dictionary* (1984).

over is simply greater than work based primarily on a specific quantum of information. Second, this conception of a core also harmonizes particularly well with life-long learning and multiple careers. Each Core course is an example of a much wider and more broadly useful category. Assume a typical current circumstance: someone who fifteen years out of school contemplates a new profession in some field in which social sciences are used. No matter what the particular profession—social work, business, teaching, and so on—the Core will already have provided a graduate with a picture of how social analysts in general study our world. More informed and valid choices should be possible. Third, the very range of the six Core categories fulfills a most important educational function. They assist in creating an atmosphere of intellectual sympathy among extremely diverse students. Those with a passion for humanistic studies will have the opportunity to appreciate the beauties of scientific reasoning and proof. And, of course, vice versa.

On rare occasions, I have known students to change their concentration as a consequence of Core studies: they were, sometimes reluctantly, forced to confront possibilities that were transformed into serious interests. That shows the Core at its best. Finally, it seem to me that there is virtue in choice, in offering a relatively sizable number of courses in each subdivision. Since they are intended to be educationally equivalent—this is a difficult ideal that we from time to time undoubtedly fail to achieve—it seems reasonable to encourage students to select the most congenial subject matter. Both teacher and student will be the beneficiaries.

Many of the hardest problems have not been dealt with here. What is the relation between "mental efforts under criticism" or "arts and habits" and curricular details? What can we really hope to accomplish with two semesters of general education science and single semesters of moral reasoning and foreign culture studies in terms of our rather lofty goals?

Let us, therefore, conclude by remembering that curriculum is only one limited aspect of liberal education. The quality of instruction and pedagogical methods—lectures, seminars, self-paced instruction—are at least as important. In addition, I believe that the faculty member as role model is a crucial aspect of liberal education. A professor with high standards and a caring personality can teach students more about ethical behavior than years of required courses.

My closest friend in graduate school had considerable difficulties in a course and requested time with the professor, a Hungarian-born economist of international reputation. They talked for a few hours, and my friend suddenly realized that it was 6:00 P.M. Of course, he apologized for taking so much of the professor's valuable time and said that, no doubt, his teacher had other more important engagements. The professor replied: "Not at all. After all, aren't we in the same profession?" These words, addressed by a famous scholar to a first-year graduate student, became legendary among my contemporaries. They taught us more about ethics and morality than many hours in the classroom, and in turn, I am sure, also benefited our future students.

Let us recall, as well, that students do a great deal to educate each other. Thus, a student body in which intellectual achievements are prized sends different messages from one where status is conferred only on varsity athletes. Course descriptions, guidelines, requirements, and such reveal only little about the inner workings of the educational process. They are necessary but far from sufficient conditions to achieve high standards of liberal education.

Many of these more human aspects of education require systematic analysis and improvement. We can learn how to teach more effectively; we can clarify goals in the classroom; we should, as faculty members and administrators, lead our lives as examples to our students. No doubt, it is also crucial for higher education to become more productive by eliminating old and inefficient ways—as urged so frequently by our many critics. And yet, I continue to believe that education in its deepest sense will always retain an element of mystery; there will always be critical components that resist quantification and scientific description, and measures of productivity. Curriculum is a skeleton. The flesh, blood, and heart has to come from the rather unpredictable interactions between teachers and students.

# 8

## Graduate Students

*Welcome to the Ancient and Universal Company of Scholars*

It is the Harvard custom to hand out individual diplomas after a large central commencement ceremony—an outdoor gathering that attracts some 25,000 spectators and that features student speeches, pageantry and song, and an opportunity to look at a few glamorous honorands. Undergraduates receive diplomas and other awards in their Houses; professional school graduates go to their campuses for a similar ceremony; and recipients of the Ph.D. proceed to a large auditorium. In that hall, it is the great privilege of the dean of the Faculty of Arts and Sciences to present each new doctor with a "sheepskin." I performed this pleasant duty for eleven years. It always was one of the high points of any academic year.

The audience consisted of old parents (no Ph.D. is likely to have young parents), spouses, and quite a few children. Professors—many of whom had become friends of the students while participating in the long march to a doctorate—were also present. Each newly certified scholar stepped on the stage and was introduced by the departmental chairman to the dean of the graduate school. That dean introduced the student to me, who then received—in order—a diploma, a handshake, applause, and much later a glass of lukewarm champagne. Many pictures remain vivid in my mind: thesis advisers hugging their students; the evident pride on the faces of parents, husbands or wives, and children; the increasing number of women; the strange fashions—old tennis shoes underneath crimson robes of silk. I also remember the courage of those graduates who had not yet found academic posts. Some stayed away; others exhibited bravado.

During my term of office, from 1973 to 1984, the job market for Ph.D.'s deteriorated with monotonous consistency. Every year seemed to bring more alarming news. "No vacancy" signs multiplied and their number was exceeded by "no tenure" announcements. In this atmosphere of gloom, I had to deliver encouraging words of greeting just before lifting a plastic glass filled with that cheap champagne. I do not clearly remember what I said during those years, although I do recall being nervous, while attempting to avoid platitudes and condescension. From the perspective of graduate students facing an unfriendly job market, could I avoid appearing hopelessly self-satisfied and smug?

At this stage, one could only express a sense of common enterprise, pride in past achievement, and hope in the future. Perhaps I should have made mention of the famous *dokuzake* (poisoned sake) case. Prewar Japanese universities operated under the constraints of a strict chair system; promotion depended on the retirement or death of a chair holder. This story was about an impatient assistant professor at Tokyo University in the 1930s. But that seemed needlessly risky just before offering a toast.

Frequently, I believed that whatever could reasonably be said came too late. The proper time to offer advice is at the beginning rather than at the end of a process. What follows are some notions that prospective or new graduate students might find helpful.

## The Setting

In nearly all universities, undergraduates are a distinct minority. The majority of the student population are post-graduates, enrolled in one of the many professional schools or in a graduate school of arts and sciences. Undergraduates are the *real* Harvard men and women. In the American system, it is undergraduate affiliation that overshadows everything else: it alone can earn the title "Old Blue" or "Trojan." I have previously referred to graduate students as cousins; probably I should have said second cousins, and perhaps even strangers in our own midst. At the great academic football rites, you will find the cousins sitting in the end zone. They come last in the assignment of dormitory space. Many lead grubby lives in some low-rent suburb far away from a central campus while eking out an existence with fellowship money and—if lucky—a working spouse.

To be an alumnus means, in the first instance, to have graduated from the college. To be sure, we make exceptions. When universities beg for money—as described earlier—all are equally welcome. Similarly, when fame is achieved, having spent a summer school at Harvard (or elsewhere) is sufficient to be regularly designated as a close member of the family. In the fall of 1988 we were quick to claim Michael Dukakis as a Harvard man, despite the fact that his graduation from our Law School does not usually confer this status. But who—except Swarthmore College—blamed us?

It would be wrong, however, to exaggerate the sameness of the graduate student population. It is extremely diverse, more diverse than the undergraduates, and it is nearly impossible to find a single denominator. Diversity has many causes: graduate students arrive socialized in various ways from their undergraduate schools; graduate education is specialized and attracts only certain kinds of individuals, committed to a particular profession and possessing certain specific talents; and each graduate school has its own culture and its own values and priorities. Most importantly, the degree of diversity is, I believe, a function of different career expectations.

Take the Big Three: Law (" . . . you are ready to aid in the shaping and application of those wise restraints that make us free");[1] Business Administration (" . . . you are well prepared to lead in the general management of people and organizations in the service of society"); and Medicine (" . . . as physicians you are ready to engage in an honorable and merciful calling"). All three faculties offer training that prepares students for successful, prestigious, and exceedingly well rewarded careers. It is true that within law and medicine, and to a much lesser extent in business administration, there is talk about *pro bono* work and service to the less fortunate. Some students begin these worthy activities while still in school and some will continue during their entire career. But student personalities are more defined by the manifest confidence in their own future. They know that society needs their services and attaches a very high price to the skills that they are acquiring. Most see their future in three-piece suits and six-figure incomes. This wholly comforting vision creates a sense of immense self-satisfaction.

Then there are the Poor Relations; they share both the noble aim of serving society and the small rewards for doing so. Education (" . . . you are well prepared to guide and serve the learning needs of contemporary society"), and Divinity (" . . . you are well prepared to foster the health and vitality of communities of faith and to help in shaping the shared values of the broader society"). Graduate students of these ancient callings tend to be older, frequently responsible for spouses and children. In understandable sorrow, they cannot fail to note that our society has a greater interest in "wise restraints" in the hands of corporate lawyers than in either "communities of faith" or "the learning needs of contemporary society." That is true,

1. The parentheses contain the phrase describing the professions during Harvard commencement ceremonies. They are spoken by the president when he awards the degrees.

indeed undeniable, if money is taken as an indicator of societal commitment. Is there a more valid indicator? Future teachers and clergymen know that the rewards of yuppiedom are denied to them, and in general they do not care. These students have different priorities, but unfortunately this does not prevent them from feeling neglected by their universities and their societies.[2]

Between the Big Three and the Poor Relations we find a very heterogeneous group of faculties: Design (" . . . [I] testify to your competence effectively to shape the space in which we live"); Dental Medicine (" . . . you are qualified for practice and research in a demanding branch of medicine");[3] Public Health (" . . . you are ready to advance the welfare of peoples everywhere by the prevention of disease and promotion of health"); and Government (" . . . you are well prepared to offer leadership in the quest for enlightened public policy and effective public administration"). What is the common denominator? Lower income expectations than Law, Business, and Medicine, but much better economic prospects than Education and Divinity. Also— with the exception of Dental Medicine—a certain emphasis on relations with or employment by the public sector.

My point is simple. Each one of these graduate schools has its own traditions, personality, and public persona. At every Harvard commencement the graduates of the Business School, who have just been awarded the MBA degree, get up and with great joy and defiance wave dollar bills. In turn, they are soundly booed by nearly all the other students. This has become a ritual of significance.

I do not feel competent to delve deeply into the professional schools. They live apart from Arts and Sciences and from the center of university life—and I know that this is a self-centered conception. I give two illustrations to support

2. In both divinity and education faculties, salaries are below university averages, scholarship money is scarce, and amenities tend to be far less lavish than in, say, schools of business.

3. When it comes to dentistry, imagination and poetry seem to have failed once again.

my point of view. Both pertain to the basic ritual of break-
ing bread. In the early 1950s, law students and arts and
sciences graduate students shared the same cafeteria, far
from the more elegant undergraduate facilities. Much was
happening in the world: the Korean War was not yet over,
Senator McCarthy was (regrettably) active, and the Cold
War was at its height. In the dining hall I tried every evening to engage law students in conversation concerning
these important events, usually without success. They were
otherwise engaged: "Let us suppose that A hits D over the
head, and then claims that it was an act of self-defense. . . ."
But gentlemen,[4] what about Klaus Fuchs? Things got so
bad that, in the graduate student council, I attempted—in
the name of civilized dining—to have a partition placed in
the hall separating law and arts and sciences graduate students. Today, I am glad that my attempt failed. Age has
made me more tolerant, and I should have taken more seriously the *mission civilisatrice* of graduate students in arts and
sciences.

Another illustration of the desire for separation from a
different prospective: the Harvard Business School operates a wonderful Faculty Club with fine food and excellent
service. In quality, the club manages to be nearly as good as
a one-star restaurant ("fair"), and that is not a mean
achievement by the standards of most university facilities.
It is also the only eating establishment in the university that
excludes professors from other faculties—except as occasional guests. Many rationalizations are suggested: the club
would be too crowded; the character would change; the
wrong people would be subsidized; and so on. Ultimately,
it is the expression of a wish not to mingle with a different
or at worst a wrong sort of person.

All this is prologue. Here the main topic is the Graduate
School of Arts and Sciences and especially its students, who
aspire to the Ph.D. degree. At every graduation during the
last fifteen or so years, when the president says " . . . with

4. I hasten to add that there were hardly any female law students in 1952.

high hope of your future, [I] welcome you to the ancient and universal company of scholars," a nervous titter runs through the large audience as these young men and women stand up, resplendent in their (rented) robes. Almost immediately the crowd bursts into vigorous applause, as if to apologize for the earlier nervous reaction. Members of the faculty cheer with particular energy. Obviously there is something special about the Graduate School of Arts and Sciences that makes us wish to cheer and at the same time to indicate concern. What is it?

First of all, the training of Ph.D.'s is a necessary condition for university status. It is what makes a university a university. Without a graduate school of arts and sciences, a university would be a college. A major university can exist without a law school, a medical faculty, or a school of business. Princeton has none of these and few will question its standing. A university can exist without undergraduates and the obvious example is Rockefeller University. But Ph.D. training is a fundamental and necessary condition— there is no substitute because it is the one activity dedicated to the survival of the university by training future generations of scholars.

Active scholars are uniquely attracted by a high-quality graduate school of arts and sciences. Faculty members consider the teaching and training of new generations of graduate students as their highest calling. They believe that working with graduate students maintains and develops their professional skills more effectively than any other activity. It may be the main reason for the great attraction of academic jobs. Laboratory scientists have told me that the opportunity to work with graduate students keeps them in the university. For them, other options would center on research in commercial laboratories, but there the principal investigator would be assisted by technicians, and that is considered a far less creative interaction.

This point can be generalized. Graduate students are the faculty's young disciples who ensure the continuity of learning. They are also the children and heirs of the faculty.

In Germany, the professor who guides a Ph.D. dissertation is called a *Doktorvater* (doctor-father) and that aptly describes the ideal. It is this ideal that sets graduate education in the arts and sciences apart from professional schools. In business, law, medicine, the main object is to train members of professions practiced extramurally. The business of graduates of a business school is business. A large majority of doctors practice medicine rather than teach, and most lawyers work in law firms. In contrast, doctoral students are trained for scholarship, teaching, and careers within colleges and universities, even though quite a few Ph.D.'s spend their lives working for government and industry. It is assumed that doctoral candidates will spend their lives within the confines of schools, dedicating themselves to "the continuity of learning." This creates a much stronger interaction between pupil and mentor. Sometimes it is possible to remain a *Doktorvater*'s loyal disciple for a very long time—one hopes, until he or she dies.[5] But both teaching and research require continual revision, and that usually takes the form of attacks on accepted ideas, frequently those very ideas proposed and cherished by your own doctor-father. A death wish against the father is a well-known academic phenomenon. To sum up: the relationship between teacher and student in arts and sciences is much more intimate than in other forms of education. A muddled outcome is predictable: happy students who bask in the warmth of familial relations, and an equal number of deeply unhappy students who feel neglected by surrogate academic parents. And many cases in between.

Currently, I have already noted, the special relationship between future scholars and their teachers is surrounded by a great deal of ambivalence. "High hope for your future" is no longer a confident prediction; instead, it has been reduced to a fervent and anxious wish. The reasons are easy to understand. Beginning in the 1970s, the market for young scholars has narrowed, and as a society we have

5. Do we need a new term: *Doktormutter* or perhaps *Doktoreltern*?

overproduced Ph.D.'s at least for the last two decades. As a result, the academic market has had increasing difficulty in balancing demand and supply. Between 1976 and 1985, only engineering (including computer sciences) had an unfulfilled demand for Ph.D.'s. Other areas—physical sciences, life sciences, social science and psychology, arts and humanities (and education)—all contained more new doctors seeking jobs than could be absorbed. The projected rate of redundancy varied from subject to subject, from a low of 11 percent in the physical sciences to a high of 67 percent in the arts and humanities.[6] Those of us lucky enough to teach at highly ranked schools hope that when a buyer's market exists, institutions with a reputation for high-quality programs will be able to do more for their graduates. A new Ph.D. from one of the top ten or twenty national graduate schools should have a better chance of capturing a scarce job than someone who has just graduated from a new and untested program. But that outcome is not assured.

There has certainly been a considerable expansion in Ph.D. programs since World War II. In 1940, 3,290 doctoral degrees were awarded in the United States. By 1980, the number had risen to 32,615. Between 1960 and 1970 alone, the output of Ph.D.'s tripled. This was the result of many new programs; expansion of existing programs could not possibly have handled such growth. In 1950–51, there were 800 institutions in the United States offering as highest level the bachelor's degree; 360, the master's degree; and 155, the doctor's degree. By 1983, these numbers were 827, 705, and 466, respectively. The extent to which the newcomers competed with the old establishment is less clear. I assume the market to be sufficiently segmented, so that major universities are relatively unaffected by this new Ph.D. production. However, that is only an assumption. It

6. American Council on Education, *Fact Book on Higher Education, 1986–87* (New York: The Macmillan Company, 1987), p. 39. Redundancy figures for the period 1976 to 1985 are projections, but similar results were obtained by various estimators. See also *The University of Chicago Record,* May 3, 1982, pp. 77–81.

is quite possible that prejudices exist in less research-oriented institutions against new Ph.D.'s who have studied in research universities. Perhaps they are seen as—in the terms of that dreaded word—overqualified and possessing some undesirable (snobbish?) attitudes sometimes justly and more often unjustly attributed to their mentors.[7]

Those students who graduate at the top of their class in any school—who are judged to be brilliant—will also have less difficulty. And, when nearly all universities are implementing affirmative action programs, belonging to an underrepresented group is another advantage. Other things being equal, women and members of selected minorities have slight advantages in securing initial positions. Despite these qualifications, the basic point remains: since the early 1970s, and at least until the middle of the 1980s, places for young scholars in all institutions and practically all fields have diminished.

There are two—and possibly three—reasons that made it increasingly difficult for the academic market to balance demand and supply. To begin with the most basic trend, higher education became less of a growth industry in the second half of this century.[8] Through the first half of the twentieth century, American higher education had undergone a remarkably rapid exponential growth, largely unaffected by economic circumstance. The number of students enrolled in college doubled every fifteen years; so, too, did the number of faculty in higher education. Because of increasing expectations of faculty training, graduate education grew even faster, with the number of Ph.D.'s produced doubling every eleven years. Over two thirds of these Ph.D.'s went into academic positions. The period of growth

7. For relevant statistics, see Burton R. Clark, *The Academic Life,* Table 3, p. 35. See also *Fact Book,* p. 106.

8. See Harvard University, Faculty of Arts and Sciences, *Dean's Report, 1977–78.* In 1899–1900, American institutions of higher education awarded about 29,000 earned degrees; in 1949–50, the comparable figure was 500,000; in the early 1980s, it stood at 1.3 million. See National Center for Educational Statistics, *Digest of Education Statistics, 1983–1984,* Table 114, p. 132.

was so smooth and prolonged that educational institutions came to think of it as the normal state of affairs.

A major change occurred some ten to twenty years after World War II. Until that time, growth in student bodies and faculties was caused almost entirely by rising levels of educational attainment. College enrollments grew over ten times faster than the college-age population. A higher proportion of students completed high school, more high school graduates entered college, and more college graduates entered graduate school.

Nowadays, these patterns have substantially changed. In our more mature society, the proportion of the population completing high school, the proportion of high school graduates entering college, and the proportion of college graduates continuing on to graduate schools of arts and sciences have been as trends fairly stable for close to a quarter of a century.

With flatter enrollment trends, the growth of higher education has come to depend more on the changing size of the college-age cohort of the population. The size of this group—influenced by a previous "baby boom"— peeked in about 1980 and is projected to decline at least through 1995.[9] This is a second reason why many observers predicted a college enrollment crisis in the 1980s. As we shall see, that is one of the bad things that did not happen.

A third adverse influence of far smaller quantitative significance has been the tendency for a longer working life. Sixty-five used to be the normal age of academic retirement, and today it is seventy. If the current intentions of the federal government are implemented, there will not be any mandatory retirement age at all as of 1994, and it is highly likely that senior professors in research universities

9. Some projections show no appreciable increases after the middle of the 1990s. See *Fact Book*, p. 4. However, the most recent and detailed research predicts sharply rising college enrollments beginning in about 1997 and lasting at least until 2010. See William G. Bowen and Julie Ann Sosa, *Prospects for Faculty in the Arts and Sciences* (Princeton: Princeton University Press, 1989), p. 42.

will attempt to remain active within their universities just as long as possible.

I realize that this proposition is not universally accepted. Some early evidence suggests that professorial retirement plans have remained unaffected by new laws.[10] My experience leads me to believe that problems will arise, especially in what I have called "Two Thirds of the Best." Better working conditions—relatively low teaching loads and most pleasant surroundings—combined with rapidly rising retirement benefits brought by every additional working year, will surely affect the plans of my colleagues.

Any increase in the actual age of retirement will raise the average age of faculty members and may also diminish opportunities for some newly minted Ph.D.'s. In 1975, the average age of American faculty members was about forty-two, and about 6 percent of them were over age sixty. In 1995, it has been estimated (still assuming a retirement age of seventy) that the average age will be about fifty-seven, with 33 percent over age sixty. Whatever one's opinion concerning the proper time for retirement—if any at all—young scholars just beginning their careers have to be somewhat concerned about the implications of these changes. Obviously the intellectual damage would be greatest in fields where knowledge is disproportionately advanced by young scholars—in the main, the natural sciences. At the same time, these young scholars should be told that the rate of retirements has far less influence on the academic market than trends in student enrollments.[11]

The academic marketplace is not only affected by long-term trends. During the working life of any scholar, shorter-term influences will be of greater significance. Current generations of graduate students are most directly affected by the expansion of the 1960s and the contraction of

10. "Expected End of Mandatory Retirement in 1990's Unlikely to Cause Glut of Professors, Study Finds," *The Chronicle of Higher Education,* December 16, 1987. These results pertain primarily to the change of mandatory retirement from age sixty-five to seventy in 1982.

11. See Bowen and Sosa, *Prospects for Faculty,* pp. 126, 159–61.

the 1970s. The net effect of these forces will determine their career prospects.

A variety of social forces led to the boom of the 1960s. In that decade, enrollment in all institutions of higher education doubled, fueled by the postwar baby boom, by veterans benefits, by the reaction to Sputnik, and by President Johnson's Great Society programs. Graduate enrollments tripled, no doubt as a consequence of prevailing optimism concerning job opportunities, combined with generous and new federal sources of support.[12]

The ensuing bust of the 1970s has been well described by President Sovern of Columbia University:

> The problems we face are rooted in a seldom-discussed phenomenon of the 1960's—the post Sputnik boom, when our universities granted tenure to thousands of younger professors. As a result, a bumper crop of Ph.D.'s in the 1970's found an inhospitable market place: the faculty jobs they sought were filled and would stay filled until the waning days of the century. Seeing their fates, many of our most promising young people went to professional schools in pursuit of other careers. Many, if not most, of a generation of top scholars were lost forever to our colleges and universities.[13]

Overproduction of Ph.D.'s—or anything else—generally sets in motion self-correcting forces that will bring demand and supply into balance. We have been living with the effects of these pressures for nearly twenty years; the level of pain is great and the possibilities of long-term harm are considerable. Until the late 1960s, the federal government contributed to the expansion of doctoral programs by funding fellowships and research programs. By 1970, the heyday of federal support for graduate study was clearly over. The number of government fellowships declined by more than 80 percent between 1968 and 1974. At the same time, private foundations phased out many fellowship pro-

12. See Michael J. Sovern, "Higher Education—The Real Crisis," *The New York Times Magazine,* January 22, 1989. See also *Fact Book,* p. 98.
13. *The New York Times Magazine,* January 22, 1989.

grams. At Harvard, the proportion of graduate students holding outside fellowships dropped from 42 percent in 1967–68 to 25 percent in 1977–78. As was to be expected, the size of the applicant pool dropped precipitously in the humanities and the social sciences and admissions fell by an even larger proportion.[14]

Lack of scholarship support is not the only problem. One also has to take into account low starting salaries—low relative to graduates of law, business, or medical schools. "When I left Law School in 1954," said Derek Bok at our 1988 commencement, "the starting salary for Wall Street firms was $4,200, while starting teachers could earn $3,600. Today, the Wall Street salary is between $70,000 and $75,000, and teachers get $17,000–$18,000, a lower pay-check in real dollars than was the case 15 years ago." And currently, the salaries for assistant professors range from $22,000 to $26,000—roughly one third of the remuneration received by beginners on Wall Street.[15]

Where is the long-term harm? Remember that graduate schools are a "necessary condition" for the faculty. If graduate students disappear or become a tiny number, we simply have no university. Scientific research, particularly in laboratories, would become nearly impossible. Professors in other areas could survive, but all the faculty need children, heirs, disciples—and scholars should not suddenly be turned into bachelors and spinsters. Universities have attempted to maintain graduate enrollments through increasing use of their own scarce resources. Even for the richest institutions they are inadequate. An unintended

14. See *Dean's Report, 1977–78.* Also Susan L. Coyle and Yupin Bae, *Summary Report 1986: Doctorate Recipients from United States Universities* (Washington, D.C.: National Academy Press, 1987), pp. 2–14. From 1970 through 1986, doctorates awarded by U.S. universities did not increase. A rising proportion of the degrees—now some 17%—go to foreigners. Government fellowship support has remained strong in the life sciences, and is weak in all other fields.

15. *Fact Book,* p. 122; the figures are for 1984–85. To be sure, some academics can supplement their income on the "outside." And how do we factor in that famous three months summer vacation? These and related issues are discussed in the next section, entitled "Professors." For now, let me say that outside opportunities are available only to a relatively small faculty group that possesses highly marketable skills.

consequence is the diversion of funds from other critical purposes—deferred maintenance, books, laboratories, and so on.

Dim employment prospects and low salaries are bound to affect quality of students now and quality of faculty later. Some will choose the academic life no matter what—individuals who are fatally attracted by the virtues and show little concern for the vices. But in the more ordinary cases, young people make rational and cautious career choices. All of us want to lead decent, well-remunerated lives, and when obvious and interesting alternatives exist, they will be selected without hesitation.

At Harvard, the greatest accolade we can bestow on an undergraduate is a *summa cum laude* degree (with highest praise). Very little has happened since World War II to make that degree easier to attain. Standards have been jealously maintained and occasionally raised, and every year only about 5 percent of the graduating class attains this exalted status. In 1964, 77 percent of these students eventually chose to attend a graduate school of arts and sciences where—I presume—they hoped to attain a Ph.D. in preparation for a life of teaching and researching. More recently, those numbers have declined precipitously. By 1981, only one quarter of our *summas* chose further education in the arts and sciences, and most recently (1987) the proportion has recovered to 32 percent. That is encouraging although it does not make up for the gains scored by law, medicine, and business.[16] And who can blame them? Who can doubt that faculty quality will eventually suffer? By now, "the best and the brightest" may be an unfortunate phrase, but it is an apt description. We do not need to attract this entire group to university work. We do, however, need our share, and that is likely to be larger than a third of Harvard *summas* and their equivalents elsewhere.

What can one say to prospective graduate students fol-

16. Figures from Harvard University, Office of Career Services, "Highlights of the Educational and Career Plans of the Summa cum Laude Graduates and the Members of Phi Beta Kappa in the Class of 1987," December 1987.

lowing our journey through this vale of tears? Oversupply, steady state, no growth, redundancy—nasty words all. Is there a more hopeful message? I think that the answer is yes, and it comes in three parts. First of all, despite the end of the baby boom, the expected enrollment crisis of the 1980s never materialized. As Harrington and Sum have shown, "This is because demographics alone do not determine enrollment trends."[17] Between 1970 and 1983, the college-age population increased by 22 percent, and college enrollment rose by 45 percent. From 1980 to 1987, enrollments still rose by 3.8 percent, although college-age population has been projected to decline 17 percent between 1983 and 1993. The rise in the number of adult students is another offsetting factor, especially the enrollment of part-time female students between the ages of thirty-five and fifty-nine. These results—entirely beneficial for future academics—seem to be the consequence of structural changes in the American economy. Mid-term forecasts indicate declining employment in manufacturing and increasing opportunities in service industries. Many of these jobs are professional, technical, and managerial, and require college degrees (" . . . young college-educated men in 1973 earned 21 percent more than their counterparts who had only completed high school; by 1986, however, this figure had jumped to 57 percent").[18] These structural changes and their accompanying income differentials could introduce new and favorable long-term consequences for the academic marketplace.

By far the most significant favorable element is to be found in the "echo effect" of the great post-World War II baby boom. As a result, U.S. birth rates have risen from the mid-1970s and will continue to rise into the 1990s. That should lead to rising enrollments, more jobs, and faculty shortages toward the end of this century.

17. Paul E. Harrington and Andrew M. Sum, "Whatever Happened to the College Enrollment Crisis?" *Academe: Bulletin of the American Association of University Professors* (September–October 1988), p. 17.

18. *Ibid.*, p. 22.

A final positive factor is the aging of the current faculty reinforced by the previously noted fall in Ph.D. production during the 1970s and 1980s, and the increasing proportion of higher degrees awarded to foreigners. Whether or not professors choose to retire between the "normal" ages sixty-five and seventy, and whatever the legal situation, at some point those in the post-World War II bulge will have to depart feet first and, on average, not too many years after reaching age seventy.

For all these reasons, many authorities foresee that "a very much better outlook for academic employment will present itself in the mid-to-late 1990's."[19] Over the next twenty-five years (1985–2009), "the number of appointments will probably equal two-thirds or more of the entire faculty as of 1985."[20] Of course, opportunities differ by fields, but on the whole, there is an optimistic consensus about the second half of the 1990s.[21] Nevertheless, it is worth recalling what was said by the Danish physicist Niels Bohr as cited in Harrington and Sum: predictions can be very difficult—especially those about the future.

## Advice of Modest Usefulness for Present and Future Graduate Students

Undergraduate and graduate students in American universities have different intellectual goals. Candidates for the bachelor's degree at selective schools are seeking a liberal education, or—to use a more descriptive phrase—a general education. They are required to choose a major or concentration, but this tends to be a somewhat casual intellectual commitment; the principal purpose is to give the student some exposure to learning in depth. What under-

19. William G. Bowen, "Scholarship and Its Survival: Demography," A Colloquium on Graduate Education in America (Princeton, December 1983), p. 13.

20. Howard R. Bowen and Jack H. Schuster, *American Professors: A National Resource Imperiled* (New York: Oxford University Press, 1986), pp. 197–198.

21. For a note of caution, see Peter D. Syverson and Lorna E. Foster, "New Ph.D.'s and the Academic Labor Market," Office of Scientific and Engineering Personnel (National Research Council), Staff Paper No. 1, December 1984.

graduates study need have no obvious relation to subsequent graduate training. It is not unusual for a literature major to attend medical school or for an economics concentrator to do graduate work in architecture. A strong liberal arts curriculum is good preparation for all types of professional training. None of this can be compared to the commitment required in choosing a field for the Ph.D. For an undergraduate, a mistaken choice is of relatively small consequence; it can always be remedied. Selecting the wrong graduate field could easily result in a misdirected and unhappy working life. Undergraduates dabble in subjects; they are dilettantes, and that is as it should be. Graduate students make lifetime commitments.

Under the circumstances, it is far more difficult to discuss graduate students "in general." Special fields dominate culture, lifestyle, morale, and future. For these reasons, it makes little sense ever to contemplate an overall reexamination or reform of graduate education. Many years ago, when I wrote to all of my colleagues concerning problems with our undergraduate curriculum, I was inundated with replies and opinions. Nearly everyone had strongly held views and welcomed the opportunity to discuss them in a large public forum. A similar effort on behalf of the graduate school was greeted by manifest lack of interest and silence. There was absolutely no desire for exchanges of views beyond departmental levels, because—I believe— disciplines dominate learning at this advanced level (English and chemistry professors saw little common ground, except perhaps the universal feeling that more money would solve most problems). General or liberal education of a non-departmental nature does not exist for postgraduate students in arts and sciences. Perhaps it should; perhaps one can find a rare instance of its existence; but it would be a great exception. Nevertheless, I will try to focus on the few commonalities of graduate student life.

Positive reasons for choosing an academic life are discussed in the next section of this book, and most especially in the chapters on Academic Life: Some Virtues, Some Vices, and those on Tenure. In those chapters, I have tried to paint an upbeat picture—to be sure, in a narrow range of schools—without minimizing the problems. The narrow range has to be stressed because the lower one moves down the scale of quality and prestige, the more virtues have to be discounted. All the listed merits will be diminished: less independence, more routine, smaller salaries, fewer good students, and so on. Of course, there may be counterbalancing attractions: location, climate, size, specific colleagues, what have you. Individual preferences are complicated. I know professors who have turned down tenured positions at the best research universities so as to remain in small colleges. Those need not be irrational choices.

With all of that in mind, I offer the following suggestions of moderate usefulness. I do not wish to discourage anyone. I do wish to stress realism.

## 1. **Enter Ph.D. programs with your eyes wide open.**

It is not all that hard to gain admission to a good graduate program, although the degree of difficulty differs by institution and field. For example, programs in the humanities tend to be rather casual in their admission procedures and may rely on high failure rates to reduce numbers to manageable proportions. Laboratory sciences, on the other hand, have to be concerned about limited bench space and are inclined to restrict entry. Some graduate programs beat the bushes for warm bodies while others routinely turn away large numbers of applicants. In general, however, competition is less severe for graduate than for undergraduate places at selective institutions. It is relatively easy to get in; for example, at Stanford, Chicago, and Yale (and others), the ratio of admittances to applications was significantly higher for graduates than for undergraduates. It is harder to get out; in 1983, the median period from baccalaureate to doctorate in this country was an unbelievable ten years.[22] It is still harder to have a successful career, defined as tenure in a "reasonably satisfactory" college or university.[23]

Getting into graduate school is not the principal hurdle; getting out may take a long time, but most people manage. The biggest problem usually comes ten or fifteen years after starting a Ph.D. program, and it is securing an acceptable tenured job. For this reason alone, it is very important to know something about the opportunities in a chosen field. Are jobs available now and are estimates about the future optimistic? Would you be satisfied with a job in industry or government if that was all that was available in your future profession? Would you be satisfied teaching in a small college located in the rural Southwest where there was no opportunity for graduate teaching, where library resources were poor, and any student with sufficient tuition money was welcome? No one suggests that you should be happy in this situation, but could you stand it? I stress these unpleasant questions because graduate students are prone to make misleading judgments based on their own experience in graduate schools. Universities that offer Ph.D. training represent, on average, the top tier of American higher education.[24] And it is in these institutions that graduate students imagine their own future. They deserve to be warned at the time of entry and also during the training period that many academic careers involve—one hopes only temporary—downward mobility.

Who should be encouraged to seek a Ph.D.? Talent to

22. The breakdown by principal areas: 7.4 years in the physical sciences and engineering; 7.9 years in the biological sciences; 9.3 years in the social sciences; and 11.1 years in the arts and humanities. These figures cover all of higher education and include professional fields as well as education, where the time period is 14.1 years. My belief is that the top institutions force their graduate students through the system with greater efficiency. At Harvard, the average from baccalaureate to doctorate is six years—long enough! See *Fact Book*, p. 141.

23. Despite previously described academic attitudes, a significant proportion of Ph.D.'s has always worked outside of higher education. A recent estimate (1984–85) shows 57% of active Ph.D.'s in the U.S. population serving as faculty members. The highest level ever attained after World War II was 70% during 1975–76. See Bowen and Schuster, *American Professors*, p. 179.

24. To complete the top tier, we need add on only the high-quality liberal arts colleges, about one hundred in number.

complete a particular curriculum is an obvious necessity, and only rarely a problem. Students should be quite knowledgeable about field requirements and their own abilities by the time they get bachelor's degrees. In any event, talent alone is no longer sufficient under present circumstances. We should also look for passion, preferably even an obsession with the proposed subject. When the market for academics was expanding at unprecedented rates in the 1960s, some people chose college and university teaching because of a vague liking for the style of life. There are amongst us clergymen who have made similar decisions: their belief in God may be uncertain, but they enjoy preaching in suburban churches and synagogues. That is inadequate motivation for this generation. The road is too full of detours and the risks of disappointment are too great. We should be looking for young men and women who find it difficult to distinguish between work and pleasure when it comes to academic tasks. If not, why not try an easier path? I see the perfect Ph.D. candidate as delicately balancing an obsession with subject and an up-to-date market survey for a particular field.[25] If I have described you, by all means join us.

## 2. Choose a thesis adviser with great care. It is one of the most important decisions that you will make as a student.

In American universities, a Ph.D. program ordinarily starts with two years of graduate course work, followed by the research for and the writing of a dissertation. The period of course work is pretty much a continuation of college. The courses may be more difficult and more specialized, but the atmosphere is familiar and comfortable. Strangely enough, grading tends to be easier in graduate courses, with an A– frequently representing the aver-

25. I have already mentioned the effect of affirmative action. Obviously one would also encourage "underrepresented minorities," i.e., women, blacks, Hispanics, and a few other categories. We know that for the foreseeable future, efforts will be made to bring these groups into the university as faculty members; any individual fitting these descriptions can and should take advantage of this situation.

age.[26] Perhaps this makes sense. For future scholars, course performance is not a reliable indicator of long-term success. The thesis is of far greater significance. So, I am urging an especially careful choice when it comes to the dissertation guide—the *Doktorvater* or surrogate parent.

Undertaking a major research project and writing a thesis is a new experience for nearly all students. They will need help in developing a project and not infrequently—especially in the natural sciences—advisers will suggest a topic. In addition, students need a reader of drafts, a critic. Very often part of the research will be financed by means of professorial grants; and a successful thesis can shape a scholar's research agenda for many years. This is intellectual guidance, and does not complete the duties of a good thesis adviser. Assisting the graduate student in finding a job is another responsibility. Is your prospective mentor someone to whom the profession turns, someone who is widely respected, with contacts throughout the country and at many different types of institutions? Professors do their own networking, and gaining entry in your field is a tremendous long-term advantage. These can be very major considerations, of far greater importance to the student entering the job market than the size or efficiency of a university placement office. Finally, and not least important, I wish to suggest a more intangible quality. If possible, one should search for a supportive mentor, someone who will extend a hand while crossing the dark valleys on the way to a thesis, and who will also be present during similarly hard times that crop up in the early stages of any academic career. One of my two thesis advisers was a paragon. All my letters were answered by return mail, typed with two fingers on an ancient typewriter. He made me feel that my work was important and that he enjoyed learning from me! During a difficult period he put me up at his house for a

---

26. The Austrian economist Joseph A. Schumpeter, who taught at Harvard in the 1930s and 1940s, is said to have given three kinds of A's: the Chinese A, awarded automatically to all foreign students; the female A, given to all women, of whom there were very few; and finally the ordinary A, for everyone else in the class.

week, while we discussed my results for many hours every day. Do they still make them this way today?

Students have difficulty in making the right choices, largely because of inadequate information. Note, for example, that the task of thesis guidance is unevenly distributed in departments. Some professors have many students while others have very few. Some have none at all. An optimal choice is not necessarily the most glamorous professor; pastoral qualities may outweigh all other considerations. In my experience, all universities are home to some teachers whose greatest contribution is Ph.D. advising, rather than writing or lecturing. These are valuable contributors to the university enterprise, who may gain modest immortality in the acknowledgement pages of books. There are supermen and women who can do it all. I have not met many. Again, the main point: make a very careful choice and do not be tempted by glitz. Find out who has the most students and why. Find out what fellow students and former students have to say. Ask questions. Ask more questions.

### 3. **Fight isolation: it is the greatest enemy of graduate students.**

Research is a lonely activity, especially when the location is a library rather than a laboratory. Few experiences in our working life can be more isolating than gathering materials for a dissertation deep in the bowels of some large library. No one can help; no human voice is heard; the only constant is that very special smell of decaying books. Am I on the right track? Could it all be a gigantic waste of time? Self-doubt grows day by day. In sharp contrast, I have always visualized the research laboratory as a community, functioning twenty-fours hours a day around support groups consisting of coffee pots, people of various ages and skills, all under the benevolent supervision of a sage scientist. Perhaps this is the slightly romantic or envious view of a non-scientist, and perhaps I have exaggerated the plight of humanists; but even if both descriptions have to be heavily discounted, there remains a valid contrast. All research has lonely dimensions because basic ideas have to originate in a single mind. Loneliness or isolation is particularly strong for graduate students in the humanities and social sciences because cooperative research is discouraged, especially when writing a dissertation: that is intended to be individual work to exhibit one's own capacities.

Isolation is reinforced by social conditions. Many graduate students are married, have family responsibilities, and live far away from campus where rents are lower. Competition among graduate students adds to the problem. They are not just trying to outdo one another in the spirit of a playful contest; their future may depend on comparative performance in classes or seminars. Who will then resist the clever putdown of a classmate in front of a professor and a seminar audience? These forces undermine student self-confidence, increase the feelings of isolation, and are in stark contrast to the more happy-go-lucky attitude of the undergraduate population.

I do not know of any general rules that can be applied to fighting isolation. Many years ago I was a founding member of the Liquidity Preference Marching and Chowder Society,[27] a small group of economics graduate students that met regularly both to study and to socialize. While it lasted we were all beneficiaries, and groups of this type should be encouraged and helped by departments. In the social sciences, workshops sometimes succeed in becoming functional equivalents of laboratories. Typically, they are built around a subfield—for example, economic history, American politics, literary theory—should have their own locations, a reading room, and be available as gathering places at almost all times for serious discussion, bull sessions, or the simple need to talk to another person at midnight when self-doubt is at its height. Of course, professors should also be regular inhabitants of their workshops, not necessarily

27. Economists will have no difficulty in recognizing liquidity preference as one of the Keynesian determinants for the rate of interest. The double entendre is obvious, as is the fact that this is—unfortunately—typical graduate student humor.

at midnight, but not only "nine to five." An especially important community-creating aspect of the laboratory is that experiments require attendance at odd hours of the day or night. Much of the work is of a continuous flow nature, and the demands on equipment also require twenty-four-hour scheduling. None of this happens very much in other fields, and I am not advocating night work for philosophy professors and graduate students. What we do need is the self-conscious search for the spirit of the laboratory outside of the natural sciences. Humanists in particular need to consider these issues. Anything that decreases the feeling of isolation deserves encouragement.

4. **When ready to take your first job, choose the best available school, even at some financial sacrifice, and even if the chances for promotion appear somewhat more dubious.**

I understand the attraction of tenure-track positions and the desire for security in an uncertain market. Yet precisely because of the current uncertainties, too many scholars in the immediate postdoctoral phase of their career may underestimate the long-term benefits that come from the most demanding colleagues and the best possible students. Challenges from both of these quarters will help the new teacher to achieve his or her full potential. It is a far more difficult goal to achieve when one is unpaced and effortlessly reaches the head of the line. Most of us benefited enormously from being challenged by our institutions—it is vital in building our intellectual muscle. Keep this in mind: in academic life the forces of downward mobility are very powerful. Searches for new professors focus on similar schools and working at lesser institutions under adverse conditions makes it progressively harder to climb the ladder. Moving up after moving down is always difficult.

The preceding pages have, somewhat inadvertently, acquired a flavor of "blood, sweat and tears." I do not apologize for gloomy warnings, because I have tried to educate, to prevent disappointment, and to take account of current realities. But a warning is only meant to put someone on guard, to prevent a mistake. It is not meant to close doors. I know many happy graduate students whose professional and personal lives are fulfilled. Furthermore, most of us do see signs of improvement in the academic marketplace: greater opportunities in the 1990s as an older generation gradually (unfortunately, too gradually) leaves the scene. Above all, in what follows I intend to celebrate—in a realistic manner—the virtues and pleasures of professorial life. I urge all graduate students to read on.

# PROFESSORS

# 9

## Academic Life

### *Some Virtues, Some Vices*

For a large segment of the population, going to work in the morning is a chore. Jobs are monotonous; discipline is imposed by machines, time clocks, and authoritarian superiors. In factories, the physical setting is unattractive and noisy. Work that is physically punishing is not confined to blue-collar occupations. As a young man some forty years ago, I spent a few months selling toys at Macy's in New York City. Twice a week, the store was open from 9:00 A.M. to 9:00 P.M., and standing behind the counter on those long days was sheer torture.

At executive levels, one encounters different forms of pain: implicit dress codes, implicit political codes, a controlled lifestyle. And people have to be concerned about layoffs, discharges later in their working life, or hopeless unemployment in obsolescent industries.

These are not, of course, universally the conditions of work. Many workers are happy in their jobs, and alienation is a tired, overused concept. Nevertheless, many go to work without joy, primarily to earn a living. It is my observation supported by some evidence that professors at good universities have a much more positive attitude toward their work.[1]

One reason may be that most of our colleges and universities are physically attractive. The very notion of campus evokes in our minds a picture of trees, lawns, and imposing structures. Campuses contain a significant proportion of the best examples of American architecture. I have spent a considerable number of years at each of three institutions—William and Mary, Berkeley, and Harvard—and I have visited many more. William and Mary is the site of the only building in this country "perhaps" designed by Sir Christopher Wren. It is a lovely, modest brick structure, housing chapel, hall, and classrooms, and overlooking an impressive sunken garden. Everything at William and Mary also harmonizes elegantly with Colonial Williamsburg; it is one of the most beautiful locations on the East Coast.

Berkeley is a campus of the University of California; state bureaucracy combined with post–World War II expansion have done much to obliterate what once was an Eden. Nevertheless, there are few more gorgeous sites anywhere. From many of its parts the great reaches of San Francisco Bay are visible; the fog can lend its own special magic to Berkeley; and many of the older buildings represent the best of late nineteenth-century California creativity.

Harvard Yard—elsewhere it would be called a campus—and its surroundings are a history of American and European architecture in three dimensions. Harvard Hall and Massachusetts Hall, built before the Revolutionary War, are still in daily use. The finest building in the Yard, the gray stone University Hall erected in the early nineteenth century and designed by Charles Bullfinch, shelters the dean of the Faculty of Arts and Sciences. In front is Daniel Chester French's idealized statue of John Harvard, in all

1. "American academics are generally happy with their choice of careers. Eighty-eight percent of them, for example, maintain that, were they to begin anew, they would still want to be college professors." E. C. Ladd, Jr., and S. M. Lipset, *The Chronicle of Higher Education,* May 3, 1976.

seasons the object of tourist attention. And I could go on to the Yard dormitories, Widener Library, Memorial Church, the Carpenter Center for the Visual Arts designed by Le Corbusier (his only building in North America).

I return to urge my point: the physical setting in which we labor matters enormously. Of this I am aware every morning as I cross the ever-changing urban squalor of Harvard Square and enter the Yard. It is an oasis; it pleases the eye and the mind in all seasons; it is a refreshing start to any working day. I think with pity of my neighbors arriving in downtown Boston to inhabit all day the synthetic atmosphere of yet another glass-lined tower.

The attraction of a campus goes well beyond architect and landscape. People like to be around universities—they enjoy the ambience. Boston, with its many colleges, has been called the youth capital of America. Psychiatrists and successful businessmen—who else can afford to pay the real estate prices?—live in Cambridge because of Harvard's presence. For them, the campus is a circus with many free side shows: museums, libraries, lectures, entertainment. Students are part of the spectacle—they set or reflect the latest in dress, music, movies, and food. To be near students—near and yet far enough away to permit occasional withdrawal—is to feel young and alive well into late middle age. It is why Palo Alto, Durham–Chapel Hill, Ann Arbor, as also Cambridge and Berkeley, have all become favored places of residence for the non-academic upper middle class.

The major aspect of the professor's work is not however the setting but the content, and here again the virtues of academic life become apparent. A friend of my father's, a tutor at St. John's College in Annapolis, when asked about his choice of occupation, said that he loved reading more than anything else; college teaching was the only profession that paid a salary for doing that. The essence of academic life is the opportunity—indeed, the demand—for continual investment in oneself. It is a unique chance for a lifetime of building and renewing intellectual capital. For many, teaching provides the greatest satisfaction.[2] For others, research is the key: it satisfies intellectual curiosity and nourishes the joys and glories of discovery.

You ask: is this not true of all occupations that exercise the mind? Is it not true of teachers at all educational levels? This is a matter of degree, but the differences are significant. In universities that emphasize research—and this is my main topic—keeping up to date can be extremely demanding and time-consuming. Modern biology, for example, has been exploding with new knowledge ever since the cracking of the genetic code by James Watson and Francis Crick in the 1950s. Its practitioners tell me that to remain abreast of current findings even in their own narrowly defined fields is almost a full-time occupation. They regularly follow these assertions with requests for reduced teaching loads—"we really do not have the time!" While thus arousing the suspicions of a dean, I know that they have a case.

Modern biology may be the most extreme example of such pressure and strain, although computer sciences and some branches of physics cannot be far behind. Nor is the phenomenon confined to the natural sciences. I completed the formal part of graduate studies in economics in the early 1950s. At that time, a knowledge of mathematics was not considered an absolutely necessary part of an economist's toolkit. By the end of the decade it was; without training in econometrics and mathematical economics, it had become impossible to read much of the professional literature. What happened in economics is now occurring in political science with the increasing use of quantitative models. Even the humanities are not immune to these revolutions, although scholars here resist change with more energy. The last twenty years have witnessed the growing influence of literary theory, semiotics, new historicism, bringing with them new constructs, a different vocab-

---

2. Only 25% of American professors indicate a strong interest in research. The remainder indicate a stronger commitment to teaching. These results are reported in the Ladd-Lipset surveys. See *The Chronicle of Higher Education,* March 29, 1976. Obviously the proportion of committed researchers will be larger in the better universities.

ulary, and non-traditional philosophical assumptions. So for the individual humanist it has become necessary to acquire new skills, to learn a new and difficult language.

These are only random examples of the pressure on academic life of research. A complementary pressure comes from graduate students. Young scholars have their eyes exclusively on the future. The "leading edge" is their ticket to success. Adherence to tradition may be dangerous. Since professors are in large measure judged by the size and quality of their graduate student followings, the incentives to be *au courant* with the latest fashions are again considerable.

Thus academic life is a world in motion. Some changes revolutionize fields of study; occasionally new subjects are born; some innovations are ephemeral and quickly forgotten. New ideas can make life miserable for the many who have a stake in the old ways, generating conflict between the adherents of the old and the new. Every scholar has to face these fundamental challenges during his or her lifetime. It is at once a burden, a challenge, and one of the attractions of academic life.

Intellectual investment is not entirely a response to challenges from others. Many scholars pursue their own ideas with little reference to peer groups. Whatever the motive, the act of research is a form of mental renewal and a great potential benefit to the individual. These challenges and opportunities can be present in some degree in other occupations, but not so often, I suspect, and I would argue that the combination of research and new ways of looking at things is a special characteristic of the university. The share of routine is smaller than in any other occupation.

Another critical virtue of academic life—I am thinking of tenured professors at, say, America's top fifty to one hundred institutions—is the absence of a boss. A boss is someone who can tell you what to do, and requires you to do it—an impairment of freedom. As a dean—i.e., as an administrator—my boss was the president. I served at his pleasure; he could and did give me orders. But as a professor, I recognized no master save peer pressure, no threat except, perhaps, an unlikely charge of moral turpitude. No profession guarantees its practitioners such a combination of independence and security as university research and teaching. Let me amplify this point.

In the early 1950s, the University of California was plunged into grave controversy by the state's insistence that all its employees sign an anti-Communist loyalty oath. Those were the days of McCarthy and the red scares. State and federal committees on un-American activities stalked the land. There was opposition to the loyalty oaths inside and outside the university, although in the end nearly everyone signed. A few professors refused and were dismissed.

The most interesting refusal was tendered by Professor E. K. Kantorowicz, a famous medieval historian and refugee from Hitler's Germany. He did not particularly object to a loyalty oath requirement—I am not suggesting that he approved it. Rather, he had a deeper objection: he did not wish under any circumstances to be classified as an employee of the state of California. Kantorowicz believed professors were not university employees subject to the usual job discipline. To be a professor was to be of a different calling. Employees work specified hours and may be paid overtime; they are given specific tasks; in most cases there is a sharp separation between work and leisure; frequently the service performed is impersonal. Does it really matter who sells you a pair of shoes?

In Kantorowicz's own words:

> There are three professions which are entitled to wear the gown: the judge, the priest and the scholar. This garment stands for its bearer's maturity of mind, his independence of judgement, and his direct responsibility to his conscience and his god.
>
> It signifies the inner sovereignty of those three interrelated professions: they should be the very last to allow themselves to act under duress and yield to pressure.

Why is it so absurd to visualize the Supreme Court Justices picketing their court, bishops picketing their churches and professors picketing their universities? The answer is very simple: because the judges *are* the court, the ministers together with the faithful *are* the church, and the professors together with the students *are* the university . . . they are those institutions themselves, and therefore have prerogative rights to and within their institution which ushers, sextons and beadles, and janitors do not have.[3]

The distinction held by Kantorowicz is most valuable. We professors have the income of civil servants but the freedom of artists. This imposes certain obligations. The formal duties imposed by our institutions are minimal, anywhere between six and twelve hours in the classroom per week during eight months of the year.[4] Yet most of us work long hours and spend many evenings at our desks or in our laboratories. We do not tell students that this is our day off, that they must seek someone else with whom to discuss their problems. We do practice our profession as a calling, considering ourselves not employees but shareholders of the university: a group of owners. "Share values" are determined by the quality of management and the product. We seek to keep those values as high as possible. None of this is to deny that we very much enjoy the calling, and believe that we are engaged in activities of high social value.

I must mention Professor Kantorowicz again, for on his death in 1963 there was an ironic twist to what I have just written. He was then a professor at the Institute for Advanced Studies in Princeton, New Jersey. The San Francisco *Chronicle* took note of the passing away of a distinguished former Californian. Besides misspelling his name (Catorowicz), an indignity that some of us get used to, the

3. Grover Sale, Jr., "The Scholar and the Loyalty Oath," San Francisco *Chronicle*, December 8, 1963.

4. Another California story seems appropriate. A professor was testifying before a state committee in Sacramento. The chairman asked: "How many hours do you teach, doctor?" Reply: "Eight hours." The chairman then said: "That is excellent. I have always been a strong supporter of the eight-hour day."

obituary said: "He was *employed* at the University of California at Berkeley from 1939 to 1950."[5]

There are yet other rewards that apply particularly to tenured members of the faculty. Sabbatical leaves are an especially agreeable custom. A university professor so favored is relieved of teaching duties every seventh year in order to allow mental refreshment. This year of refreshment is accompanied by a reduction in salary, but research or other grants on many occasions make up the shortfall. Faculty members love sabbaticals. Projects can be completed, sites visited, colleagues in distant places consulted. Professors tend to be enthusiastic travelers and their way of life encourages this natural proclivity. For the best among them, the reference groups are thoroughly international. In addition, a significant proportion of research topics require travel and foreign residence.

My own case may be only slightly untypical. I lived in Japan for nearly five years as a soldier, graduate student, teacher, and researcher. I spent fairly long periods lecturing, researching, and consulting in the United Kingdom, Indonesia, and Israel. And I have lost count of the foreign countries in which I have attended conferences. Since these activities combine business and pleasure, they can be viewed as fringe benefits. University professors at major institutions are among the leading "frequent travelers" in this country—I should think immediately behind pilots, flight attendants, professional athletes, and on a par with salesmen. Abuses do exist, and some of my friends, with heavy sarcasm, have been referred to as the "Pan American Airways Professor of Biology," the "Swissair Professor of Physics," or the "El Al Professor of Sociology."

In a recent study of academic mores, the novelist David Lodge—who first noted that the three things that have revolutionized academic life in the last twenty years were jet travel, direct-dialing telephones, and the Xerox machine—describes our periodic gatherings this way:

5. San Francisco *Chronicle*, September 13, 1963.

The modern conference resembles the pilgrimage of medieval Christendom in that it allows the participants to indulge themselves in all the pleasures and diversions of travel while appearing to be austerely bent on self-improvement. To be sure, there are certain penitential exercises to be performed—the presentation of a paper, perhaps, and certainly listening to the papers of others. But with this excuse you journey to new and interesting places, meet new and interesting people, and form new and interesting relationships with them; exchange gossip and confidences (for your well-worn stories are fresh to them, and vice versa); eat, drink and make merry in their company every evening; and yet, at the end of it all, return home with an enhanced reputation for seriousness of mind. Today's conferees have an additional advantage over the pilgrims of old in that their expenses are usually paid, or at least subsidized, by the institution to which they belong, be it a government department, a commercial firm, or, most commonly perhaps, a university.[6]

The alleged abuses can be more apparent than real. In 1984, my former colleague Carlo M. Rubbia won the Nobel Prize in Physics. A Harvard professor and high-energy physicist in search of new particles, he required the services of a large accelerator. None was available in Cambridge, Massachusetts. Other sites in the United States proved unsuitable, and so Rubbia shifted his activities to the European Center for Nuclear Research in Geneva, Switzerland. Every two weeks or so he traveled abroad to carry out experiments, spending many days away from Cambridge. A clever individual, Rubbia purchased a string of the cheapest APEX tickets every seven days or so and used them on a staggered basis, thereby circumventing the requirement that the user remain abroad more than fifteen days. I am told that the people at Swissair got to know him so well that an upgrade to first class virtually became automatic—long before the Nobel award. On my own rather frequent trips to the West Coast I usually spot a colleague or two on their way to SLAC—the Stanford linear accelerator.

6. David Lodge, *Small World* (New York: The Macmillan Company, 1984), prologue.

Closely connected with sabbaticals and travel is another generally positive feature of academic life—at least from the point of view of the faculty. Along with professional independence, the absence of bosses and the light nature of formal obligations have been mentioned. (Informal obligations when taken seriously, and that is the normal case, are demanding and time-consuming.) The professor controls his or her time to an unusual degree, and it is generally accepted that some time can be used for "outside work." The long vacations are available for that purpose. In addition, at Harvard and elsewhere a professor is permitted to spend one day a week on non-university activities.[7]

"Outside work" can take many forms and at the margins is extremely difficult to define. Public service is generally encouraged, although with disagreement as to what fits under that rubric. There is an evident difference between campaigning for a political candidate and testifying as an expert before a congressional committee. Still, public service—for example, unpaid leave from the university for one year or more to take an assignment in Washington—is favorably viewed.[8]

For some, though by no means the preponderance of the faculty, there is also the opportunity of earning additional money from extramural activities. In one highly unusual case at Harvard, a professor became a part-time salesman in Filene's basement. Consulting for private industry is a more common and remunerative activity. Some have successfully started companies. My late colleague, the distinguished economist Otto Eckstein, founded DRI, a highly successful economic forecasting enterprise. At least five biogenetic firms have been started by Harvard professors. Many professors go on lecture tours and a few have the

7. To enforce this rule is impossible: try to define "one day a week." Surely vacations are not included. How about weekends? In any event, surveillance is impractical and objectionable. As usual, one has to rely on the sense of obligation of the individual.

8. The Harvard rule permits no more than one year of leave under ordinary circumstances. Public service is the only exception, when a two-year leave is permitted. These rules differ significantly from place to place.

skills to give concerts. In certain faculties, notably at the Business School, corporate board memberships are readily available. It is even possible to make a fortune by writing, and Professor *emeritus* J. K. Galbraith has been the outstanding example at Harvard during the last three decades.

There are significant negatives associated with outside activities to which I will return, but a word is needed now. The ability to sell our services beyond the walls of the academy is closely correlated with the institutional label we are able to use. It helps to be at a famous university: economists would say that we derive a rent from such association. Since outsiders have some difficulty in making independent judgments as to talent, they, sometimes unwisely, put much faith in labels—a Harvard professor. The individual sells his institution at least in part. Also, only a relatively small proportion of a faculty possess skills that are readily marketable on the outside. Leaving aside the professional schools as belonging to a different universe, sizable extra earnings come primarily to scientists, economists, and a few other social scientists. A successful history or English text will earn money, but such opportunity is far less available than imagined. I am aware of no reliable figures on this entire topic, but my guess is that in Harvard's Faculty of Arts and Sciences, only about one third of the members earn 20 percent or more of their salaries on the outside. Many fewer will exceed that 20 percent by a large margin. In considering the financial aspects of university life, for most people the salary must be thought controlling.

**The View from Below**

Some of my colleagues—especially those on probationary appointments without the boon of tenure (see chapter 10)—may take a different view of our profession and its pleasures. They will consider my words to be smug and self-satisfied, written in praise of those who have "made it," and out of touch with younger scholars still climbing the ladder or with those who may never reach the top. These feelings are understandable, even though no one starts out as a tenured professor, and all of us have experienced some of the same agonies. What does change from time to time is the state of the academic market during the early years of a career. For example, the 1950s were a mediocre decade for job seekers; good positions were hard to find. I easily recall my last year as a research student in Japan (1957–58). Having already acquired a wife and child, I desperately awaited a job offer from home. Berkeley finally came through in the late spring—it was my only offer. By way of contrast, the 1960s were absolutely outstanding, as universities in all parts of the country expanded in the wake of Sputnik and the Great Society. Demand was so strong that standards for appointment probably declined. Government cutbacks in education and general stagflation created disastrous job markets for academics during nearly all of the 1970s and the first half of the 1980s. Many of the finest young scholars had difficulties in being placed. Currently the situation is getting better as the postwar generation of professors reaches the age of seventy and as institutions of higher learning benefit from a general improvement in the economy. Obviously the mood of young faculty members competing for positions and promotions is closely related to their own opportunities in the academic marketplace. A few geniuses or near geniuses will always be in demand, but the mood of individuals even with outstanding talents will be greatly affected by the number of vacancies at the top.

Strengths and weaknesses of market forces are not the whole story. As a consequence of an "up or out" or probationary system (described in chapter 10 on Tenure), the environment will always appear cruel to the "junior faculty." The very use of that term creates a condescending atmosphere. Those so-called juniors all hold the Ph.D. or similar advanced degrees. They are adults, mostly in their thirties, and not infrequently internationally recognized authorities in their subjects. Their technical competence and command of the latest research tools is often superior to that of their senior colleagues—largely a result of having been trained more recently. In terms of teaching, research, advising, or committee assignments, they perform exactly the same duties as their elders; in truth, junior professors are routinely given the least desirable assignments. They are assigned unpopular required courses, equally unpopular student advising, and classes that meet at eight in the morning or late Friday afternoon. And finally we come to the basic oddity of the non-tenured faculty's position: they do exactly what the senior faculty does, only for half the pay, less status, fewer amenities, and an uncertain future. It is a most unusual and alienating situation.

In an army—to cite the example of another hierarchical organization—the officer corps is divided into company grade, field grade, and general officers, all with different pay and privileges. These reflect seniority, duties, and responsibilities. Commanding a platoon and commanding an army are not the same thing. To do the job properly, a general needs more staff than a lieutenant. A law firm comes closer to a university department, with its division between associates and partners. Even here the academic situation remains unusual, because associates in law firms often assist or work under the supervision of partners. That is not at all the situation in a university. An assistant professor does not assist anyone; an associate professor is not anybody's associate. These are merely designations for independent scholars who receive low pay and little secretarial help, while performing the same tasks as full professors. To outsiders—as well as many insiders—all this has to appear quite exploitative.[9]

9. Some of my colleagues may object to this description. They will claim that tenured professors have more burdensome administrative duties inside and outside of the university. Many serve on national committees and are active in a variety of academies and professional societies. Senior professors will also point to their heavier load in guiding Ph.D. theses. Although individual situations differ, I reject the average validity of these claims. Administrative duties are benefits as well as costs, and one is rarely forced into these tasks. The same is true of national service. Furthermore, not all professors have many Ph.D. students, and when they are numerous, their presence is certainly taken as a sign of one's own intellectual excellence. The one clear difference is that the non-tenured members do not participate in the labor-intensive work connected with promotion to tenure. Surely that is not a sufficient discrepancy to account entirely for the cleavage between the two groups.

As if all of this were not sufficient, we add one more blow that creates the deepest of all psychological wounds: explicit rejection frequently occurring at the end of a six- to eight-year term. At Harvard, in the Arts and Sciences, rejection happens in approximately eight out of ten cases. Proportions will vary, but in institutions that are included in "Two Thirds of the Best," retention is never routine. Furthermore, failure to be promoted to tenure is not the consequence of a casual act. It does not come about because some faceless authority forgets to renew a contract or cites plausible reasons of, say, economic hardship. On the contrary, rejection is carefully calculated, determined by close associates, and it is even public. From that point on, the scholar is marked with a scarlet letter, always having to explain the basis of a presumably mistaken negative judgment. In every case with which I am familiar, the result is a scar that may not even be wiped out by the award of the highest professional honors.

Why would anybody, apparently so smart, be dumb enough to permit him- or herself to be placed in the situation of a junior faculty member? Are they masochists? Not at all: theirs is a reasonable choice because the pain of the early years is outweighed by the rewards of a tenured career. What economists call "revealed preference" tells the story: non-tenured faculty members want most of all to be professors at good universities; other attractive alternatives are clearly second choices. These so-called victims of exploitation are strong believers in the virtues of academic life as revealed by their attitude and, above all, actions.

Although based on impressionistic evidence, I believe that observers of the university scene will agree that the very best graduate students and junior professors want to remain in the academy. This is certainly true in arts and sciences; to a lesser degree it applies also to professional schools. Economics can serve as an excellent example because it is a field whose skills are used inside and outside of the university.

A number of Harvard graduates in economics have made distinguished careers in banking or government, or perhaps international organizations. Some have made large fortunes. When their names and achievements arise in conversation, there is likely to be an undertone of sorrow: "Rubinstein owns a quarter of Manhattan, and is regularly consulted by the President of the United States. I remember him as a pretty bright young fellow. Too bad he wasn't quite good enough to become a professor at Berkeley." Rubinstein may not share these feelings, but I think they fairly represent academic attitudes of all ranks. I have also known a number of students who—during the lean years of the 1970s and early 1980s—took lucrative posts in business. At the first good opportunity they were happy to resume academic careers.

In fact, most non-tenured professors eventually receive permanent posts somewhere, but not necessarily at the institution of initial appointment. When the academic market is strong, it is still not possible for a few top schools to provide posts for all talented scholars. At those times, however, a junior appointment at—for example—Harvard, Stanford, or Chicago pretty much guarantees an excellent post at some reasonable university in the United States. At other times, tenure at a good place can be a more elusive goal. During the 1970s there developed a class of academic journeymen whose members never climbed "up" and were always shown the way "out." They became permanent visitors, and without a doubt some left the professoriate for other more welcoming occupations. I do not know of any firm estimates concerning the size of this unhappy cohort. Personal observation leads me to believe that the number is not large. Achieving tenure is not an unrealistic expectation, although many younger scholars at the most highly ranked universities may have to move down a notch in order to gain security. That improves quality on a national basis and is one reason for the growing number of centers of academic excellence in our country.

An additional refinement is useful. The supply of academic talent can be—in my view—divided into two broad categories: those with great comparative advantage for teaching and research (sometimes manifestly unfit for other types of work), and those possessing more general talents (individuals who can do a variety of other things just as well). The first group is easily seduced by the attraction of university life. They love knowledge in depth and playing with ideas; they hate the time clock and want to be their own bosses; they may prefer books and ideas to human beings. They may be repelled by what the *Harvard Crimson* calls "The Real World." All of us have known many examples of this type; it is almost the accepted caricature of a professor and does contain a few grains of truth. The second group will join the pool of academic talent only when the financial sacrifice is not too great. When the market is strong, they are pleased to be part of our company; when it is weak, and professional alternatives exist, they will look far beyond ivy-covered walls. Relying only on people whose "fire in the belly" is exclusively academic may not lead to a sufficiently large pool of talent. It is one important reason for us always to remain concerned about the attractiveness of our working conditions.

"Up or out" is a brutal slogan and the root cause of non-tenured misery. While a necessary and entirely defensible practice, it is not an especially friendly sign of welcome. Where tenure track is practiced (see chapter 11) and where social Darwinism is slightly more muted, there may be less anxiety among the probationary ranks, but probation is a trial and, by definition, the outcome is uncertain. All true, but surely there is no need to glory in the suffering that is inflicted on our younger colleagues. A university term appointment need not be the moral equivalent of a fraternity initiation in which most pledges are rejected. "Up or out" can only be justified as a way to raise the quality of tenured appointments, and a gauntlet of putdowns and petty humiliations administered to prospective candidates does not improve performance.

For those of us who are permanent shareholders in the university, there are two duties *vis-à-vis* our non-tenured co-workers that are only rarely performed adequately or gracefully. First, we have to be able—at all times—to put on their shoes. Where they pinch should enable us to understand the anxieties, pains, and occasional neuroses that afflict this group. Looking at the world from their perspective will encourage more thoughtful, supportive, and sympathetic attitudes. It should also greatly diminish petty annoyances. The other duty—and this is a matter of plain self-interest—is to create circumstances that will allow these scholars to attain maximum possible intellectual growth during their term. Needs will vary with the times in which we live, with our fields, and various other special circumstances. In my experience, our best universities do not always fulfill this duty at a high level of excellence. I would like to make a few modest suggestions.

Some things are now being addressed: improving the circumstances of two-career couples by providing day care and job-placement assistance for spouses. In some areas of the country, housing subsidies are crucial. All these are expensive and obvious steps.

Far less well understood and only rarely put into practice is the principle that *professional fringe benefits should be independent of professorial rank.* As I have already pointed out, the unusual aspect of our hierarchy is that members perform essentially the same tasks without regard to rank. Then why should full professors be advantaged in terms of secretarial assistance or research help? Or laboratory equipment? Or money for travel to conferences?[10] A greater stress on equality for these benefits—a redistribution of resources— would help younger colleagues reach their full potential and improve the chances for internal promotion. In turn,

10. To make my meaning clear, I have no problem whatever with allocating offices on the basis of seniority. That is a matter of cosmetics: the quality and quantity of work is relatively unaffected. (That is not true of studies in libraries; these could affect quality and quantity of research.) Secretarial or research assistance has a much more direct bearing on professional activities.

that would raise morale and cost efficiency: internal promotion is far cheaper than bringing in a "star" from outside.[11]

My last suggestion is the most difficult to put into practice; perhaps it is also the most important. Academic departments need to provide young scholars with a sense of community, with mentors—with seniors who take the role of colleague seriously. Although assistant and associate professors are not anyone's assistants, they can at least be treated as associates, and not as transients. A good academic department should resemble a family: supportive, guiding, and nurturing. At its best, the department can become a partner in the progress of its younger members, helping each one to attain their capabilities.

None of this will eliminate the pain of eventual rejection. The chances remain very high that it will occur. But surely the pain is lessened and can gradually be transformed into pleasant memories. These memories will positively affect future generations of students who may be tempted by academic careers. To transform a vicious into a virtuous circle is possible.

This introduction to university life from the professorial point of view has already referred to tenure a number of times. Academic security of employment is an important and frequently misunderstood subject. An elaboration of this topic is my next entry.

11. An internal promotion always applies to a relatively young scholar who shows promise. The bargaining power of that individual is bound to be lower than that of an established star at a rival institution.

# 10

# Tenure:

## *The Meaning of Tenure*

I learned long ago that the overwhelming majority of non-academics view tenure with deep suspicion. Most recently *The Economist*[1] described tenure as a promise to professors that "they can think (or idle) in ill-paid peace, accountable to nobody." Somehow we, in academia, are getting away with something; that is the general feeling. Lifetime tenure induces laziness, stifles incentives, and directly contributes to lack of performance on the job. It is a prescription for going to seed. There is a belief as well, that the custom is immoral—even un-American! To these dim views might be added the widely held undergraduate opinion that their favorite teachers are systematically denied tenure, as well as the conviction of some non-tenured younger faculty members that they are smarter and more qualified than the old bastards who deny them promotion. That is the bill of particulars.

1. "The Tenure Temptation," February 28, 1987.

I may have overstated these feelings, but not by much. For a number of reasons—to be dealt with later—they are surprising. In the United States, academic tenure has a legal and social history going back to the 1920s, and there is no need to describe it here.[2] I am interested in the present, not in the history. Even then, a general definition and description is difficult. In 94 percent of colleges and universities in the United States,[3] *some* professors hold their jobs for "life"—i.e., until the stipulated retirement age—and in general, cannot be removed by the administration except for gross neglect of duty, physical or mental incapacity, a serious moral lapse, or grave institutional financial stringency. There is the additional requirement that the discharge of a tenured professor, a rare event, entails some form of due process. Of course it is also possible to seek enforcement of tenure contracts by means of the courts.[4] I stress *some* professors because the award of tenure usually involves a probationary period, typically lasting from three to eight years.[5]

Tenure frequently is tied to rank. Professors and associ-

2. A great deal of useful information is contained in the Commission on Academic Tenure in Higher Education's *Faculty Tenure* (San Francisco: Jossey-Bass Publishers, 1973).

3. A survey conducted in 1972 revealed that "tenure plans are in effect in all public and private universities and public four-year colleges; in 94 percent of the private colleges, and in more than two thirds of the nation's two-year colleges, public and private. An estimated 94 percent of all faculty members in American universities and college are serving in institutions that confer tenure. . . . A substantial number of institutions—most of them junior and community colleges—operate not under a tenure plan but under some form of contract system." *Ibid.*, pp. 1, 10.

4. I cite below *all* that is said about tenure in the Harvard *Statutes*:

Professors and associate professors are appointed without express limitation of time unless otherwise specified. All other officers are appointed for a specified term or for terms of unspecified duration subject to the right of the University to fix at any time the term of such an appointment.
All officers who hold teaching appointments, as defined from time to time by the Corporation with the consent of the Overseers, are subject to removal from such appointments by the Corporation only for grave misconduct or neglect of duty. Officers who hold professional or administrative appointments are subject to removal from such appointments by the Corporation for grave misconduct or whenever, in its opinion, their duties are not satisfactorily discharged.

5. In some medical schools, the probationary period can be ten to twelve years.

ate professors normally have tenure and assistant professors, instructors, and lecturers typically do not.[6] The situation is further complicated because in institutions of higher education there are likely to be various forms of security of employment. Junior faculty members—instructors and assistant professors—are given term contracts. Many researchers, some teachers and administrators are the beneficiaries of appointments "without limit of time": a presumption of continued employment. At Harvard we have sometimes, informally, used the term "industrial tenure" for this group, implying the prospect of long-term jobs unless there is a basic change in the needs or finances of the university. *Academic* tenure, however, is quite special and different. No president or dean can have it in those capacities. It is a privilege of the professorate—and for them alone. With it should come the right to choose the path of one's own intellectual development. As dean, if I had said to the president that financial and educational matters had become boring, and that I intended to use the next few years to focus on the quality of Harvard's football team, he would no doubt have insisted on my immediate resignation—despite his rather well-known youthful enthusiasm for athletic sports. As a tenured professor, I can tell my chairman that I plan to change my specialization from Japanese economic history to Soviet economic studies. So long as I am competent to carry out my intentions—so long as I can become competent in a reasonable period of time—the chairman will be unable to thwart my newly chosen path. Remember the two crown jewels possessed by every tenured professor at a top school: independence and security.

Let me now try to state the affirmative case for tenure as one of the necessary virtues of academic life. The first habitual line of defense is *tenure as the principal guarantor of academic freedom,* ensuring the right to teach what one be

6. At Harvard, in the Faculty of Arts and Sciences, only full professors have tenure.

lieves, to espouse unpopular academic and non-academic causes, to act upon knowledge and ideas as one perceives them without fear of retribution from anyone. Few professors will treat the need for this type of protection lightly since our country has a long history of professorial persecution for naked political reasons. In my own lifetime I have seen the ravages of McCarthyism and other kinds of witch-hunts.

As a group, university teachers are probably less conventional—less conformist—than the average population, thereby attracting suspicion as corrupters of youth. Conservatives seem especially fond of this view. Professors also tend to be verbal and visible and are trained in the advocacy of ideas. Passions easily reach a boiling point in universities and can attract a great deal of attention. Protection may be as much needed from inside as from outside assault.

Administrations, with or without external pressure, have been known to attempt to enforce their own versions of orthodoxy. I must admit that if I had been a university president during the turmoil of the late 1960s, the temptation to fire certain faculty members would have been almost irresistible. I am thinking not of unpopular ideas or speech, but of sit-ins, violent disruptions, and other forms of uncivilized behavior, especially on the part of those who should have been examples to students. Looking back, I am glad that tenure, and more importantly, the tradition of academic freedom provided a defense against those with my hot temper and base impulses.

Nothing can diminish the need for academic freedom; its absence has reduced universities to caricatures in many parts of the contemporary world. The difficulty lies in making a tight connection between academic freedom and tenure. Do not young non-tenured teachers need protection just as much or even more? It is sometimes suggested that a corps of senior (tenured) unafraid colleagues serves as guarantors of liberty for all. This is not convincing. To be at all effective, this mythical corps would have to be united precisely when freedom is threatened and controversy abounds, and that is a pipe dream. We need not theorize. During the early 1950s a number of Harvard instructors and assistant professors became victims of McCarthy-style political pressures. Some term appointments were prematurely rescinded; a few left "voluntarily" rather than facing investigation of their political opinions or affiliations. The same was true everywhere else, and I do not recall that their elders organized an effective defense anywhere. Of course, liberty for some is better than liberty for none: one has to recognize that tenure helps the maintenance of academic freedom.

And yet the United States is a considerably more tolerant country now than, say, twenty-five years ago. We are less provincial and more indulgent; some would say more (or too) permissive. The fact is that the range of socially accepted behavior and thought is exceedingly wide. Our courts are also more activist in defending individual rights. For all these reasons, academic freedom may not be especially threatened at this time, although a retrograde movement is always possible. It does not seem to me very likely in the near future, but who am I to make a forecast?[7]

Another line of support for (working) life-time contracts is a group of reasons that I will call *tenure as a source of internal discipline.* Granting tenure is costly for institutions, departments, and colleagues. Once awarded, a university obliges itself to pay a relatively high salary for a long period of time—on average, I would think for at least twenty-five years. Academic departments grant membership for the same length of time, and they have to be concerned about the costliness of mistakes. Once in possession of tenure, stripping someone of a professorship becomes virtually impossible. And who wants a mistake for a colleague for

7. "Few crusades have ever been more successful than that for the right of the modern faculty member to be secure in his or her belief and expression. We should not be misled in this matter by our committed tendency to fight battles that are already won." Speech by John Kenneth Galbraith, University of California at Berkeley, March 27, 1986. One could possibly also think of safeguards short of lifetime contracts that would effectively protect academic freedom. For example, grievance committees with impartial membership.

twenty-five years! Of course, generations of students are also concerned: departmental errors of judgment have a direct effect on the quality of their education. An important and salutory consequence of high cost in many different senses is that the existance of tenure encourages departments and those who review their actions to make tough decisions that would otherwise be all too easily avoided. Thus tenure is a major factor in maintaining and raising standards; electing life-time colleagues becomes a matter of utmost seriousness.

But why go down this road in the first place? Because without long-term obligations, our sense of internal discipline would be much weaker. The temptation to extend an individual's employment many times for "one more year"—just to avoid inevitable unpleasantness—could become irresistible. It cannot be an accident that professions in which collegiality is important use systems that approximate academic tenure very closely. Law firms are the best example: partnerships resemble professorships, and the discipline of selection is improved by the implied length of commitment. Both law firms and universities avoid periodic and perpetual reviews of partners or tenured professors. These would be time-consuming, divisive, and destructive of the collegial ideal. Once is enough: at the time when partners are chosen or when tenure is offered. But that "once" has to be subject to extraordinarily rigorous standards.

There are other traditional arguments in favor of tenure. The practice is said to contribute to institutional stability; those with the security of tenure are expected to judge others more fairly or professionally and not on the basis of personal competitive advantage; an "up or out" system—a corollary of tenure—prevents the long-term exploitation of teacher-scholars in junior ranks.[8] All of these points are valid to some degree, though they seem equally reasonable

8. Although an "up or out" system could exist without giving tenure.

in other forms of employment, ranging from the Japanese factory to an American hospital. For me, the essence of academic tenure lies in the consideration of one more reason.

I have in mind *tenure as social contract:* an appropriate and essential form of social contract in universities. It is appropriate because the advantages outweigh the disadvantages. It is essential because the absence of tenure would, in the long run, lower the quality of a faculty. And faculty quality is the keystone of university life. The best faculty will attract the ablest students, produce the finest alumni, generate the most research support, and so on. Unlike most other sectors of the economy, the possibilities of technological (and organizational) progress are more limited in higher education. Substituting capital for labor does not appear especially promising, and nearly everything hinges on the quality of people.

Our professional lives, as I have already attempted to show, can be described as a "good deal." There are comparatively few unpleasant routines; for many of us, work approaches pleasure in pleasant settings. There is, however, another aspect that has to be considered. Our jobs—as senior professors at major universities—require high intelligence, special talents, and initiative. These attributes are in general demand: business, law, medicine, and other professions are looking for people with similar characteristics. And some of these careers promise, at considerable risk, far greater financial rewards. At the point of career selection all of us faced a variety of choices, and nearly all were potentially more lucrative than teaching. The current (1988–89) average annual salary of a full professor in Arts and Sciences at Harvard University is about $70,000. That is one of the highest averages in U.S. universities. Average age of tenured faculty is about fifty-five and the average professor is a recognized world authority in some subject or other. Assistant professors, all with Ph.D. degrees, start at about $32,000. Lawyers, fresh out of school, will be hired by New York firms with annual compensation of about $70,000. What Teddy Roosevelt said in 1905 is still valid:

> . . . I appreciate to the full the fact that the highest work of all will never be affected one way or the other by any question of compensation. . . . But it is also true that the effect upon ambitious minds can not but be bad if as a people we show our very slight regard for scholarly achievement by making no provision at all for its reward.[9]

Choosing higher education still involves a trade-off. The cost is economic, and that burden is shared by the family. Benefits are not in the narrow sense material, and one of the most essential is tenure. In my view, tenure carries the implication of joining an extended family; that is the social contract. Each side can seek a divorce: the university only in the most extraordinary circumstances and the professor as easily as a male under Islamic law. It is not an uneven bargain because the university needs its share of talented people, and professors trade life-long security and familial relations for lesser economic rewards.

That was how I interpreted tenure as dean, and I had many occasions to put this social contract interpretation into practice. My door was open at all times to colleagues, and I tried to place at their disposal Harvard's resources in personal as well as professional matters. Problems of alcoholism, divorce, long-term illness all came to my attention and were, I hope, approached in a family spirit. In Arts and Sciences we had no detailed sick-leave policy for professors; it was dealt with informally and with great generosity. One of my teachers had a stroke and was incapacitated for about six years. The faculty simply kept him on the payroll. Perhaps poor business practice—but excellent family practice.

I do not wish to leave the impression that membership in

---

9. Address by President Theodore Roosevelt at Harvard University, June 28, 1905. I would like to thank Professor Robert J. C. Butow for calling this quotation to my attention.

the tenured faculty family is only another, slightly more generous form of health insurance. It is a much broader vision; in reality, a state of mind. For example, when special opportunities arose, rules were cheerfully broken or reinterpreted in favor of the individual. A tempting invitation from abroad might mean the need for travel funds or extra leave time; a new research idea could call for seed money; one was always able to approach faculty resources through the dean. Not everyone got what they wanted, but the dean would try to help, while loudly proclaiming that his actions in no ways constituted a precedent.

Am I, with excessive sentimentality, urging an inordinately paternalistic interpretation? Not if one thinks of professors as shareholders without bosses, and not as employees. The dean is *primus inter pares,* a colleague temporarily running the show before being replaced by another peer. His actions are not favors granted from above. Instead, they are investments in the general welfare, and therefore in the high quality of the family enterprise: in those with permanent membership who form one set of owners.

There is one other aspect of tenure that should be mentioned when we emphasize "extended family" and "ownership." Having the assurance of a position until retirement obviously removes one of the main fears faced by many workers in our society. Far more significant, the tenure system seen as a social contract also means that aging does not bring overt loss of respect. The rights of the individual are secure and do not change until retirement. Even after retirement, most universities continue to extend valuable privileges to *emeriti:* scientists retain (reduced) laboratory space, others are given offices, and the use of all common facilities—libraries, clubs, etc.—continues. These are expensive habits—some would label them bad management—and one has to admit that there are abuses.[10] Nevertheless, the possibility of aging with dignity is enormously

10. At Harvard, for example, a large proportion of scarce Widener Library studies are assigned to retired professors who hold them for life. Many of the holders use them very little, while more active younger scholars wait years for available space.

attractive and exceedingly rare in our country, and relatively insignificant abuses are a small cost.

I am sure that a number of my colleagues at Harvard and
elsewhere will be tempted to dismiss the social contract
interpretation of tenure, especially if they are under fifty. It
is fashionable for outstanding and well-known younger
scholars to say that they do not care and never worried
about tenure, particularly after they have attained that status.[11] These individuals feel extremely mobile and know
that if they so desire, another school will enter an attractive
bid for their services. Some may have great difficulty in
seeing the faculty as an extended family. Whatever comes
to them is interpreted as inalienable rights or the just recognition of individual merit. These are our counterparts of
young movie stars, men and women blessed with great
beauty and desired by studio and public. Just as aging stars
find fewer parts—the number of John Waynes is very limited—so does mobility decline steeply for professors in
their early fifties. One can perhaps always go somewhere
else, but the range of choices becomes greatly constrained.
And even though the family may give most to younger
members, recognition of its value is probably more developed among older constituents.

I have attempted to describe the precious characteristics
of the academic social contract—to me the essence of tenure. The "real world" has its own ways of motivating and
inspiring loyalty in their various communities. Higher economic welfare has already been mentioned, and specific
embellishments are stock options, extremely generous retirement plans, golden parachutes, club memberships, and
other imaginative arrangements. Furthermore, tenure or
near tenure is certainly not restricted to higher education.
Federal judges, many civil servants, and primary and secondary schoolteachers all participate in similar arrangements. And that is why I have always been puzzled by external suspicion of this academic custom. At bottom, it has to

11. I have hardly ever heard anyone without tenure dismiss the possession of
same.

be related to the special academic combination of great freedom—small formal obligations—*and* security. That is what arouses distrust: no nine to five, no assigned place of work save a few hours in the classroom, and the assurance of a monthly check! A perfect prescription for laziness unless work and pleasure are highly correlated—and they are.

But there are also other, more external, factors that induce discipline. Peer pressure has already been alluded to a number of times. Few occupations produce as many regular and public judgments about their membership. Our books are reviewed, rarely without a few drops of acid; our articles are refereed and sometimes rejected; and grant applications fail from time to time. Memberships in academies, offices in learned societies, name chairs, and in many instances salaries openly signal where we stand in relation to others. Students are an additional spur. Lecturing to nearly empty classrooms will deflate even the largest ego and poor—often biting—student ratings have been known to change the habits of more than one professor.[12] The pressure to produce quality research in adequate quantity and to teach well is strong and comes from many directions; dismissal or non-renewal of contract is not needed as reinforcement. The notion that tenure fosters deadwood is false—especially at top rank universities. The combination of tenure and low quality is dangerous and admittedly may perpetuate mediocrity or worse. To repeat: that is not an issue for the type of schools discussed here.

It is true that a large tenured faculty presents peculiar problems of management, especially if threats, fear, or direct orders are a preferred managerial tool. Instead, the emphasis has to be on ‘consensus and persuasion—on a democratic and participatory style.

12. A sanitized quote from a recent *Course Evaluation Guide* published by the Harvard Student Committee on Undergraduate Education: "Professor X seriously handicaps [the course]. [The] reportedly lifeless presentations emphasize material irrelevant to the course and rush through the difficult, important topics, much to the consternation of students. Instead of explaining their [scientific] meaning, Professor X merely writes formulas on the blackboard, in what students cite as a typical example of [a] shallow approach."

# 11

## Tenure:

### *A Model Case*

While nearly everyone seems to have an opinion about the pluses and minuses associated with academic tenure, very few inside or outside the university understand the process, the goals, or the standards. For this reason I thought it might be interesting to describe an illustrative tenure procedure. As usual, my examples come from Harvard Arts and Sciences, and our procedures are not at all typical. That is not so important. The goals and standards of our research universities are very similar, and that gives these examples wide applicability.

The number of tenured posts at any university is limited by a budget constraint. Tenure creates fixed costs for any enterprise, and in a private university these costs have to bear a reasonable relation to income generated by endowment gifts and student tuitions. (In a public institution, the ultimate guarantor of tenure is the taxing power of the state.) At Harvard, a newly created professorial chair would currently require the net capital addition of about $2 million; the resulting perpetual income stream will barely cover a senior professor's salary and fringe benefits—and the price of a chair keeps rising. Junior (non-tenure) faculty slots are variable costs: their number can be controlled in the short run. Although the occupants do have term contracts, they are of relatively brief duration and only rarely exceed five years. At this time Harvard Arts and Sciences is the temporary home of about two hundred junior professors and about one hundred lecturers. The numbers tend to fluctuate, reflecting teaching needs and finances. By the standards of most research universities, the tenured proportion at Harvard is low—slightly under 60 percent. At many institutions where getting tenure is easier or where faculty expansion has displayed a more cyclical character, the proportion can easily reach 90 percent. And that does lead to structural rigidities.

As this is written, the Faculty of Arts and Sciences is the permanent home for slightly under four hundred tenured professors. They are assigned to some fifty departments and degree programs, and a continual, slow process of internal reapportionment reflects a variety of forces. New fields and sometimes new departments require senior leadership. For example, area studies (Japan, China, Middle East, Soviet Union, etc.) were hardly known before World War II; now Harvard boasts a large corps of these practitioners. Today there are also departments of Biochemistry and Molecular Biology, a significant group in computer sciences, a Department of Statistics, and one of Afro-American Studies—all of relatively recent origin. Sometimes donor interest will expand certain fields by means of new restricted gifts. Recently, our faculty acquired chairs in scientific archeology, and in modern Greek and Australian studies. We were delighted to enrich our programs with these additional resources, even though these subjects may not have represented the highest internal priorities. Lastly, the apportionment of tenure posts has to reflect the changing interests of undergraduate and graduate students. Demand by consumers of instruction and research guidance has to be taken into account, and that is why there are, for example, more professors of political science and biology than of Acadian or the history of science.

At any one time, I would estimate that some forty tenure decisions are in various stages of consideration. For the most part, vacancies arise when senior professors retire, die, or resign, or when new permanent posts are created by planned expansion or unexpected donation. The completion of junior faculty terms can also stimulate departmental requests for additional tenured posts. Faced with the threat of losing a talented and desirable young scholar as mandated by the practice of "up or out," departments will frequently request an in-depth tenure review. Retirement certainly is the most common origin of tenure vacancies at Harvard and elsewhere. Death and resignations before reaching retirement age are relatively rare occurrences. Professorial life is too pleasant: during my term as dean, there were years without premature death or tenured resignation for jobs at other universities. Unfortunately, not all years were so blessed; on a few occasions a small number of our best people chose to go elsewhere.

In any academic department, nominations for tenure are a counterpoint to all the trivia of daily routine. A permanent commitment to a colleague or a tenured invitation offered to an outsider represents a supremely important investment and frequently a gamble. The professional reputation of individuals associated in a discipline depends, to a considerable extent, on the quality of the group (department): being a member of an excellent department enhances individual reputation and increases professional opportunity. At the very least one hopes that a new member of the club (department) does not lower the average; ideally the aim is to raise the average.

Prevailing rules and market forces also require that decisions are made early in the career of the candidate. Nearly all universities have some form of "up or out" rule that prevents young scholars from remaining in junior ranks beyond seven to ten years.[1] The market, especially in subjects that are "hot" or for individuals who generate their own heat, induces its own competitive pressures, and the chance of keeping or getting a rising star may depend on the timeliness of an offer. During my term as dean, the youngest person awarded a tenured post was a twenty-six-year-old astrophysicist from Princeton. The famous mathematician Charles Louis Fefferman was tenured as a full professor by the University of Chicago at the age of twenty-two. In general, promotion comes at an earlier age in the natural sciences, slightly later in the social sciences, and latest in the humanities (see note 4, p. 196).

For these reasons, questions relating to new tenured members are the most common topic of departmental deliberation. (Possible exceptions are salaries and space.) Whom shall we attempt to promote? Who can be lured to our university? Who shows or does not show promise? Will the administration authorize a position? That is the nature of the discussion.

For my typical and imaginary Harvard case, I will choose the Department of Economics since it is my own base. It is a large department, about thirty tenured professors and about fifteen junior members. Size is a loose function of a number of variables. With some regularity, economics is the largest concentration (major) in Harvard College. The basic course in Principles of Economics enrolls close to one thousand students, and that raises the demand for teachers of the subject. The number of concentrators has varied, but economics has always attracted many undergraduates. Some would say that this is due to the small intellectual demands made on students—many Harvard athletes are among our graduates. Others, with more charitable inclinations, would stress that economics is excellent general and

---

1. Just as, in the army, being passed over for promotion means "early retirement," only in our world the decision comes after a much shorter interval and the person involved will, in all probability, find a post in another, frequently less prestigious school.

even rigorous preparation for law and business, very popular choices these days. Interestingly enough, and for no known reason, the size of the major varies inversely with the business cycle and may be one of our more reliable leading indicators. The department also runs a large, successful, and demanding Ph.D. program. Its popularity is no doubt closely related to the inherent fascination of the subject, a visible group of professors, a university of high reputation, and not least the existence of job opportunities for economists.

There is one other reason for the large number of economists in the Faculty of Arts and Sciences. Many Harvard alumni become successful businessmen. Once they have achieved financial success, the university will engage in relentless pursuit urging them to provide tangible evidence of gratitude to alma mater. And since their achievements are primarily economic, they tend to think kindly of the subject and to offer new chairs to the department. Sometimes there is a contrary motivation that paradoxically yields the same result. After years in the world of business, these alumni are convinced that they were taught irrelevant and false doctrines—oftentimes, they believe, tinged with left-wing prejudices. Now the motive becomes the salvation of future generations from a similar fate, and chairs are still offered, sometimes proposing tags and terms that mention free enterprise, emphasis on policy studies, and the like.[2]

For all of these reasons, the Economics Department can expect to recommend a new tenured appointment at least once every two years, and more usually once a year. It is common to confront two or even three vacancies in a typical academic year. Attempting to fill these posts, either by internal promotion or by inviting a scholar from another institution, is the key collegial task of those economists who

2. As the Russians say, it is not nice to "spit in the soup." I do not urge fewer positions in economics. I would point out, however, that subjects vary in their attraction to donors. Anything with the real or perceived promise of practicality has an enormous advantage. To raise funds for the teaching of foreign literature is, alas, much more difficult.

claim membership in the department. It takes time—frequently more than a year—the stakes are high, and the process entails pleasure and pain.

As I have already indicated, the discussions have an ongoing character and emphasize two slightly contradictory considerations: what fields within the discipline need to be strengthened (macro- or microeconomics, industrial organization, economic history, etc.), and regardless of field, who is the brightest, most interesting, and promising economist available. Both aspects matter, although in the end the special fields cannot be ignored without hurting the graduate and undergraduate teaching mission of the department. Candidates are discussed, papers read, letters soliciting nominations are written to colleagues all over the world, lectures heard, and slowly a consensus takes shape.

Although individual professors will enter these debates with their own preconceptions and prejudices—pushing one's own students is a widely recognized weakness that can bring disastrous results—the debates tend to be remarkably open and democratic. In some fields—economics is a textbook example—there does arise a serious intellectual difficulty. When subjects change rapidly and new techniques emerge, it grows harder for older professors to judge the young. For example, my own background, training, and competence does not allow me to read current mathematical economics. In making choices in that field, I have to take what my colleagues say on faith. Generalists are an endangered species in modern universities; nearly all of us are highly and narrowly specialized.

What has been described up to this point is the usual situation in most research universities. A number of Harvard peculiarities can be mentioned. First, not all departmental citizens take part in these deliberations. Participation is limited to members of the so-called executive committee, those professors with tenure. Junior faculty are excluded so as not to be placed in a condition of conflict of interest—after all, they are candidates for present and future openings.[3] They are only informally consulted. The same applies to staff and students, but on grounds of lack of competence. Professional qualifications are the main issues, and neither staff nor students have the training to make valid judgments. (As we shall see, student evaluation of faculty teaching is considered at a later stage.) None of this is really very strange by national standards. I mention it only because students, in general, feel that they should have a greater voice in tenure decisions and that is a question we will eventually have to address. Also, at some institutions, the non-tenured faculty has a voice. For example, when I was at Berkeley in the 1960s, one designated junior professor served as a member of the executive committee in the Department of Economics.

A more noteworthy Harvard peculiarity relates to the scope of all tenure searches. When an opening exists, any Harvard department is instructed to ask itself: who is the best person "in the world" fitting the job description? If the best person is—in the opinion of departmental colleagues—one of our own junior members, he or she will be nominated for promotion. If it is an outsider, he or she will be invited. If the best person declines, the offer is then made to the next best person. A position may also be left vacant if high-quality candidates are not available. Of course, I am describing an ideal, and practicalities do matter. "Best" is, to some degree, a matter of taste. The "best" may also be over sixty years old, and that might not be a reasonable departmental investment. Furthermore, when the "world's leading authority" is a foreigner, emigrating to the United States may present insurmountable barriers. Sometimes visas are difficult to obtain; American salaries trail the levels in some European countries; most important, perhaps, are the difficulties associated with leaving a familiar setting and culture for an unknown environment. At Harvard, some years ago, we appointed a celebrated

3. See chapter 15 on University Governance: Seven Principles to Ensure Reliable Performance.

student of Italian literature who had to communicate with the dean (not me!) through a translator. He resigned after a few months. Language is not commonly a barrier, but it does happen.

Whatever the realities, ideals matter, and the concept of subjecting all permanent appointments to worldwide competition sets Harvard apart from most other American universities. The system, at least in principle, gives no advantage to young—possibly qualified—scholars already at Harvard; indeed, their individual chances for promotion are slim. There are many more junior faculty members than any realistic number of tenured vacancies, and competing against the largest possible universe loads the dice against internal candidates.[4]

To describe competing philosophies of searching for tenure candidates is difficult. They vary enormously. The Harvard practice of looking widely with an excess supply of non-tenured professors on the scene describes most of the Ivy League and a number of other private universities. It is one end of the spectrum. Some schools, including a few Ivies and many of our most famous state universities, use a tenure-track system. According to this practice, every junior post can, if desired, be converted to tenure. It is a limited presumption of tenure when the probationary period (usually seven or eight years) is completed—a presumption, *not* a guarantee. But the possibility of promotion is never excluded on grounds of lack of vacancies. Furthermore, when the question is finally argued and decided by

4. A few Harvard facts will provide some perspective. At the time of their first tenure appointment, the present faculty averaged thirty-seven years of age, and 54% were advanced internally. The group appointed since 1973 has averaged forty-one years of age, and 39% have been internal promotions. Clearly a decline, but 39% is not a negligible proportion. Yet individual chances of promotion for junior faculty are very slim because the pool of about two hundred people completely changes its composition every six or seven years. Thus the individual's chance falls to below 10%.

The proportion of internal candidates for promotion approved by the president exactly matches the rate of approval for external candidates. Fully 55% of candidates submitted to ad hoc committees in recent years were age forty or younger (56% in the natural sciences, 54% in the social sciences, and 38% in the humanities). And 77% of these younger nominees were approved in the ad hoc process. See Harvard University, Faculty of Arts and Sciences, *Dean's Report, 1979–80.*

departments and administration, the test is not "best avail-able in the world" but achieving an internally defined stan-dard of performance. That standard can be very high; in theory and in specific instances, both standards could pro-duce the same choice, although in general tenure track is a more forgiving test. When the job market is tight, young scholars are powerfully attracted by these positions.

Tenure track has some obvious advantages. The system probably raises the quality and morale of the non-tenured faculty. Young scholars tend to be risk-averse, especially when the academic market is weak. They will choose jobs where the possibilities for advancement are the firmest. A greater emphasis on internal promotion is also economical: bringing established outsiders from competing universities is the most expensive way to renew a faculty. The accent on youth associated with internal promotions is another ad-vantage. On the other hand, what I have described as the Harvard system may have the slight edge in terms of stan-dards for senior appointments. Competition for positions is keener and the range of candidates is greater. My sense is that some version of tenure track is the wave of the future, driven by considerations of cost and morale—two powerful and valid concerns.

At some institutions, the presumption of tenure is so strong as to become a virtual guarantee following a brief probationary period. Here one thinks especially of places with strong faculty unions. One of my friends served as dean of the Colleges of Liberal Arts and Sciences at a un-ionized Catholic school in California, where—according to him—all denials of tenure were routinely pushed to arbitra-tion. The collective bargaining agreement concerning ten-ure qualifications was so vaguely worded that the univer-sity's denials were never upheld by the arbitrator. A particularly puzzling feature of these proceedings bases tenure and/or promotion only on an individual's applica-tion to a dean. In making his decision, the dean is forbid-den—under threat of an unfair labor practice charge—to seek any information or opinions from currently serving members of the faculty; no union member can "manage" (judge or supervise) another member.[5] This sad situation does not conform to my vision of tenure as a desirable social contract. It runs counter to all the previously enumerated virtues of academic life and leads to a form of employment security designed to encourage academic mediocrity.[6]

Let us return to our "typical" Harvard case. The Economics Department, seeking to attract a new tenured specialist in the field of, say, industrial organization, has reached a preliminary consensus: a scholar in his middle thirties, a full professor at a rival university. Youth is a definite asset because the average age of tenured professors is near fifty-five. A young man or woman will bring fresh views, up-to-date technical training, and the promise of being a mentor to a new generation of graduate students. Innovative approaches to the field and command of the latest research techniques are especially desirable. There is an unstated feeling that our resident experts are slightly beyond their prime.

Now, the departmental chairman has the duty of composing and sending what we call a "blind letter." This letter

5. *Collective Bargaining Agreement Between the University of San Francisco and the USF Faculty Association* (1981). Here are some excerpts:

> Chairmen are elected by [the] Faculty Association Members, not appointed by the Dean.
> The parties understand that the University should not assign and . . . Faculty Association Members should not accept responsibilities that, if accepted and performed, could be construed as being management functions and that would thereby invalidate the essential differences that exist between parties to a collective bargaining agreement. Examples of duties that the University should not assign and the Members should not accept include such personnel responsibilities as hiring, evaluating, recommending for tenure and promotion, assigning duties . . . and such fiscal responsibilities as budget development and management.

A most unbelievable set of provisions that reduce, by their own actions, members of an honorable calling to membership in an academic proletariat!

6. Most curiously, the bargaining agreement at this institution defines the university as being the president and other administrators. The faculty is defined as "members of the bargaining unit." Students are not mentioned. What a strange picture of a university! The agreement also contains the following amusing sentences: "All Association Members are required to attend the annual Commencement exercises in cap and gown. Permission to be absent from these exercises may be given by the Association member's Dean."

says that the Economics Department proposes to make a tenured appointment in the field of industrial organization, and lists the top five or six candidates, normally individuals of similar ages. The preliminary departmental choice is not revealed—hence the characterization "blind." Those receiving the letter, leading scholars in the field here and abroad, are asked to rank and evaluate the candidates, to comment on the general comprehensiveness and quality of the list, and if at all possible to suggest other names. A special plea is made for the inclusion of minority and female names.

At Harvard and elsewhere, there is a lot of skepticism concerning blind letters. It is believed that in our small, gossipy world, recipients will be anything but blind: they will have no difficulty in identifying the department's choice. That may be true, but I also know that inquiries concerning a specific person produce primarily praise. There is no context, being the bad guy is never pleasant, and these days the fear of leaks and open files affects all responses.[7] A list of names invites a more nuanced, a more subtle reply. We are all pretty good at reading between the lines and at understanding damnation with faint praise.

If the replies to the blind letters are satisfactory—the candidate ranks at or near the top of most replies, or some poor evaluations can be explained as idiosyncratic—the department confirms its judgment with a formal vote. A simple majority is not always considered a sufficiently strong departmental endorsement. On the other hand, unanimity is not necessary. A few negative votes do not invalidate a case for tenure.

Now the dossier moves to the decanal level. The dean and his principal academic advisers will study the file—search letters, blind letters, *curriculum vitae*, departmental case statements, and so on, and determine whether or not the candidate merits further, more searching examination.

---

7. It has reached the point where some requests for "confidential" evaluations are simply not answered, except perhaps on the telephone. A great loss to the academic profession because we so depend on the frank assessment of individuals.

In nearly all cases, the dean does decide to proceed to the next higher stage because questions and doubts—if any— are disciplinary and professional, and as such entitle the department to have its arguments heard by experts. Once the dean has made a decision to move forward, he will require each member of the departmental executive committee to provide a confidential explanation of his or her own vote. An experienced dean knows all too well that departments frequently present a somewhat misleading impression of enthusiasm and unanimity. Professors are not immune from group-think or pressure exercised by a few charismatic individuals. Private and confidential letters provide a superb check on the extravagances of official case statements.

The next phase entails the appointment of an ad hoc committee and begins the participation of Harvard's president. Each tenure procedure gives birth to an ad hoc committee chaired by the president with the dean as one of the members. It is the committee's task to advise the president on the proposed tenure recommendation. De facto, the final decision rests with the president; de jure, approval has to be given by the Corporation and the Overseers.

A special characteristic of Harvard ad hoc committees is their composition. In addition to the president and dean, there are typically five other members. Three participants represent the special field of the candidate—in this example, industrial organization—and all of them are distinguished scholars from other universities. That is done to give the president the most neutral advice possible, unaffected by local friendships or prejudices. An additional two members are generalists from inside Harvard but not members of the department making the recommendation. Our sample candidate is an economist, and therefore the generalists are likely to be social scientists. Obviously the composition of the committee, and especially the choice of outsiders, can affect the outcome. Departments are asked for their suggestions, and invitations are issued in the name of the president. In reality, this difficult and controversial task is

entrusted to a special assistant of the dean, in my time a
senior professor of philosophy, and a man of remarkable
erudition and fairness. It is he who had to make certain that
every ad hoc committee contained recognized, impartial,
and wise experts; no simple task. No effort or expense is
spared in luring the right arbiters to Cambridge. For example scholars from overseas are not infrequent participants.
Still, when—as sometimes happens—the outcome dis-
pleases a department, blame will all to often be attributed
to unrepresentative or allegedly incompetent committee
composition.[8]

An ad hoc meeting is a formal proceeding that resembles
a trial. Participants gather in Massachusetts Hall at 10:00
A.M., and hear brief presentations by the dean and president; they will already have read the dossier. Three classic
questions are always considered. First, is the candidate (de-
fendant?) of sufficient quality to be offered tenure at Harvard? Secondly, even if the answer to the first question is
yes, can we do better? And thirdly, is the choice of special
field optimal in view of the department's current membership?

One set of questions is in nearly all instances pointedly
omitted at this and all earlier stages of the review procedure. Is the candidate a nice person? Will he or she be a
pleasant and cooperative colleague? To introduce such
considerations would almost certainly be considered bad
form. I have always imagined that in other types of collegial
association—for example, law firms or medical group practices—these are considered legitimate issues for open discussion and action. I would not like to suggest that they are
ignored when academic departments make their choices or

8. In a recent speech filled with reminiscence my colleague, Professor J. K. Galbraith, said: "[A Harvard ad hoc committee] is presumed to bring a detached,
even judicial, judgement to bear. Ever since my own appointment, I have wondered about the efficiency of this device. I was then asked by my departmental
chairman to give him—to present to the committee—the names of scholars of
high eminence who would be favorable to my appointment. I unhesitatingly
obliged." (Obviously procedures have been tightened during the last forty
years—if Galbraith's account is accurate. Concerning that point, I have some
slight doubt.) Speech by John Kenneth Galbraith, University of California at
Berkeley, March 27, 1986.

when review committees render judgments. One can hint, make oblique jokes, or express private reservations, and in our small world these acts can be significant. However, I have almost never heard someone simply say: "I do not want Professor X as a permanent colleague because she is an awful person who will poison the atmosphere in our department and that explains my strong negative vote." This would not be good form because our ideal points entirely to the cerebral. We seek the best scholar-teachers, and if they happen to have abominable personalities, why then we claim joyfully to suffer in the name of learning.

To be sure, there is an element of cant in this custom; but there is also a large degree of reality. I have witnessed too many choices that cast aside obvious character and personality flaws in pursuit of scholarly excellence. The price of such action can be very high, and this form of behavior is, I believe, an American university peculiarity. Our British colleagues, for example, seem to make sure that their final selections are more "clubbable."

At ad hoc meetings, departments are represented by about four positive witnesses. All professors who voted against the appointment are also invited to appear. As the witnesses arrive at twenty- or thirty-minute intervals, they see the membership of the committee for the first time. Until that point, the identities of the panel (except, of course, for the president and dean) are kept confidential to prevent unseemly advance lobbying. The questions begin. Why candidate A rather than Professor B? Have the witnesses studied the major relevant articles and books? Is the department's choice too immature or too mature?—one or the other will inevitably be alleged by someone. (Of course, the law requires us to avoid age discrimination.) What explains the subtle negative remarks of world authority C? The atmosphere is juridical, a bit tense, and slightly nervous, especially for the departmental advocates. Harvard's president is a lawyer and easily adopts the style of a prosecutor. Others join this spirit and create, perhaps too easily, a panel of devil's advocates. These are not ordinary, dry academic committee meetings. Sparks fly quite often. I have seen distinguished older scholars treating one another with icy courtesy only barely masking contempt. Once, a witness gave an illustration by name of what, in his opinion, would have been a most unworthy appointment. A member of the committee turned a deep shade of red: his name had been used as the example! After that I always made certain to introduce all members of the committee to the witnesses.

It is not at all unusual for positive witnesses to turn slightly negative under the stress of interrogation. I have also heard professors explain in great detail that they are more eminent than the candidate, who is nevertheless the best available choice. One time I asked a colleague who was testifying whether he truly believed that the nominee was a first-rate scholar. He hemmed and hawed, and later berated me for asking an embarrassing question. But I have said enough to indicate the seriousness and difficulties of the occasion.

A word or two about a perennial controversy: the evaluation of teaching. At Harvard, and all other major universities, a professor has to be a researcher and a teacher. Few do both equally well, but high minimum standards must be set and maintained for each activity. It is far easier to evaluate excellence in research. The fruit of research is publication, a tangible product subject to continual peer review. Book reviews, citations, and the amount of work generated by one's ideas yield a great deal of reliable evidence. A tenure dossier and an ad hoc committee are well equipped to render opinions in this area. Teaching ability is more subjective, and evaluation and measurement are less certain. Despite a widespread view that teaching ability is ignored by research universities, the tenure review process also deals with this aspect of the candidate in some detail. The dossier has to contain a special letter from the chairman of the department providing all relevant information. This includes student evaluations, occasionally letters from graduate students, reports of class visits, and similar materials. As dean, I felt that simply by listening to faculty gossip—a serious task for any dean—and by studying available evidence, for example, the annual course evaluation guide published by the student Committee on Undergraduate Education, it was not all that difficult to gain an accurate sense of a colleague's teaching abilities or—perhaps as significant—enthusiasm for the task. Certain code words immediately alert an experienced pair of ears to trouble. "Good in small groups" almost always means a lousy teacher.

The main point is not to make unnecessary compromises. There are occasional geniuses whom one would want to have on a faculty even if their customary mode of communication took the form of grunts and mumbles. The power of their ideas and value of their research contributions—presumably communicated in print—triumph over all other defects. A university should make a place for these people; a college cannot. But genius is, by definition, rare even on the faculties of our great schools, and luckily some who might fit that description are outgoing personalities and wonderful teachers. Most of us, and especially those of us who become tenured university professors, are extremely competent; the majority are creative. Those qualities are not sufficient to forget our dual obligations and privileges—teaching and research. We must learn to do both very well, otherwise a lifetime contract should be denied. And that does happen. Teaching is an art, and not all of us are blessed with the same amount of natural talent. Yet teaching can also be taught by the use of a variety of highly effective modern techniques that include expert counseling and practice videotaping sessions, consciousness-raising seminars featuring famous teachers, and similar devices. At Harvard, the Danforth Center for the improvement of teaching has helped many faculty members to reach a higher level of pedagogical performance.

By now the committee is at lunch in the formal dining room of the mansion that until recently was the residence

of Harvard presidents. A few glasses of sherry have been
consumed, some professional news and polite chit-chat ex-
changed while drinking the soup. This pleasant interlude
does not last long, because the president is anxious to
begin the discussion. During the morning he has heard
conflicting testimony: the candidate is young and perhaps a
lifetime commitment is premature; some feel that a better
person has been overlooked; one member of the Economics Department has chosen to offer negative testimony
pointing to the candidate's alleged misuse of statistics.
These questions have to be resolved. The president goes
around the table asking each member of the committee to
state their initial views, starting with the distinguished outside guests. This is followed by a general discussion.

One hopes for clarity and consensus, and more often
than not they do occur. At other times, strong debate takes
place and sharp divisions of opinion remain. There are no
votes. The procedure is entirely advisory, and each individual offers his or her personal advice. A final decision is
made by the president of the university; he is the only one
with that authority. He can follow the advice of the ad hoc
committee or ignore it—the choice is his. Of course, the
choice is his within certain reasoned limits. A university
president cannot govern without faculty cooperation.
Quirky, unreasonable, and unexplained judgments will not
be sustainable for a long time. All of his decisions have to
consider the political consequences. In the overwhelming
majority of cases he does follow the committee's advice,
especially when it is clearly stated. It is also the case that
most candidates presented for appointment eventually
meet presidential approval. The figures vary greatly from
year to year, but my guess is that the annual failure rate
rarely exceeds 10 percent. None of this should be interpreted as signs of a meaningless procedure. The committees are composed of experts and their advice should be
ignored only in exceptional circumstances. Most candidates meet approval because departments interpret turn-

downs as a criticism of their collective judgment, and weak cases have a strong chance of falling by the wayside before a committee is called to order.

At 2:00 P.M., four hours after first convening, the president brings the session to a close, normally without announcing a decision. The president and dean together stroll back to their respective offices, and in easy cases the decision is settled before the short walk terminates. They may agree, in rare cases, that the department's case lacks merit; sometimes the president will authorize the dean to make an immediate offer. At other times, there are more conversations and attempts may be made to gather additional evidence. Other experts are called, new letters are written. Sometimes weeks go by before a final decision is made.[9]

That is the end of a long story. I have told it in such detail to show readers that the granting of tenure is serious business. I know of no private corporations or professions that search for people with equally rigorous and objective standards. The depth of inquiry and exhaustive character of the examination of candidates put the tenure process in American universities in a class by itself. At Harvard we may have reached a point where we are never entirely satisfied with any new appointment after lovingly inspecting every conceivable weakness, every intellectual wart and pimple of a prospective colleague. Most of us, however, remain convinced that the quality of the Faculty of Arts and Sciences is maintained and improved by the steps I have just described.

What occurs at Harvard is not exactly duplicated elsewhere. Few, if any, university presidents play as great a role in the appointment process. Harvard's Derek Bok consid-

---

9. The Harvard Way is not without its risks. A major defect is the length of time between "informal approach" (when a candidate discovers that he or she is being considered) and a formal offer. Six to nine months is a normal time span, and a lot can happen in that interval. Some scholars resent the uncertainty of the waiting period and the notion of undergoing an exhaustive review. Others are tempted to use the possibility of a Harvard offer to bargain with their own institutions, and once their conditions have been improved they lose all desire to move.

ers this role to be the most important and interesting part of his job. It is the most direct way for him to control the quality of the faculty, and demands a considerable time commitment: on average perhaps twenty ad hoc committees in Arts and Sciences alone every year. Harvard's complete reliance on outside specialists is also unusual. At most other universities, external evaluations primarily take the form of letters, while review groups are more heavily weighted with insiders. In my view, these differences matter far less than the similarities. Each university has its own ways, and I have naturally used the example of Harvard. What unites us is the careful, in-depth, national and often international search for tenure candidates. That is a meaningful and powerful bond.

## Some Further Doubts

Until now I have mainly accentuated the positive aspects of the system. I also wish to consider some criticisms that have not yet been mentioned. To start with, there is the well-known allegation that the system tends to exclude innovation while perpetuating established specialties and approaches. In the words of one social critic:

> Organization measures wisdom in accordance with what is already believed; it accepts as wise action what is already being done. Intellectual quality is assessed in accordance with what most resembles the beliefs and methods of those making the decision.
>
> Faculty control of appointments *can* sometimes be a means to self-perpetuating quality. It can more especially be a means to self-perpetuating mediocrity. And in a world of change, it can be a powerful tendency to academic obsolescence.[10]

This is a serious charge not so much because of its validity, but rather because of an implied theory concerning the sources of academic innovation. Who should be the in-

10. Speech by John Kenneth Galbraith, University of California at Berkeley, March 27, 1986.

novators? Who should decide what innovations to adopt? Who, in fact, spearheads most academic innovations?

This accusation is aimed at the departmental form of organization used in nearly all universities. Departments are, without a doubt, a favorite whipping boy in and out of the academy. They are seen by some as inherently conservative structures that prevent interdisciplinary approaches and the appointment of mavericks.[11] An additional complaint is that departments ignore students—particularly undergraduates—and run largely for their own convenience, i.e., as a club in the bad sense of the word. The relation of these adverse circumstances to tenure is obvious. Departments, as we have seen, initiate the process. Higher authority can approve or reject, but in nearly all cases the range of choices is determined by a department that represents an established discipline.

As one who has suffered at the hands of departments for many years, my appetite for developing a stirring defense is small. I have witnessed the decline of fields owing to internal dissension and petty jealousies. From time to time, "great men" have been given an opportunity to impose their will with extremely detrimental results. Many times I found myself in disagreement with departmental taste for new members—I believed the choices to be too conservative—and their educational policies. In very rare cases (four times in eleven years) I was forced to place departments "in receivership," essentially to declare the enterprise intellectually bankrupt until reorganized. I have also observed my share of departmental arrogance *vis-à-vis* students, younger members, and all manner of deans.[12]

11. There is, of course, nothing inherently superior about interdisciplinary approaches or mavericks. The results are what count, not fashionable buzz words, and by that standard the score would favor discipline rather than interdiscipline. Very few Nobel Prize winners in the natural sciences or economics have been mavericks.

12. A recent T-shirt for sale in Harvard Square tells the story. It shows the Harvard seal, and on top the word "History" in brackets—in our jargon, meaning "not offered this year." Where the word *veritas* normally appears, we find "gone to France."

Yet most of these criticisms miss the point even if we do not reject—as one should—collective guilt. Departments are a necessary and efficient form of organization because their members are better equipped than anybody else to judge quality in their subjects. Of course they also make errors and sometimes need prodding from higher levels. At Harvard, and at other universities, the most valid opinions concerning the future of, say, chemistry or fine arts is to be found in the collective wisdom of those respective departments. Administrative opinions are far more likely to be flawed and overly influenced by trendiness. That is why so many departments become centers of innovation, transforming themselves incrementally with periodic infusions of new blood. And that is also why old departments quite regularly produce offshoots (new departments), give birth to new fields, change requirements, and so on. None of this is easy or rapid, nor does it get the publicity of occasional decanally inspired innovations such as a new core curriculum. In the long run, however, the inner core is quality of the faculty and not a particular curriculum, and it is well served by departments.[13]

Two related doubts also are on the minds of our critics: mistaken choices despite or because of careful (and conservative) procedures, and the tenure-related inability to get rid of deadwood. These problems are not unique to universities, although they may be more important because of the almost absolute job security attached to a tenured post.

There are two kinds of mistaken choices (of course, besides those resulting from possibly wrong criteria): someone selected who turns out to be a disappointment, and

13. My impression is that the absence of departments has done very little to remove the abuses normally associated with their existence. That applies even to the quantity and quality of interdisciplinary work. As an example, I cite the current situation at the University of California at Irvine. Here we have a school of social sciences deliberately established in 1964, from the outset without departments. Whatever its current status, few will claim that the structure at Irvine has produced interdisciplinary or educational results that stand significantly above the average of its peer institutions.

someone not selected who, with the benefit of hindsight, should have been chosen. Both situations certainly occur. We have failed to appoint young scholars who eventually performed dazzling feats of research. We have appointed professors whom we believed to be future leaders of their fields and who have in later years been failures. We have—I hope inadvertently—appointed disastrous teachers. But these could be unavoidable mistakes; perhaps we made the best choices with the information available to us at that time.

These are subtle questions and there is no scientific evidence available to prove that the type of tenure selections described here result in conservatism, wrong choices, deadwood, and poor teaching; it is equally difficult to prove the opposite. I have, however, participated in over two hundred tenure selections (ad hoc committees), and I have had to live with the consequences of those choices as administrator and colleague. In my opinion, the system works well—not perfectly, but better than conceivable alternatives. Outright mistakes are rare: disappointments usually come with early warning signals, but we may proceed anyway because choices are limited. The greatest risks are a consequence of our inability to predict the future—not, I wish to stress, our difficulties in evaluating current achievements comparatively. Scholars develop at different rates. Some hit their stride late; others shine very early, only to dim after age forty. These risks are truly unavoidable in a system that acknowledges a social contract between professor and institution.

And do a significant number of university professors "idle in ill-paid peace, accountable to nobody"? In my experience, this is the smallest problem. I have seen misdirected energy, too much outside activity, as well as the pursuit of research that will yield few valuable results. I have noted the redirection of professorial activity toward administrative assignments. But the label "deadwood" would apply only to under 2 percent of a major university faculty; that is my totally unscientific conclusion.[14]

Another issue of growing debate is retirement. A necessary condition of a smoothly functioning tenure system is a reasonable and clearly determined retirement age. Sixty-five seemed fine to me, though the current practice of age seventy is workable. The prospective absence of mandatory retirement will, I think, necessitate the modification of tenure.[15] The reasons are simple. On the one hand, the incentives for professors to retire may be small; on the other hand, forcing colleagues—one's peers—into retirement at some undetermined point following a long association is awkward, distasteful, and impractical.

That incentives for retirement are small seems inherent in the upper echelons of academic life. I have repeatedly stressed limited formal obligations, and moderate income levels. To these factors add that tasks are physically undemanding—no heavy lifting, few set hours. Why would anyone leave voluntarily, especially if this step inevitably brings with it some reduction in income? The danger is clear: after a certain age, as energy declines, the proportion of formal obligation to total effort will inevitably increase until the two are identical.

No institution interested in preserving quality can tolerate a growing gerontocracy that necessarily brings with it declining productivity. The disastrous effect on young scholars surely needs no elaboration. If ever mandatory university retirement is deemed to be age discrimination, an alternative mechanism will have to be found to accomplish the same purpose. The introduction of term contracts and periodic tests of competence and performance seems

14. I also believe that those within the 2% should not simply be ignored, as perhaps happens too often. Early retirement is an excellent option, and deans—after and only after seeking a lot of advice—should find no difficulty in signaling by means of salary policy and distribution of other benefits.

15. At present, federal law still permits colleges and universities to retire tenured faculties at age seventy. That will no longer be possible after 1993, when those schools will be treated like other businesses in which mandatory retirement is prohibited.

logical. None of this is horrible in theory, but the practice would either be hellish or inefficient. How can one possibly expect neutral and tough verdicts involving associates of a working lifetime? My prediction is that the vast majority of contracts would be renewed—as happens in most contract systems already,[16] accompanied by the certain decline of quality. Older professors could increasingly keep out the young, and that is bad. Lesser opportunities could lead the young to be ever less interested in academic careers—a sad picture. A far better method would be to restructure retirement in such a fashion as to diminish the economic benefits of extra lengthy service while lowering the financial risks of retired life. A combination of defined benefits and indexed pensions might work well for institution and individual.

16. See *Faculty Tenure,* p. 12.

# 12

# Burnout, Envy, and Other Forms of Pain

When my own thesis adviser, the economic historian Alexander Gerschenkron, retired over a decade ago, *The New York Times* ran a story under the headline: "Harvard's 'Scholarly Model' Ending Its Career."[1] Obviously a gentleman who deserves our undivided attention. During World War II, Gerschenkron, a refugee and not then holder of a regular teaching post, worked in a northern California shipyard as a flanger. During his "exit interview" with the *Times,* he said: "I seriously considered staying in the shipyard. I liked the contact with the anonymous mass of Americans. And the work doesn't follow you at night into your dreams. Is scholarship pleasure or pain? If someone cuts your leg off, you know it's pain, but with scholarship you never know." In some ways, a surprising assessment at the end of an exceptionally successful scholarly career.

I can offer a personal example that makes a similar point. As a dean, my activities would consist of seeing many peo-

1. June 19, 1975.

ple, shuffling papers, writing letters, and chairing innumerable committees. Frequently these activities did not result in measurable progress or benefit, but I always returned home at night convinced that my time had been used productively. What is the basis of this constructive illusion? The difficulty of measuring executive output, and the natural tendency to give oneself the benefit of the doubt.

As a scholar-teacher, my feelings of accomplishment and progress are necessarily cyclical: there are regular troughs and a few peaks. Take writing a book—the classic professorial task. One cannot—at least I cannot—write for eight hours a day. In common with others, I set aside a period of the day for writing, say, the morning. And some mornings it does not go well at all. I sit and stare at the yellow pad, make too many trips to the coffee machine and bathroom, yearn for telephone interruptions, and by noon have little to show of any value. Instead, I am frustrated and feel guilty. Frustration is the product of temporary failure; guilt comes from holding the gift of independence and freedom, with an assured salary, and using it so badly.

Here we have the great paradox of our profession: a significant virtue (freedom) that is so easily transformed into a vice (guilt). Therein lies the impossibility of distinguishing pleasure and pain. Both sensations are very personal. We are not members of a large symphony orchestra protected in our occasional ineptitude by fellow players and a skillful conductor. While we can, to a limited degree, hide behind the names of our institutions—some provide more protection than others—in the end we stand alone either in front of the class or on the printed page. In the world of the faculty, reputations are made and destroyed on a highly individual basis.

Business is quite different. If the American automobile industry is accused of producing a low-quality car, it is not easy for the management and labor of General Motors to feel that they play no contributing role in this assessment. By contrast, I am certain that attacks on Harvard education seem very remote to most of my colleagues. They will believe that criticisms are directed at others, and pay close attention only when their personal reputations are involved. Of course, emphasis on the individual has its good and bad sides. Good: success does not need to be shared; bad: failure cannot be shared.

What are the major factors that make up the darker side of academic life? Perhaps none are unique, but they do appear in special guises. I will discuss the following broad categories of evil: burnout and boredom, getting old, and envy.

Compared to most other careers, the working life of a professor does not incorporate clear progress or stages once the great hurdle of tenure has been overcome. And that is a major contributing factor to boredom and burnout. Once a lifetime contract is awarded—say at age thirty-five—the individual faces over thirty years of unchanging duties: to contribute new research results and to teach students. The fundamentals are set and do not alter, because ours is a collegial enterprise of "owners" with equal rights and responsibilities. The organization is not conceived in terms of group vice presidencies, foreign branches, or the leadership of a team effort. Per tenured professor—and compared to business—the number of available administrative posts is very limited, and in any event their real and perceived advantages are small.

Over the course of a career, it is common for research interests to change significantly. Students also change from year to year and supply new stimulation. That suffices to keep most of us active and interested; but a minority inevitably will lose enthusiasm. Different factors account for this troubled group. In some instances, a brilliant creative mind can deteriorate; more frequently entire fields leap forward in new ways and leave behind those unable to change. Sometimes established subjects become dull and routine, and boredom affects all practitioners. There are also individual dead ends that appear only after many years of intellectual investment, creating deep anxiety and pessimism about one's intellectual future. Some scientists have trou-

ble in keeping up with their graduate students because
fields change so quickly; some humanists give up because
they are not sure that anybody cares about their work.
None of these categories includes the "deadwood" problem so often mentioned by opponents of academic tenure.
For the moment, I am not considering individuals who have
retired voluntarily while collecting salaries—those who
have simply stopped trying.[2] I am concerned with those
who experience difficulties in creating an appropriate
rhythm for their working life.

Frustration in research can make classroom activities unattractive. If in our own minds the field has become dull,
how can it be made interesting to students? If we have been
overtaken by others, how can we have the confidence to
teach the next generation of scholars?

These are extremely delicate topics, and their discussion
is avoided as much as possible in universities. It is as if we
all lived in glass houses and no one wished to throw the first
stone. As dean, I knew virtually every senior member of our
faculty—about four hundred individuals. With only one exception, none ever told me that his or her research was of
lessening value or at a dead end. Every Harvard scientist
with whom I discussed research assured me that his or her
work was going very well, and suggested that their greatest
achievements were in the future. Age in no way changed
these forecasts. That simply cannot be true, and some who
made the projections knew it all too well.

We contribute to the problem of burnout by steadfastly
refusing to recognize that life does have stages that require
adjustments. For example, I believe that younger members
of the faculty should take primary charge of graduate instruction. They are up to date and most specialized in their
knowledge. Graduate training should emphasize depth and

2. Some years ago, Stanford University attempted to develop an early retirement
system for these individuals. I was told that a dean approached one obvious candidate and assured him that Stanford's generosity would permit immediate retirement at half-salary. The professor declined, pointing out that, after all, he was
already retired on full salary.

sharp focus, as well as the technical and theoretical frontiers of a subject. These qualities are the forte of scholars in their early post-Ph.D. years. The older members of the faculty should, in my opinion, be more active in the teaching of undergraduates, where the latest specialist wrinkles are less important than wisdom. Our undergraduates come to college to receive a liberal education, and their most effective teachers will approach even quite specific topics in context and broad perspective. Life experience is a valuable part of the liberal arts no matter what the subject.

I am certainly not suggesting that it is desirable for this division of labor to be rigidly observed. A great many older professors remain first-class graduate teachers and—equally important—the graduate students want them in the classroom, and especially in the laboratories. Furthermore, as Ph.D. thesis advisers, the most famous senior names bring advantages in the form of job prospects. It is also true that some of the finest undergraduate instructors are young men and women just out of graduate school. I still think that my point deserves more attention than it has ever received in universities. A gradual shift toward undergraduates as a teaching career progresses makes sense and might save some professors a lot of frustration, while being good for students. It does not happen easily or naturally because of counterproductive prestige factors, and the refusal to recognize a desirable pattern of change in long-term intellectual activities. Professors measure success in terms of disciplinary recognition, number of graduate students, size of grants, and the like. The fundamental yardstick remains the same for some thirty-five years, and that is not a good idea. This may also, in part, explain the many unhappy retirements among professors. Throughout their working lives they claim to want more time for their "own work," and when that becomes possible between ages sixty-five to seventy, the removal of teaching obligations, committee assignments, and departmental votes is frequently greeted with open resentment. The answer may be that the activity now most suitable, research, is least congenial at that age, because the most original work is so often done by the young.[3]

Next, I turn to the category previously labeled "envy." I have chosen that unpleasant word to describe an array of characteristics especially prevalent in the academic world: envy of colleagues in other fields, and envy of those earning more than we do in other occupations. To be envious afflicts a large proportion of humanity. However, the trait is particulary well developed among academics because of deep conviction concerning our own worth and resentment at lack of recognition by "others": i.e., university administrators, the public, the government, students, nearly everyone.[4]

According to an American Association of University Professors survey, the average annual salary of full professors in doctoral level institutions (for the academic year 1984–85) was $44,100. For assistant professors, the figure was $26,480.[5] Somewhat depressing salary levels when we consider the qualifications of these individuals. But the numbers are slightly misleading. Our three thousand colleges and universities are too heterogeneous, and averages mean little. For Harvard Arts and Sciences, the tenured salary for professors during that same year averaged slightly over $60,000.[6] Similar levels will be found in the top thirty or so research universities in the United States. Is this good or bad? Compared to what? A very difficult question. For example, in 1935 a full professor at Harvard earned around $8,000 a year; on that income, a servant and a cottage in

3. In 1965, on his sixty-fifth birthday, a group of former students presented Alexander Gerschenkron with a volume of essays in his honor—a *Festschrift*. Instead of thanking us, his remarks on that occasion were almost resentful. He wished that we would eventually be subjected to a similar unpleasant experience.

4. That may be a reason why it is sometimes difficult to convince professors to give to charity. The feeling seems to be that they are subsidizing society simply by practicing their chosen profession. It is a characteristic that we allegedly share with physicians.

5. *Fact Book*, pp. 122–23.

6. Salaries in business, law, and medical faculties are much higher. Informal discussion with fellow deans leads me to estimate a difference of 20% in favor of these professional schools.

Maine were easily attainable. The equivalent would be $59,000 in 1984. A period of over forty-five years has brought almost no improvement; furthermore the current tax burden is heavier and (legal) tax avoidance is problematical for those whose incomes consist largely of salaries. Servants are long forgotten; cottages in Maine quite rare.

Take another example. The present annual salary of a federal district judge is $89,500; a senator or representative receives the same amount; a member of the cabinet gets $99,500. These numbers are close enough to be comparable to top academic-year salaries, but they become less attractive as a yardstick when we realize that civil servants have suffered the steepest income declines in recent years. Between 1969 and 1984, while academic salaries declined slightly or at best stagnated, the purchasing power of congressional salaries fell by 39 percent; district court judges registered minus 32 percent. In my opinion, judges and congresspeople are grossly underpaid. Unfortunately, that is not an opinion shared by Ralph Nader and large portions of the general public. Note that during the same time span, the purchasing power of baseball players increased by 466 percent, and that of corporate executives by 68 percent. As Senator Paul Simon (Democrat, Illinois) said to the Federal Commission on Executive, Legislative, and Judicial Salaries: "The weakest player on the Chicago Bulls basketball team, who spends most of his time on the bench, is paid substantially more than the person who makes the country's laws."[7]

Are our laws more important than the kind of education received by our children or the quality of the basic science produced in our laboratories? Are legislators and educators less valuable than basketball players? Is the size of income a measure of social worth? Why do bus drivers in some of our large cities earn more than non-tenured university teachers? It would be easy to raise many more ques-

7. As reported in *The New York Times*, August 9, 1985.

tions illustrated by a whole array of statistics. We do not need to do so to make our point. In real terms, professorial (and public service) salaries have risen little in the postwar period while the incomes of professionals and business people have shown large gains. Consequently, the relative standard of living of academics has suffered—relative to doctors, lawyers, executives, and similar occupations. There are trade-offs described in my section on the virtues of academic life, but family needs create great pressure when the usual reference groups so obviously outperform one's own calling. The net effect is some envy: a feeling of being insufficiently appreciated by society, and a less than wholly attractive picture for those considering an academic career.

A far more serious problem is what I will call internal envy. It has two roots: the philosophical premise of collegial equality and academic reality. The tree that is nourished by this root system can, on occasion, bear poisoned fruit.

Arts and sciences encompass most of the traditional subjects of higher education: the humanities, and the social and natural sciences. Suppose one were to ask a president or dean, are all these subjects of equal importance? Are some more valuable than others? The answers would very much depend on the type of school. For example, state colleges with strong undergraduate professional programs may judge "importance" and "value" in terms of student enrollments; resource allocation in publicly funded schools tends to be enrollment-driven. That would tilt the scales in favor of business, engineering, biology, and economics. Humanistic studies would have to be assigned a lesser place.

Other deans and presidents might wish to consider the demand and supply of trained personnel. Some academic disciplines are in demand outside of universities, and that leads to strong competitive pressures. A case in point is the rapidly growing field of computer sciences and its parent subject, electrical engineering. Everywhere, students at all levels are flocking to computer science courses; it is the hot subject of the decade. Simultaneously, there has been a great industrial expansion requiring a growing number of highly trained specialists. The result is a shortage especially of applied (as opposed to theoretical) computer scientists, because these individuals are needed in industry, universities, and government. (Keep in mind that industry and government have no obvious need for Ph.D.'s in English, history, or Celtic literature.) And, of course, the market works quite well. A growing demand for an inadequate supply of skilled people raises salaries, and industry has little difficulty in almost pricing these experts out of the academic market. But we cannot do without them, and so they have to be placed in a special category—paid a premium wage, accorded special working conditions, and in a certain sense declared to be "more important."

Academic subjects with practical value give their practitioners considerable financial and non-financial rewards. Because science is deemed vital to our national defense and technological competitiveness, government and industry sponsor research in these fields. Those who profess sponsored subjects receive many advantages: summer salaries, student assistance, travel funds, better offices, modern equipment, and so on. We should also note the psychological benefits that derive from research sponsorship or a high market price for particular skills. It is a tangible sign that someone cares—that there is demonstrable value in the intellectual product.

I am not suggesting that every professor neatly fits into one of two categories, beneficiary of outside interest and therefore manic, or lack of outside interest and therefore depressed. Although reality is more complicated, this division is a useful first approximation. I believe that the postwar years have created a dual structure (a dual economy?) in universities.[8] In the "modern sector," we find scientists

8. Before World War II, government and private research sponsorship was virtually unknown. It is amazing how many scientific discoveries were made at that time with only tiny research budgets.

and many social scientists. Benefits are not equally distributed: at the moment, biology is treated more generously than other sciences (expenditures on health are popular and profitable); support of natural sciences dominates funding of social sciences (hard science is better than soft science); and within social sciences, economics generally is the favorite child (it is the hardest of the soft sciences). I will not attempt to explain or defend this pecking order, except to note that it can be the cause of some envy. These would be the rather gentle disagreements among the "haves."

To understand the real meaning of envy we have to look at the "have-nots" in the "traditional sector": a large residual category of fields generally, and somewhat inadequately, described as the humanities.[9] We are, in fact, dealing with two lifestyles and living standards. The traditional sector has lower incomes, older facilities, fewer secretaries, and a dearth of modern status symbols: word processors, computers, butcher-block furniture, private little kitchens and washrooms, even something as primitive as push-button telephones. As dean, I was always aware of these differences; to me they did not appear minor. A letter from a scientist arrived on personalized stationery, perfectly typed by a secretary. A phone call to that gentleman's office might reveal that the secretary had an English accent: an indication of membership in a high caste. When the professor of Chinese sent a letter, it was likely to be written in his own hand or imperfectly pecked out on an ancient typewriter. His phone was answered by machine or, more likely, by no one at all.

These differences are not created by the university; to eliminate them is beyond its power. The flow of research funds is determined by government, industry, and philan-

9. Humanists may believe that they have a near monopoly of suffering and neglect. Yet there are branches of the natural and social sciences that also bear relative deprivation. For example, the use of scientific museum collections (botanical, zoological, and geological) is no longer required by most leading-edge researchers. Molecular and cellular techniques are crowding traditional systematists. Those charged with maintaining these institutions for a future time when they may well be in great demand fully share feelings of envy.

thropy, and by priorities and fashion. The greater the flow of research monies, the more opportunity for amenities: secretaries, conferences, travel funds, summer salaries, and so on. In my lifetime, neither priority nor fashion has favored even the broadest definition of humanistic studies. (A possible exception is the study of certain languages deemed critical, from time to time, by the Department of Defense.) The simple fact is that some skills or occupations command higher salaries and receive a larger share of public and private resources. An institution can attempt to mitigate the differences—to minimize the gap—but eliminating the dual structure is out of the question. This would require raising everyone to the level of the most favorite specialties, and that would be well beyond the means of all universities.

There is still another complication to consider: the advent of the professional superstar. Until now we have discussed specific categories that confer advantages. But privileges can also be acquired *ad personam:* extra money, extra space, extra leave . . . extra whatever is available. It is a peculiarly American phenomenon, and derives from fierce interuniversity competition. Despite my belief in the virtues of institutional competition, it seems to me that we are excessively fond of statistics, measurement, and ratings.[10] Who is number one in this league or that; who leads at the box office; who is slipping in business? These are the type of questions that preoccupy public opinion and the press. They are also on the mind of American universities, because attracting a superstar has a powerful influence on ratings and external image. Make no mistake. There is a price, and it is paid in the currency of envy.

10. Our "national pastime" of baseball provides ample evidence of this proclivity. No sport produces more statistics per minute of action.

# 13

# The University as Marketplace

The focus of pain discussed in the previous chapter from the perspective of the individual professor is, to a considerable extent, a direct consequence of market forces. We have, quite consciously, opened our institutions to the influence of markets. Positive results have already been noted. These are in keeping with the American way of life. Problems also emerge.

We are a society in continual transition. Regions once prosperous turn from industrial heartland to rust belt; areas that in the past were swamps and desert are now the rich sun belt. Neighborhoods also seem to be in perpetual motion. When I was young, Amsterdam and Columbus Avenues in New York City were inhabited by lower-income people. Today they have been gentrified, and are the home and playground of the "yuppie" class. In the United States, a "good address" is ephemeral; we are not noted for stability.

Similar tendencies can be observed among our universities. For example, just before World War II the roster of leading American institutions of higher education had a familiar ring. It would include members of the Ivy League, Chicago, Berkeley, Johns Hopkins, MIT, Wisconsin, and others. Today those universities are still leaders, but they are challenged by a group of newcomers that have entered or are determined to enter the circle of top ten or twenty. Stanford, UCLA, Texas (Austin), and NYU all fit into this category. So do a number of schools in the Big Ten. In recent years, I have noticed that at Harvard we worry more about the lure and power of Stanford than about the attractions of Columbia and Yale. Twenty-five years ago, my former colleagues at Berkeley were inclined to look down their erudite noses at UCLA—that raw, somewhat showy place "so suitably" located in Los Angeles. These feelings of self-satisfaction have today been replaced by healthy respect. A few years ago Texas created a stir by liberally sprinkling $100,000 plus offers throughout the country, and they succeeded in attracting a few extremely distinguished scholars.[1] And when it comes to applied mathematics and fine arts, the leading position of NYU is acknowledged by all.

American universities exist in the real world, where leaders are challenged and sometimes forced to make room— even be replaced by—newcomers. For us, the comforts of Oxford, Cambridge, the University of Tokyo, and the University of Paris do not exist. At all times there is a group of universities clawing their way up the ladder and others attempting to protect their position at the top. If one believes in the virtues of competition, as I do, one would stress the benefits of the system. That a large proportion of the world's leading universities are located in the United States I have already in part attributed to the effects of inter-institutional rivalry in my discussion of "Two Thirds of the Best."

1. This began before the oil price collapse. Amazingly enough, the figure of $100,000 no longer sounds all that impressive.

The contrast with Great Britain, already mentioned, has been beautifully described by Christopher Rathbone:

> In contemplating the manifest sense of permanence and stability of an institution like Oxford, Americans feel the existence of some basic institutional wisdom they miss in their own universities. Part of this impression is due to the self-sufficiency of a place like Oxford. Very simply, Oxford is not obliged to compete. There are no challengers perpetually ready to depose Oxford from its preeminent position. Much of the strength of Oxford's institutional integrity comes from its own self-assurance, from being able to take itself and its exalted position for granted. Oxford, then, unlike its American counterparts is not out to prove itself. As an establishment institution Oxford is an unalterable fixture in the life of the nation. This lends self-composure and dignity.[2]

It may be true that Oxford is preeminent among British universities, but that is no longer the most exacting standard. Not having the obligation or opportunity to compete may be one of many reasons for the relative decline of British universities since World War II. Rathbone continues:

> The condition of being able to stand outside the field of competitive institutional combat is a blessing shared by no American university. The only possible exception here is Harvard. Even if its position were anything like as secure as Oxford's, Harvard's behavior as an institution within the consortium of the nation's elite does not exhibit anything remotely resembling Oxford's sense of security, but then Harvard is incessantly obliged to spar with envious challengers. The capacity to take one's reputation for granted is invaluable precisely because it permits the atmosphere of calm in which the mind is truly free.[3]

The contrast between Oxford and Harvard—symbolic of a contrast between American and non-American institu-

2. "The Problems of Reaching the Top of the Ivy League . . . and Staying There," *The Times Higher Education Supplement,* August 1, 1980.

3. *Ibid.*

tions—is elegantly stated. I am not entirely certain about the relationship between calm and a free mind. Excessive calm can lead to the wrong kind of mental freedom; some would call it sleep.

How does an American university rise in reputation and esteem? Money is a sine qua non, and for private universities the size of endowment is a fairly reliable indicator of prestige. Fair—but far from completely reliable. As the tables on pages 229 and 230 indicate, all top twenty institutions are research universities (the richest college is Smith, and it is ranked number 31). Size of endowment drops off very quickly: Chicago's capital fund (number 11) is only 23 percent of Harvard's (number 1). To claim that Harvard is, in some sense, four times better than Chicago would be sheer nonsense. Three public universities are found among the top ten—the Texas, Texas A & M, and California systems—but their endowments per student are very small. Of course, state universities have access to tax revenues, and size of endowment becomes less meaningful. By the standard of endowment per student, Rice would rank ahead of Yale, Stanford, Columbia, and Chicago. That will not sound right to experienced quality rankers. A survey conducted a few years ago among college presidents determined the following sequence of university quality, emphasizing undergraduate programs: 1. Stanford (5); 2. Harvard (1); Yale (4); 3. Princeton (3); 4. Chicago (11); 5. Duke (27); Brown (28); University of California at Berkeley (10); 7. University of North Carolina (74); 8. Dartmouth (19). The numbers in parentheses show the institution's position on the endowment list, and once again indicate a weak correlation.[4] None of this is surprising. Endowment is only a very imperfect measure of either wealth or disposable resources. In Harvard's Faculty of Arts and Sciences, endowment income

4. See "America's Best Colleges," *U.S. News and World Report,*" November 25, 1985. The endowment ranking for Berkeley actually applies to the entire California system.

## Endowment—Top 20 Institutions

| University | Endowment (in Thousands) |
|---|---|
| Harvard University | $4,018,270,000 |
| University of Texas System | 2,829,000,000 |
| Princeton University | 2,291,110,000 |
| Yale University | 2,098,400,000 |
| Stanford University | 1,676,950,000 |
| Columbia University | 1,387,060,000 |
| Texas A&M University System | 1,214,220,000 |
| Washington University | 1,199,930,000 |
| Massachusetts Institute of Technology | 1,169,740,000 |
| University of California | 1,122,160,000 |
| University of Chicago | 913,600,000 |
| Rice University | 857,155,000 |
| Northwestern University | 802,670,000 |
| Emory University | 798,549,000 |
| Cornell University | 725,096,000 |
| University of Pennsylvania | 648,528,000 |
| University of Rochester | 556,908,000 |
| Rockefeller University | 542,765,000 |
| Dartmouth College | 537,272,000 |
| Johns Hopkins University | 534,809,000 |

*Source:* Copyright 1988, *The Chronicle of Higher Education.* Reprinted with Permission.

only covers slightly over 20 percent of annual expenditures. Other assets—buildings, real estate, art works, etc.— are omitted when calculating the wealth of universities, as are tuition payments, government grants and contracts, and annual giving. Even if all resources were correctly evaluated, they would not constitute an adequate measure of quality.

By far the most dependable indicator of university status is the faculty's degree of excellence that determines nearly everything else: a good faculty will attract good students, grants, alumni and public support, and national and international recognition. The most effective method

## Largest Endowments Per Student

| Private | Students | Amount |
|---|---|---|
| Rockefeller University | 119 | $4,561,100 |
| Princeton University | 6,264 | 365,800 |
| Harvard University | 16,235 | 247,500 |
| Mount Sinai School of Medicine | 494 | 234,300 |
| California Institute of Technology | 1,850 | 221,100 |
| Rice University | 3,986 | 215,000 |
| Swarthmore College | 1,312 | 210,400 |
| Yale University | 10,504 | 199,800 |
| Grinnell College | 1,253 | 181,000 |

| Public | | |
|---|---|---|
| Virginia Military Inst. Foundation | 1,592 | $49,400 |
| Oregon Health Sciences University Foundation | 1,141 | 33,300 |
| University of Texas System | 90,000 | 31,400 |
| Virginia Commonwealth University | 1,553 | 27,700 |
| University of Virginia | 16,823 | 23,700 |
| University of Delaware | 15,918 | 18,400 |
| University of Cincinnati | 24,962 | 10,200 |
| University of Pittsburgh | 26,953 | 8,200 |
| College of William and Mary | 6,951 | 8,100 |
| University of California | 146,429 | 7,700 |

*Source:* Copyright 1988, *The Chronicle of Higher Education.* Reprinted with Permission.

to maintain or increase reputation is to improve faculty quality.[5]

One path to higher standing is frequently called "growing your own." Improved selection in junior ranks should eventually raise average senior quality levels. It is a slow and risky strategy. To predict future achievements of young teacher-scholars is hard, and the confirmation of positive or negative judgments can take many years.

5. Although the analogy may make some readers uncomfortable, a faculty can be compared to a baseball team—the university president as owner, the dean as manager, the faculty as players, and students, alumni, etc. as spectators. To have a consistent pennant winner requires money and excellent players. These can be produced by a farm system (junior faculty) or purchased from other teams (superstars).

A far more attractive strategy when one is in a hurry, as we usually are, is to entice proven performers from other universities. The move of a professorial superstar from one institution to another can result in instant recognition.

It is also a very costly way of achieving laudable goals. Superstars in all fields command enormous financial rewards, and are smart enough fully to exploit their market power. They are capable of demanding new buildings, large laboratory facilities, special (reduced) teaching obligations, "kitties" of discretionary money in six figures, sinecures for spouses, purchases of expensive homes, and much else. A typical superstar package in the sciences is likely to cost between $2 and $4 million—not much by the standards of professional sports, but a staggering amount in terms of university budgets. Add the nagging fear that the object of all this affection may turn out to be an "extinct volcano," a superstar who is over the hill, and it is easy to understand why deans negotiate with sweaty palms and brow.

With this in mind, let us return now to the premise of collegial equality and to the darker side of academic life. Obeying the laws of demand and supply is a great temptation: they are simple and clear indications for specific action. The number of first-rate molecular biologists available to universities is limited because of demand for their services in industrial and government research. Market forces raise their wages considerably beyond average academic levels, and that is that. A professorial superstar in any field is the functional equivalent of a baseball pitcher who regularly wins twenty games and we should recognize that those individuals are scarce. The laws of demand and supply tell us that this type of scarcity commands large financial rewards. Simple? Not at all.

Economic rationality works well when a "bottom line" is unambiguous. That may occur in business when ownership is clearly identifiable. Whether we are thinking of a baseball team or a factory, stockholders or individual proprietors, it makes sense to manage the institution in such a way as to satisfy those who are entitled to the fruits of the bottom line. I am not suggesting that this is easy. One has to consider products, technology, time horizons, risks, employee satisfaction, and many other problems. Nevertheless, it makes sense to reward individuals in proportion to their contribution to a clearly measured pool of profits. The twenty-game winner deserves to earn more than a .200 hitter because his contributions are more likely to result in a pennant, and that means large profits for the owners. Similarly, the manager of a highly successful division of a large corporation can justly claim rewards that are not available to those who are in charge of losers.

But what is the university's bottom line and who are the owners? In simplest terms, we teach and educate students, and produce research. Some professors have many students and others very few. In rare cases, a few professors may have no students. Since students are the major source of tuition income, it might appear attractive to reward star performers who hold forth in blockbuster courses to audiences of five hundred or more. They produce a lot of tuition income—far more than their salaries.

There exist at least two major difficulties with this policy. A great classroom performer may not be a top-notch researcher, and that would have to be considered. Far more significant, the opportunity and capacity to attract large student audiences is subject-specific. To follow bottom-line reasoning would mean that those subjects attracting vast number of pupils are, somehow, more important and valuable. As already mentioned, the largest course in Harvard College most years is Principles of Economics. Nearly one thousand students are normally enrolled, annually yielding some \$3 million of tuition income.[6] Does this mean that economics is more important than Middle Eastern languages or thermodynamics? Obviously, that de-

6. In 1988–89, tuition was \$12,310; students take eight half courses per year; and Principles of Economics is a full year course.

pends on one's conception of importance. Economics is popular at universities because the course fulfills certain distribution requirements; because students believe it helps them understand the world in which they live; because many aim for graduate business and law school where the subject is viewed as good preparation. Surely the study of Arabic or physics fulfills equally laudable purposes.

Any experienced academic leader—president, dean, chairman—will know that this line of reasoning is a meaningless parody and can only have destructive consequences. Of course student demand for instruction has to be satisfied, but it is only part of a larger mission. Our task is also the preservation and interpretation of culture, indeed, the continual reinterpretation of culture. We transmit the great traditions from one generation to the next. We nurture subjects and approaches that may not be in current demand, or that seem irrelevant to contemporary concerns, because we know that there is often very little relation between truly important and currently fashionable ideas. I am quite sure that the solution to some of our present-day dilemmas will invoke insights and knowledge possessed by thinkers hundreds of years ago. And we are the keepers of those treasures. I once told President Bok that even if there were no students at Harvard who wished to study Romance languages—at that moment not our most popular subject—we have the obligation to keep the department alive. Why? Because the classics of French, Spanish, and Italian literature are a priceless heritage. To lose their living influence is tantamount to sinking back into the dark ages.[7] A university cannot be run by cost accountants

---

7. This stirring paragraph is taken more or less verbatim from a fund-raising speech given some years ago. After its publication, I received a number of letters from chairmen and professors of Romance language departments containing words of praise. Indeed, some who communicated with me had posted copies of my speech on their bulletin boards. I was not singling out their subject for special praise—that was their mistaken assumption; it was only one of many possible examples.

or as a commercial enterprise responding only to changing markets. That is bad for us and worse for the societies we seek to serve.

Many of us understand that the market sends false signals if the mission of the university is taken seriously, and yet we cannot ignore internal and external pressures. The signals are false because the ranking of scholarly subjects in order of importance is so flawed. We have to make choices, and to allocate resources. Pragmatic decisions will favor fields and individuals, but they are not obviously related to the intrinsic intellectual value of individual activities.

Take the improbable comparison of Sanskrit and computer sciences. Surely there is no need to dwell on the importance of computers: students in large numbers demand to be taught; every pundit tells us that these machines are transforming our lives; the subject is still new and great forward strides are expected in the next few decades. Every university has to meet these needs. The number of computer scientists on university faculties is estimated to grow exponentially in the near future. They will command high salaries and receive special privileges, reflecting market power. Their letters will surely be "word-processed" by secretaries and perhaps expedited by electronic mail. Lucrative private consulting arrangements and generous graduate student support should be the norm. And the rigors of teaching are likely to be relieved by professional gatherings—all tax-deductible—in exotic resort settings. Teaching loads will not be excessive; competition will see to that. Without these comfortable arrangements, it would simply be impossible to attract those scientists to campuses. Their opportunity costs are high. Working at IBM or Bell Labs duplicates nearly all attractions of university life at equal and more frequently higher income levels.

Sanskritists find themselves in a rather different situation. In the United States there are only seven departments of Sanskrit, most of them very small. At Harvard—where the budget, when I was dean, supported one professor and one associate professor—for a long time the department did not even rate an office or a full-time secretary. According to my informants, fewer than fifty individuals teach the subject in North America. Although not many students need instruction—employment opportunities for specialists are extremely limited—individual professors have to offer a large variety of courses, ranging from teaching the basic language to the reading of advanced texts.

I will not argue that we need to expand the teaching and research of Sanskrit; demand and supply seem to be in balance. However, I would contend that it is vital for the language and literature of this major civilization to be studied at some universities; that the few individuals who do so may derive great benefits that we cannot measure—benefits that go beyond the preservation of culture.[8] No one can claim that the intellectual contributions of the individual Sanskritist are less valuable to the university enterprise than those of the computer scientist. We are all common laborers in the vineyards of the arts and sciences—preserving, discovering, teaching. The particular fields that we choose to till yield different crops: apples and oranges! To open the mind of one student in a small esoteric class may do more to change the world than the explication of timely material in front of crowds. That has to be the academic ideal, but—to borrow a Marxist phrase—contradictions abound.

For me they became particularly vivid when my replacement as dean was selected. He turned out to be a brilliant economist, thirty-nine years old, winner of the prestigious J. B. Clark Medal awarded by the American Economic Association to the most outstanding member of the profession under forty. During his relatively short career he had gained a full professorship, a named chair, an international

8. The physicist J. Robert Oppenheimer studied Sanskrit as a Harvard undergraduate. Did it make him a better scientist? Who can say? One might also ask whether one can understand modern India without a critical appreciation of its classical texts.

reputation, and very decent remuneration. His distinctions were entirely deserved; any institution would be lucky to have him as a member of its faculty.

As chance would have it, his undergraduate roommate at Princeton was also on our staff in the Department of Near Eastern Languages, and he happened to be an acquaintance. This young man—he and the new dean were exactly the same age—taught Persian, Arabic, and some other languages and literatures. His accomplishments as a linguist, grammarian, and teacher were acknowledged by his colleagues at Harvard and elsewhere—to be sure, a small group. He held the untenured rank of Senior Preceptor (language teacher), with little security, low status, and an exceedingly modest compensation. Chances for professorial tenure were not so good. The market for specialists in Persian is not booming. Both careers perfectly illustrate our dilemma.

Contradictions that nourish the darker side of our life are not confined to distinctions between fields. The superstar phenomenon has the same effect. Why it exists has already been explained, and the consequences are subtle. Most of us recognize the power of markets, the need for big names to enhance departmental reputations, and the glamour of great prizes. At the same time, we are aware of the fuzziness of the bottom line, and this makes questionable all departures from egalitarian practice.

These are some of the sources of our discontent. On balance, I believe that the virtues of our customs and arrangements are far outweighed by the vices. To make certain that this remains true or—if necessary—becomes true is a major responsibility of academic administrators. They face the difficult, nearly impossible assignment of maintaining the delicate balance between outside pressures and internal ideals.

# GOVERNANCE

# 14

# Deaning

Academic administration, as we shall see, is a very peculiar art. "Deaning" is the form of administrative servitude with which I am most familiar, but my experiences are more broadly applicable. Academic paper-pushers of all sorts should have no trouble in recognizing themselves.

As time passed and I acquired more seniority as an administrator, a number of friends and acquaintances sought my counsel concerning the attractions of deaning, provosting, and even presidenting. In nearly all cases they had already made up their minds to accept an administrative position—although they did not necessarily admit that, even to themselves. My friends were not in need of counsel—it was too late for that—but they were in need of a picture depicting their own future. Sometimes I gave a crash course in academic administration. In my own mind, I called it "Quacks of a Lame Duck": I had the nerve to become an instructor of these subjects only at the very end of my term. What follows might be a set of lecture notes.

The dean of a faculty of arts and sciences has to become

familiar with the entire spectrum of "non-professional" learning from anthropology to zoology. (Provosts and presidents have to include professional learning as well.) In my case that meant exciting new encounters with natural scientists, humanists, and social scientists outside of economics. These were not casual encounters, because the dean has to understand warmly and sympathetically what animates these scholars. Decanal knowledge cannot be scholarly understanding; perhaps it is no more than "executive understanding." Nevertheless, it is a vastly enriching experience.

The dean is likely to be the person who knows more members of the faculty than anyone else—usually by first name. He will also get to know students, staff, policemen, buildings and grounds workers, alumni—in short, a significant part of the entire university community. No ordinary professor can have as wide a circle of friends and associates; few will have the opportunity to make so many enemies. Even though deans do not always encounter individuals in the most auspicious circumstances—there are too many conflicts and disagreements for that to be the case—I still consider the possible range of friendships to be one of the great rewards of deaning.

To leave the impression that deaning is only a positive experience would be misleading. As administrative head of a faculty of arts and sciences, I had to face the difficulty that my responsibilities were not related to any standard description of a profession or field. "Arts and Sciences" is not a subject. The deans of law and medicine, for example, continue to function as lawyers and doctors and do not lose touch with their peers. That could not have been my experience. Being a dean of arts and sciences means that one is entirely engaged in administration, and most of the issues have nothing to do with your own discipline. That applies even to economics. When I was a student, the question "Have you ever met a payroll?" used to be asked of fledgling economists in somewhat mocking tones. Well, I did meet a payroll for many years and during hard times, but *that* is not what economists do or care about.[1]

In chapter 3, I have already described the decanal day. The essence of that message should be repeated. Both professors and students have in their possession uninterrupted time. Time to write, read, think, dream—and to waste. A dean's schedule—any administrator's schedule—could not be more different: half-hour appointments lasting nearly all day and not infrequently beginning with breakfast. Indeed, most meals acquire an official character. Learning to make little speeches while eating is essential. Once I compared myself to a dentist: twelve to fourteen interviews a day, frequently accompanied by pain. That resulted in an angry letter from an official of the dental profession!

None of these things is very peculiar. Those in charge of anything will have many friends and enemies. Leaders of large groups cannot hope to go beyond "executive understanding"—typically skimming memoranda prepared by assistants—and that is the opposite of professional expertise. Finally, running an establishment of significant size will inevitably move beyond most standard descriptions of fields. Arts and Sciences is no more diverse than General Motors or the Department of the Interior. The oddities of academic administration lie elsewhere.

A few years ago I went to see the motion picture *Amadeus,* a study of two musical lives: that of the genius Mozart and the journeyman composer Antonio Salieri. Somewhat surprisingly, I found myself rooting for Maestro Salieri, *Hofkapellmeister* (musical director or administrator) at the Hapsburg court, who might be considered almost a villain. I came to sympathize with Salieri, who seemed to be in the position of a typical dean. My heart went out to him because the "Amadeus Problem" is with us today, especially in universities.

According to the film—the story employs a good deal of

1. Perhaps those who keep choosing economists for administrative posts should keep this fact in mind.

artistic license—Mozart's character is infantile and fundamentally unpleasant. His behavior is atrocious and selfish, but his musical gifts are divine. Seemingly without effort, Mozart composes symphonies and operas of supreme beauty. In contrast, Salieri is a good man of average talent. His long life has been devoted to the glory of God and emperor. His works are the product of sweat; none will ever have the touch of genius. Salieri's initial reaction to Mozart is friendly, but when the latter mocks him, the feelings become hostile—even threatening. At one point, the miserable *Kapellmeister* turns to God in bitter complaint: his years on earth have been consecrated to good deeds, and yet inspiration and creative powers have been awarded to the childish and despicable Mozart. Is that justice?

Every academic administrator at an excellent university must have, on occasion, shared Salieri's desperation. Our constituencies are inhabited by extremely talented scholars, including some who merit the label genius. A significant proportion own difficult and childish personalities (remember that temperament is ignored at time of appointment). Great scholarship, even great teaching, is in my experience often combined with quirky character traits. Nice guys don't necessarily finish last, but it would be hard to argue that they are especially well represented among the frontrunners. Shortly after I became dean, one of Harvard's greatest scientists requested an appointment. The prospect was exciting. I knew the gentleman only casually and looked forward to meeting someone whose name figures most prominently in the history of twentieth-century discoveries. Perhaps it was naive to expect a combination of Einstein and Arrowsmith; in any event, that was not to be. During the course of the interview, wishing to take back an inspirational message to my children, I (perhaps inappropriately) inquired about this man's sources of scientific inspiration. A reply came without the slightest hesitation: "Money and flattery." My disappointment was profound, but I came to realize that this scientific genius understood

all too well all that deans had to offer. Salieri: you are one of
us.

Another aspect of our special culture is the expectation
of reticence. Openness is an admired feature of American
life, and that includes the university. Ambition is tolerated,
even encouraged. Hard work is respected. We have never
followed the ideal of the English amateur, an appearance of
idleness disguising energy. These straightforward, attractive characteristics vanish in the choice of deans, provosts,
and similar academic executive officers. In business, can
you imagine someone repeatedly declaring their unavaila-
bility for the post of CEO or COO while secretly hoping—
perhaps campaigning—for the appointment? It might happen in rare instances. With us it is the rule. It is always bad
form for a professor to admit the desire for administrative
office. One of our clichés says: anyone who really wants
these posts should be disqualified. Governance is a form of
class treason, a leap from "we" to "they," and a betrayal of
our primary mission—teaching and research. For this reason also, it is crucial—once a decanal or similar post is attained—to give evidence of continual suffering. Colleagues
will offer condolences (congratulations would be a breach
of manners) and the incumbent must always publicly yearn
for a speedy return to laboratory or library or classroom,
no matter what his or her real state of happiness.

Let us be candid about another rarely discussed matter.
Administrative duties bring considerable long-term financial advantages. Extra stipends and various fringes—for example, official residences—are common perquisites of joining the governance apparatus, and former deans and
presidents are usually treated with more than average kind-
ness even if their performance has been barely adequate.[2]
This may explain why, in fact, these appointments are
rarely turned down.

2. A frequently missed point: administrative stipends become part of pension
calculations. A decade of these payments can make a considerable difference at
time of retirement.

Yet another peculiarity is our persistent refusal to recognize the value of experience as preparation for academic administration; the higher the office, the less attention is paid to demonstrated executive qualities. One can get the impression that no previous experience is wanted. Harvard's current president came to the job after a three-year term as dean of the law school, a rather limited horizon. The immediate past president of Yale was a professor of Renaissance literature. His successor brought with him one and a half years of service as dean of Columbia's Law School. My own successor served as chairman of the Economics Department for less than a year. The current and highly successful president of New York University brought very little related work experience to his important assignment. I also fit this pattern. Three years of service as a departmental chairman, and heading a number of faculty committees, did not constitute a meaningful training program for taking charge of 1,000 teachers, 8,000 students, 6,000 employees, and budgets eventually exceeding $200 million.

These practices are not irrational. Compared to other institutions, a university does not possess an available pool of experienced administrators preparing for advancement. On the contrary, the "natural" selection process—i.e., awarding tenure—rejects all evidence except that pertaining to research and teaching. Furthermore, those who are selected for scholarly reasons and then, prematurely, drift into low-level administrative assignments are not admired by their colleagues. High office—deans of faculty, presidents, etc.—brings a certain grudging respect; low office brings only thinly disguised disapproval. A professor who willingly becomes an assistant dean or assumes charge of a summer school is considered tired of research, over the hill, desperate for a little money, or all of the above. Now we can begin to understand why previous experience carries so little weight. Choosing the most talented, capable, and respected persons necessitates consideration of a much larger group. Indeed, from a certain point of view, premature administrative indications may be a negative characteristic.

Given the unusual situation in universities—if you will, a corps of senior executives or tenured professors whose expertise lies outside of administration—one might ask: why not turn to professionals? After all, running an enterprise, balancing budgets, supervising building maintenance, raising money, developing personnel policies—none of these is directly related to research and teaching in any field, with the possible exception of business administration. Would it not be sensible to leave these rather distasteful, vulgar tasks to hired help?

In general, I believe that is a prescription for disaster. The technical skills of the executive—reading balance sheets, estimating discounted present value or debt capacity, and similar arcana—are trivialities compared to understanding the fundamental nature of the university. And this has to come from inside experience acquired by long hours in library, laboratory, and with students. Early in my non-scholarly career, a senior professor said to me: listen to gossip, that is what all good deans do. It took me some time to appreciate his deep wisdom. Obviously my older friend did not want me to be concerned with recent scandal or cocktail party conversation. As I came to realize, he urged me to keep my finger on the pulse of a complex organism by listening. Who was doing the best work in a department? Which fields were especially promising? Was a certain research center declining in quality? One can learn the answers to these and other questions by paying attention to constructive gossip, provided that the listener has a trained ear. In nearly all cases this will be done most ably by someone steeped in the culture of universities. The clash of cultures can be illustrated by a good story that may be apocryphal. When Dwight D. Eisenhower was president of Columbia University, he retained a military aide as befitted his rank of general of the army. The young major used to sit outside his Low Library office. One day an elderly, typically rumpled professor arrived to keep an appointment. The aide looked him over with a stern eye and said: "Button up, doc, you're going in to see the general."

## Helpful Hints for Academic Administrators

### 1. Never be surprised by anything.

Among the charms of office are increases in unexpected events. A professorial life normally is tranquil and sheltered; few people will know your name. Neighbors or postmen may wonder why you spend so much time at home, but in general they have more important things to think about. To be a university teacher brings the opportunity of following a pleasant routine: mornings working in a quiet office, teaching classes no earlier than 10:00 A.M.—students won't show up earlier—long lunches, and afternoon seminars, all carried out in comparative anonymity. Facelessness is not an option for the major administrator. Your name appears in the press with regularity; your habits, behavior, and decisions become matters of public discussion; and many odd letters will cross your desk.

In 1976, the following job application arrived from Algeria:

Dear Sir:
   I have the honor to ask you to consider me for the post of professor in any suitable faculty.
   I have nine PhD's. I have studied at Cambridge University. I have spent eighty years in the United States. I have known many American students. I have worked as a neurologist in many psychiatric hospitals of your country. I have studied geophysics and many languages, including Egyptian, French, Dutch, English, Chinese and Japanese.
   To tell you more about myself, I was the friend of a number of American presidents (George Washington, Roosevelt, Abraham Lincoln). I am a veteran of the Civil War. I have worked with Metro Goldwyn Mayer. . . .

At this point I stopped reading and sent the application to my friend, the provost of Yale. Our sister institution is especially famous for its humanistic studies, and I had the feeling that the gentleman from Algeria would find New Haven a more congenial environment.

More recently, a letter came from the Midwest.

Dear Sir:

We need your cooperation for a serious problem that involves all the Harvard College professors. We were watching the Phil Donahue T.V. show and he had two prostitutes plus two women who were trying to help the prostitutes as guests. The prostitutes stated that lawyers and college professors were the majority of their customers. They stated the men wore perfume and jewelry and all the college professors came not only from Missouri but Massachusetts. They stated all the Harvard College professors came to St. Louis, Missouri each week because of the large choice of hotels. . . . Dirty college professors stay in Massachusetts.

I attempted to reassure the lady who wrote this letter by telling her that Boston hotel capacity had doubled in recent years, and expressed the hope that dirty college professors would henceforth be less inclined to travel.

Sometimes, the general public will make truly original and helpful suggestions. From Brooklyn, New York, there arrived the following epistle signed by a gentleman with the (self-awarded) title of Special White House Adviser on Homeless Missiles.

Dear Dean of Faculty:

As your title suggests that you obviously have a fully endowed natural faculty of foresight and are clearly in full possession of all your faculties, I should like to suggest a suitable alternative to the Guaranteed Student Loan Program.

As a modest proposal, I suggest the creation of a student MX Missile Loan Program, i.e. students would receive loans based on the number of hours spent monthly driving MX missiles from one rocket launching site to another.

Such a program would enable students at your institution to serve God, missile, country and their own education—all at the same time. . . .

My reply included a profound expression of gratitude. However, I had to point out that missile sites were largely located in the West, and student travel expenses would make the plan less attractive for Harvard. Unfortunately for universities with more favorable locations, I believe that our government may decide to keep the missiles stationary.

Of course, these are all "kook" letters: sometimes amusing, not infrequently nasty and obscene, and most often pathetic. But they do illustrate an inevitable feature of administrative existence. A call to lead a faculty, college, or university is uplifting. We think of great decisions and debates about the philosophy of education. We may see ourselves speaking for "the humanities"—or "science" or what have you—to the nation and perhaps even the world. We do not know ahead of time that in reality life will be a rollercoaster taking us from the sublime to the ridiculous five times a day. High-minded topics are part of the job, and that is foreseen and predictable. But would anyone believe that the choice between two- and three-track storm windows for dormitories took many hours of negotiation between that Olympian figure, the president of Harvard University, and his principal acolyte, the dean of the Faculty of Arts and Sciences? Or that because the temperature in a large lecture hall was 40 degrees and the microphone inoperative—all in front of seven hundred students of English literature—the dean would be publicly accused by two professors of inflicting intolerable pain and downgrading, even killing the humanities? You had better believe it!

## 2. Learn the value of being vague.

As a group, academics are intolerant and critical. In their work, they are used to giving and receiving strong criticism. Precision of thought and expression is a quality that elicits admiration. Not surprisingly, professors have a certain contempt for politicians—compromisers, talkers, windbags. I do not believe that many deans share these simple-minded views. Over the years, I have developed profound sympathy especially for politicians attempting to survive in a democracy. From time to time, I would cast envious glances at a variety of totalitarian models of governance ranging from Albania to North Korea. How much easier to be an effective leader in that milieu; no wonder those chaps stay in office forever, or at least until they get shot.

We, on the other hand, live in the world of special interests. Student concerns are political, sexual, social, and occasionally academic. Each topic is backed by a pressure group with a detailed agenda. The Faculty of Arts and Sciences is divided into some fifty departments; every department has its own program and will concentrate on little else. Denying a request—usually an appropriation—and citing considerations of general welfare is not going to make a favorable impression. And then there are alumni, the government, the press, the town (as when it rhymes with gown), each one in pursuit of a few objectives. Alumni desire reasonable athletic teams, academic excellence, faculty sympathetic to whatever their politics happen to be, and granting admission to their children. The government wants to purchase research without paying its full cost. It also wants to prevent the free flow of scientific information in the name of too vaguely defined national security. The town wishes the university to pay taxes, to have it build houses for the poor, and to prevent the building of more dormitories. Representatives of the press are anxious to replace universities altogether, particularly as purveyors of lectures on public morals.[3] Picture the dean (president,

3. In this connection, a tribute to the *Boston Globe*: I suggest a special self-righteousness award. One of its favorite editorial topics has been poor university performance in implementing affirmative action programs, notably at the tenured level. The irony of having these admonitions published under a *Globe* masthead containing not a single woman or minority member was evidently lost on this group of (white) gentlemen.

provost) as a seal with a gigantic ball labeled SPECIAL INTER-
ESTS precariously balanced on his nose.

The democratic politician—and that is what we are too—
understands that vagueness is the quality that produces
maximum approval. Specificity inevitably leads to a strong
negative reaction—somewhere. Recent presidential campaigns introduced some powerful slogans: "getting government off our backs," "standing tall," "knowing who
you are," and that great gem—"read my lips." As long as
we do not explain what any of this means (the obvious
answer is nothing), these phrases result in harmless good
feelings.

A specific illustration of the general principle may be
useful. During the last few years the United States has been
subjected to a national debate about education. Reports by
various commissions have been greeted with approval by
the media and educators. We are urged "to do better," to
improve the skills of our students, to raise the standing of
teachers. But the commission documents contain few details concerning implementation, and very little analysis of
the structural problems of American public education.
How do you reform a system controlled by twenty thousand independent and local school districts? After all, that
is the most important practical question. Despite the lack of
answers, nearly everybody applauds.

By way of contrast, some years ago Harvard University
changed its undergraduate curriculum. Our debates and
conclusions were closely monitored by press and public
largely because the national debate was just starting and we
are always highly visible. We were precise, and provided a
great amount of detailed implementation. Our results were
greeted with much criticism (and some welcome praise);
nearly everyone could object to something. That is the
price of specificity in an age of the pet peeve. I am not

These lines were written three years ago. Two women have been added, now
accounting for 1/10th of the masthead. The racial composition has remained
unchanged.

suggesting that vagueness is always desirable, but on occasion it does have its uses.

### 3. Memorize the correct definition of the adjective "responsive": giving response; constituting a response; answering.

Here we have one of the most misused words of the American English language—especially on campuses. The young, and many not so young, have convinced themselves that to be responsive is the same thing as saying yes. Those of us over forty should know that a negative reply is just as responsive; no administrator can afford to forget this.

I emphasize this seemingly minor grammatical point because of the extraordinary difficulty in disposing of issues in a university. Our society is a very unusual mix of generations. Nearly half the citizens of Arts and Sciences—I have in mind primarily our 6,500 undergraduates—are between the ages of eighteen and twenty-two, and they turn over every four years. As a group, students have short memories, and the same issues arise year after year as new student leaders reach the limelight. New leaders will, with considerable regularity, accuse administrators of not being responsive to their demands, even though a clearly negative reply was given annually for the past decade. Faculty members have longer and rather unforgiving memories; eventually they will get even. You may need a colleague to serve on an important committee: perhaps support is required for a controversial vote. If you notice a lack of cooperation, recall that eight years ago you—quite reasonably—turned down this person's request for better parking or additional leave with pay.[4] In the eyes of your colleagues, you had

4. These are not outlandish examples. When the student revolution erupted at Berkeley in 1964, the faculty provided rather lukewarm support to President Clark Kerr. Many reasons for their attitude were discussed at the time. Faculty discontent with newly instituted parking fees was believed to be an important factor.

been unresponsive. Administrators cannot afford to forget *anything,* least of all the meaning of yes and no.

**4. Consider that "no comment" is often the most appropriate reply to a question. There is no obligation to talk to the press. Avoid doing anything that you would not wish to see published in a newspaper; you will fail, but it is a worthwhile goal.**

All academics like to see their names in print, on book jackets, articles, and even in newspapers. For most professors, this is a positive experience; at worst a harmless event. Writing books or articles is evidence of scholarly productivity, and an occasional bad review is quickly forgotten. We can always take revenge by writing nasty reviews ourselves. Many colleagues seem to take particular satisfaction in publicly commenting on world affairs in the daily press. That is an especially pleasurable and riskless activity: no one will remember what was said one week later (today's newspaper is used to wrap tomorrow's fish), world affairs are unaffected by what experts say, and relatives are impressed by evidence of one's authority. The ultimate form of this indulgence is the numerous public service or political advertisements published most often in *The New York Times*. The average signer is a professor presumably seeking to influence a matter of important public policy *and* to see his or her name on display—usually in print of microscopic dimensions. In fact, these advertisements have no discernible effect on anything, except perhaps on the balance sheet of *The New York Times*.

Academic administration operates under entirely different circumstances. Now the task is to keep one's name out of newspapers or to have it used only when it serves an institutional purpose. There will be no need to pursue reporters with offers of opinions or background information. They will be the hunters and you the prey, and sometimes it makes sense to avoid capture. Freedom of the press concerns the right to print what one knows to be true, and not the right to know everything. Discretion is a quality that all deans, presidents, and provosts have to possess or acquire in a hurry.

In 1974, the scientific community at Harvard was disturbed by an incident that, unfortunately, has become more common in recent years. A series of biological experiments performed by an assistant professor and a brilliant undergraduate helper promised results of absolutely major significance. People started talking about the next Nobel Prize and it was rumored that a mentor of the junior faculty member had already poured the champagne. What followed was a bad surprise for all those involved—except perhaps one individual. In the wake of initially successful results, no one was able to duplicate the experiments. And that has remained true to this day. What happened? No one will ever be certain, though the main suspicion fell on the undergraduate assistant, who in a different matter was discovered to have forged letters of recommendation for himself. We may assume either that there occurred a most unlikely fluke or that someone fabricated scientific evidence.

This sad story hit the front page of many newspapers, damaging the reputation of science in general and Harvard in particular. I was especially disturbed by the premature celebrations and publicity. It seemed to me that in modern biology there existed excessive competitive pressure: a field moving forward with enormous, exciting rapidity offering fame and fortune to those who win by no more than a nose. This atmosphere is extremely well described in James Watson's remarkable *The Double Helix,* and maybe that is the way it has to be. As a layman, I yearned for a balance between the *The Double Helix* and (yes!) *Arrowsmith*—that selfless young researcher peering at the test tube late at night in his laboratory, thinking of mankind rather than white tie and tails, Stockholm, and shaking hands with the king of Sweden.

In that somber mood, I was walking to my office on December 29. The university was closed, the Yard deserted. And then I saw a familiar face: a reporter for *The New York*

*Times* who had on occasion written nice things about me. Naturally I was disposed to be friendly and we chatted about the scientific incident just described. The reporter told me of his intention to write an interpretive article for the Sunday paper, and we continued with our conversation—certainly it was not an interview. In this relaxed setting, talking informally to someone who had put my name into print favorably, I made a big mistake. I mentioned excessive competition among scientists, and then—unable to resist a clever, arresting description—described some biologists as "the worst sort of scientific Sammy Glicks."[5] This remark was printed on Sunday and attributed to "an influential Harvard administrator." I was mortified and slept very little that night. My own stupidity was obvious: I had violated a rule of good administration.

On Monday morning, the chairman of the Biochemistry Department—a wise and renowned scientist whom I admired, respected, and liked—hand-delivered a letter. The last sentence said: "I consider this slanderous statement by an administrator of my University a grave insult to the Department of Biochemistry as well as to me personally." The temptation to duck, to claim ignorance was great. I might well have attempted to follow that foolish path. In the end, circumstances led me along a road of greater virtue. My boss, the president, to whom I confessed, gave me a stern Protestant lecture that said come clean. Furthermore, I recalled making the same clever remark to some of my associates. Lastly, a reference to Sammy Glicks had a certain ethnic flavor that fitted me better than anyone else.

I asked to meet with the members of the Biochemistry Department. After acknowledging my mistake and apologizing, we had a candid and spirited exchange of views. They heard my concerns and complaints, and I acquired a better understanding of their circumstances. We parted friends, and many years later—after my departure from

5. See Budd Schulberg, *What Makes Sammy Run.*

office—they gave a dinner in my honor. No other department did that.

## 5. Cultivate the art of asking people for money; your career may depend on the results.

Fundraising will always be a principal obligation of senior university administrators, no matter what is said when presidencies and such are offered to naive candidates. In the jargon of the trade, one must learn to become a "closer": somebody who can shift from polite, frequently awkward preliminaries to asking for a seven-figure gift. It gets easier with practice.

I have been told that when Derek Bok was offered the presidency of the university, the Senior Fellow of the Corporation told him not to worry about fundraising. He knew that if Harvard did its job well, financial problems would solve themselves. I wonder how often Mr. Bok recalled this hilarious bit of advice as he rose after dinner, dog-tired, in some distant city to deliver yet another speech: "I am delighted to be with you in Los Angeles, Chicago, Kansas City, Atlanta . . ."

Fundraising will always be the leitmotif of academic life. Rich or poor, public or private, college or university—there is never enough money to go around. Annual giving, capital campaigns, alumni relations, donor cultivation, are activities subsumed under the euphemism "development." They are all about money and become second nature for administrators. Nearly all of us could or should be able to deliver a polished appeal for nearly any activity in our schools two minutes after being awakened without warning at 3:00 A.M. The size of the audience would not matter; having an undistinguished plate of chicken *à la* king set on one's lap might strengthen the Pavlovian response.

Fundraising is necessary, but it is much more than a necessary evil. I grew to like it, and never ceased to be amazed by the loyalty and generosity of our alumni, or by the intelligence and probing minds of many foundation officials. Asking for money is an excellent way to test the free market, a most effective method of surveying the feelings and priorities of any constituency. "Development" is a form of education for the giver and receiver. Making the case and convincing a potential donor of its validity is healthy for all concerned. One of my letters on behalf of our annual giving campaign was returned from Midland, Texas, by a graduate of the class of '48 with the following note: "Harvard is a spent institution in a doomed country, both long overrated. Just try to make the best of it." Fortunately for us, and for the country, his views were not representative. Personally, I much prefer the equally improbable question posed by that great nineteenth-century benefactor, Henry Lee Higginson (1834–1919): "Did not all that really mattered in the world depend upon enlarging the influence of Harvard before it was too late?"[6]

Many members of the university community have great trouble in asking for money. All too often, visits whose intent is well understood by all parties lead to no conclusion—positive or negative—because it is so difficult to say: "We hope that you will contribute at least one million dollars in support of our supreme effort to maintain the excellence of the university." An hour of polite conversation goes by all too quickly, and few individuals will make big gifts without being asked. Being Jewish, and therefore raised in circumstances where asking for and giving to charity is considered routine, is very helpful. Understanding and practicing *chutzpah*[7] is equally useful.

During a capital campaign that raised over $350 million for our Faculty of Arts and Sciences, I had spent many hours with John L. Loeb, the well-known financier and philanthropist, who had made numerous magnificent contributions to Harvard in the past. My purpose was to secure what in the trade is known as a "leadership gift": I hoped

6. Cited in Seymour E. Harris, *The Economics of Harvard* (New York: McGraw-Hill, 1970), p. 272.

7. Yiddish for supreme self-confidence, nerve, gall.

that he would be willing to endow *fifteen* junior faculty positions, requiring nearly $10 million. That was not a small sum, even for Mr. Loeb. He is a gracious person, very much a "gentleman of the old school," and full of affection for Harvard. Our meetings were pleasant, at least from my point of view, and the moment had arrived for me "to close." For this decisive occasion, I asked President Bok to come along. Having the top man at your side is an inestimable advantage—nearly a prerequisite for securing major gifts.

Our meeting took place in New York City at the Four Seasons Restaurant. We ate—I clearly recall—very expensive and delicious hamburgers. As the conversation gently evolved toward specific dollar amounts, our host inquired: "Are you asking me for five million?" I replied: "Not quite, sir. My hope is that you will agree to give ten million, so that others would be inspired to give five million." John Loeb frowned, his face darkened. "Henry," he said, "that comes close to *chutzpah,*" and then he added rather unexpectedly: "By the way, do you know how to spell that word?" I indicated my ability to do so by grabbing a napkin and reaching for my pen. Suddenly the president of Harvard University snatched the napkin from my hands and printed CHUTZPAH in large block letters on the paper, and gave it to Mr. Loeb. *(O tempora! O mores!)* After carefully folding the napkin into a small square, Mr. Loeb placed it into one of his vest pockets. The meal quickly came to an end and we shuttled back to Boston. A few days later there arrived the most welcome news that the Loeb gift would be around $9 million. We had established that the value of *chutzpah* is approximately $4 million.

6. "**Do not separate yourself from the community . . . do not judge your fellow man until you have been put in his position.**" (Hillel in *Sayings of the Fathers*.)

This is excellent advice because the temptation to separate is great, and its consequences disastrous. It is all too easy for the administrator to forget what the world looks like from the perspective of professors—especially junior professors—and students. A senior administrator becomes a symbol of his or her university, and it is dangerous to confuse privileges of representation with personal entitlement. All of a sudden, you will entertain on a grand scale, perhaps in an official mansion, without spending your personal funds. Remember that the money for this comes from the university: right out of the pockets of students, professors, and alumni. To be sure, they are the beneficiaries; but they are also paying guests and you are not the generous host. When traveling to other schools— especially abroad[8]—you may be met by limousine, treated to banquets, and offered gifts. You may get invited to address large audiences at commencements while receiving an honorary degree. Do not consider these tokens of honor as personal recognition; those go to thinkers, creators and other great researchers. Our recognition is entirely derived.

The dangers of separation from the community—colleagues and students—should be easily understandable. They are similar to the problems currently faced by many American managers. Distance from peers results in poor information; in the inability to hear constructive gossip. That gap also undermines administrative authority, which should be based on the principle of *primus inter pares* rather than on rank and commands. Most serious, perhaps, is the resulting difficulty of getting hard or unpopular decisions

---

8. In my experience, foreign universities—particularly those located in non-Western countries—are the most ostentatious in their treatment of dignitaries. A real problem in terms of reciprocity for Americans. The head of a Saudi university told me that he received money to purchase a new Cadillac every other year. I told him that the president of my university drove a twenty-year-old VW Bug. Inverse snobbery perhaps, but a strong symbol nevertheless. In the People's Republic of China, as the leader of an academic delegation, I was entitled to a suite in all hotels (the others had only rooms) and transportation in a hand-tooled Red Flag limousine the size of a 1936 Rolls-Royce. The most exquisite advantage was domestic first-class travel on Chinese airlines. There was absolutely no difference between first and coach class—same seats, food—but a curtain separated the two compartments.

accepted. This will happen more easily if "we are all in the same boat" is not a farce.

## 7. Never underestimate the difficulty of changing false beliefs by facts.

Many Harvard alumni afford a perfect illustration of this proposition. Today, the average size of classes is smaller than twenty years ago, and yet a large proportion of our graduates are convinced that their time was educationally more intimate. Currently, over 90 percent of our senior faculty teach at least one undergraduate course per year. The firmly held belief that Harvard professors do not teach undergraduates is not the least bit weakened by these statistics. It seems very tempting to cling to the belief that Harvard—or any other place—reached its peak just when one was a student: ten years ago or fifty years ago, it does not really matter. (Recall the words of John Buchan!) In our particular case, these convictions have held true for 350 years, and perhaps we need not be overly concerned. My point, however, is more general. When given the opportunity—in the absence of incontrovertible scientific proof, and sometimes even then—people believe what they wish, and empirical evidence does not lead to quick altering of cherished positions. From an administrator's point of view, there are no easy lessons that follow. I cite it as one of the unavoidable difficulties of our existence.

## 8. Learn to think big—especially when dollars are the measure.

One of the greatest shocks for new academic administrators—almost by definition individuals with little previous experience—is the amounts of money casually tossed about. Universities are big enterprises, and the sums correspondingly sizable. The annual budget of the Faculty of Arts and Sciences currently is over \$300 million; Harvard

University's budget is more than $700 million. The size of these sums is hard to comprehend for a typical professor who thinks in terms of his own salary, perhaps the purchase of a house, and views a research grant of $100,000 as very big. Making multi-million-dollar judgments is an acquired habit; in the early stages, it inspires sheer terror. I mean, it takes some time to become comfortable with an energy bill of about $8 million, a phone bill of over $1 million, and individual laboratories that can easily cost $4 million.

It was my misfortune to become dean in 1973 just as the faculty's financial situation started to deteriorate. We were producing large annual deficits and I had promised my "bosses"—the president and the Corporation—to eliminate them in three years. In those early days, I sat in my office until late in the evening concerned about "small sums"—say, painting a few classrooms—lest we run short of cash. Some time elapsed before I realized that a year and a half would pass before the consequences of a fiscal decision became apparent, or that small economies based on household practices will not affect deficits of $3 million. Two conclusions emerge. New administrators tend to err on the conservative side; they find it difficult to leap from their own petty circumstances to the big picture. At the same time, thinking frequently in sums of seven, eight, or even nine figures makes it rather more difficult to focus on the problems of paying for the children's summer camp. A mildly schizoid attitude is helpful.

# 15

## University Governance:

### *Seven Principles to Ensure Reliable Performance*

Governance concerns power: who is in charge; who makes decisions; who has a voice, and how loud is that voice? These are always complicated and contentious questions, especially in higher education. The reasons are clear. To begin with, universities and colleges are schools for adults, and the requirements of schooling and adulthood can be difficult to reconcile. Secondly, universities in America are often seen as agents of social change, as producers of research that could affect policy and also as places where entry or membership confers life-long advantages on selected individuals. It is understandable that many people are anxious to influence some of these outcomes. Thirdly, in our country colleges and universities can also be wealthy foundations as well as large enterprises that use their resources for a wide range of purposes more or less related to education. Universities are large employers; they manage sizable investment portfolios, own residential real estate, operate restaurants, gift shops, campuses abroad, and much else. How wealthy foundations and enterprises dispose of resources is of legitimate concern to all sorts of people, inside and outside of their walls, and they demand a hearing. Finally, nearly all of higher education—public and private—receives funds or subsidies from taxpayers. (Somewhat over 20 percent of Harvard's budget come from government funds.) Taking money from the public means that representatives of the people, including the press, have a legitimate interest in how authority is exercised by the recipients.

In considering issues frequently associated with university governance—my interest is primarily in internal, academic questions: should students participate in faculty meetings, should faculty have a voice in investment policy, who should determine academic requirements, and similar matters—I have found the principles outlined below to be useful. I am quite sure that they apply to other types of organization, and I view none to be overriding or absolute. As a whole, however, they make sense to me.

## The First Principle

*Not everything is improved by making it more democratic.*

I shudder as I write this sentence. No doubt future generations of students and colleagues will have additional proof of my deeply reactionary leanings. Even so, this principle is not placed first for nothing.

The United States and a few other countries attempt to practice political democracy. Although practice may fall short of the philosophical ideal, "one man [person], one vote" describes the legitimate goal of our political life. Formally, every vote is of equal weight and most of us believe that in our relations with government more is better than less democracy. There are those who believe that power should be distributed more equally as well in other spheres of our existence. For example, the economy could be made more "democratic" if the distribution of income were less skewed, and I believe that would be a very good thing.

A strong belief in the value of political democracy is not inconsistent with the practice of less democratic ways in other areas of life. Families are not usually run on democratic principles; neither are armies, hospitals, or most workplaces. Formal or informal hierarchies are in place: some voices are more powerful than others, and we know from experience that the functioning of these institutions is not necessarily improved by distributing power more equally.

Most social institutions have both democratic and hierarchical characteristics, and that applies to American universities. As a generalization, I would suggest that the relations *between* major university constituencies—faculty, students, staff—are hierarchical; *within* constituencies, relations tend to be more democratic. Even this proposition leaves me slightly uncomfortable, because of the many distinctions that prevail within groups. Some faculty members are tenured; others are not. Non-academic positions include senior vice presidents earning six-figure salaries and groundskeepers mowing the lawn for quite a bit less. These voices do not carry the same weight. Even students are not in any sense a homogeneous category. After all, this label attaches to seventeen-year-old freshmen and heads of families attending professional schools.

The most basic force creating hierarchy in all education is the interaction between students and teachers—the constituencies for whom the university primarily exists. Universities are schools attended by students seeking knowledge from teachers;[1] graduate students might be described as apprentices being trained by masters in their subject; all students are judged and certified by those more competent

---

1. I do not intend to suggest that teachers are the only source of knowledge. Students learn from books, from each other, and in many more mysterious ways. Nevertheless, the role of teachers has been *central* in nearly all systems of education.

than themselves. I am obviously describing an unequal or undemocratic teacher-student relationship, but it should not imply student oppression or the arbitrary exercise of authority by teachers. It means neither ignoring the rights of one nor unreasonable privilege for the other. Hierarchy does imply that some views predominate, and not on the basis of majority opinion.

Democratizing universities can have many meanings. One might be concerned about how the faculty governs itself or the prerogatives of faculty *vis-á-vis* administration, and much else. In recent years, especially since the 1960s, the issue of democracy has acquired another by now well-recognized meaning: more power for students, probationary members of the faculty, and non-academic employees in the setting of university policy. An extreme example were some of the decisions made by the Harvard faculty when a new Afro-American Studies Department was created in 1969. As a result of intense student pressure, building occupations, and open threats, the faculty voted that six undergraduate students—about one half of the total membership—would be placed on the committee charged with the job of designing the department. Three of these students were to be elected by the Association of African and Afro-American Students, a student political organization without open membership (you had to be black to join). All the student members of the committee were entitled to vote on tenure and term appointments. In other words, black undergraduates received the same privileges and responsibilities as tenured faculty.[2] The result was a brief period of chaos. Fortunately for us, most faculty members soon regained their senses. Within a few years, these tasks—inappropriate for students anyhow—were entirely removed from undergraduate hands. Other institutions here and abroad took rather longer to return to sanity.

The limiting case exists in some European universities where the practice of "parity" was born in the 1960s. Power

2. See Henry Rosovsky, "Black Studies at Harvard," *The American Scholar* (Autumn 1969).

over virtually all decisions came to be equally shared between students, faculty, and employees *(drittelparität)*—and not infrequently the government. The educational results have been disastrous. Academic standards declined and a sense of mission was lost. Much earlier I mentioned the Dutch experience, and it can once again serve as an example. The Dutch government amended university governance and instituted a version of parity in 1972. Within a few years, many of the better research institutes had lost their professors. This was especially true in the sciences, where escape to industry was possible and inviting.

Excessive democracy—and by that I mean parity, unclear lines of authority, and similar forms of administrative paralysis—may not be an accidental outcome. It can be the understandable reaction to arrogance and abuse of power by those in charge—administrators, professors, or ministry bureaucrats. In other words, excessive democracy could be brought about by insufficient democracy—the movement from one extreme to another. That is how I would interpret what happened in German universities during the 1960s. Reasonable hierarchy can never mean lack of accountability (see the Seventh Principle). I am not attempting to define the optimal degree of university democracy. My point is much simpler: more democracy is not necessarily better.

### The Second Principle

*There are basic differences between the rights of citizenship in a nation and the rights that are attained by joining a voluntary organization.*

As American citizens, we are equal in terms of political rights after reaching the age of eighteen, provided that we have not been convicted of a crime. For most of us, citizenship is not a voluntary act. We control neither our birthplace nor the nationality of our parents. When citizenship is elected rather than acquired by birthright, there may be some limitations. As a naturalized American, I am prohibited by the Constitution from becoming President—in my case only a minor inconvenience but not, perhaps, equally insignificant for Henry Kissinger, or former Secretary of the Treasury Michael Blumenthal, or New York banker Felix Rohatyn.

Membership in a university community or university citizenship is quite different. It is always acquired by application and/or invitation and that should legitimize constraints. Just as corporations can sell restricted shares that no one has to buy, and clubs can enforce certain rules[3] since no one is forced to join, so can schools offer positions or admission with limited rights. The optimal degree of university democracy need not—and in my view should not—follow the model of national citizenship. Accordingly, students are invited to study and not to govern the university. Faculty members are invited to teach and do research and to set educational policy in their sphere of knowledge.

Indeed, faculty rights are also limited. Some areas of governance and policy are properly deemed beyond faculty jurisdiction, usually for reasons of lack of specialized competence or conflict of interest. These matters are generally considered the responsibility of trustees. I do not wish to suggest that restricted rights mean no rights. Everyone should be able to express opinions freely, and mechanisms for "voice" or "input" for all groups are more than merely desirable—they are mandatory if we wish to create a just university. My present emphasis is only on limitations and on rights that should not be presumed to be the same for all groups.[4]

---

3. But not *any* rules. Just because an association is voluntary does not give it the right to violate our laws. Thus racial and in some instances gender barriers are prohibited in private clubs of certain size.

4. For a denial of the validity of the first two principles, I refer the reader to Robert Weissman's "The Hidden Rule: A Critical Discussion of Harvard University's Governing Structure," issued by Harvard Watch on December 7, 1987, under the auspices of Ralph Nader. Mr. Weissman and I agree on very little. He is certainly not disposed to draw a distinction between the rights of national citizenship and university citizenship.

## The Third Principle

*Rights and responsibilities in universities should reflect the length of commitment to the institution.*

During my years as dean, I made a statement to a group of undergraduates that became notorious and provoked much student hostility. I was addressing the role of various groups in our community and said: "Remember, you—the [undergraduate] students—are here for four years; the [tenured] faculty is here for life; and the institution is here forever." This banality came to be interpreted by the student press as a sign of my arrogance and insensitivity to the legitimate claims of youth. It was frequently reprinted, usually underneath one of my particularly unattractive pictures. Eventually, a movie poster appeared on campus that announced in big letters: "Remember you are here for four years; Dean Rosovsky is here for life; but Diamonds are Forever." Obviously I had made an impression, but not necessarily of the right kind.

Why should a longer time horizon increase one's voice? That is certainly what I was saying to students, *not* because of their youth, but rather because they are transients. Almost all forms of organization recognize that long association (past and prospective) gives special competence and deserves recognition—up to a point. Anyone can outlast their welcome, but other things being equal, most forms of enterprise respect and reward seniority. We do so because length of service is an indicator of experience and loyalty, and a certain sign that short-term exploitation is not a goal of the individual.

Universities encounter a special problem: the mixture of constituencies assures that those with the shortest time horizons will outnumber everyone else; those with the least knowledge and experience are a majority. Consider, for a moment, the vast divergence of time horizons in a typical university. Undergraduate students—about 6,500 at Harvard—get their degrees in four years and depart. Graduate students—some 10,000—on average stay for slightly less time if we include professional education. Some students attend part time or are enrolled in special programs; the latter may come only for a few weeks. There are over 50,-000 students in this category. Former students become alumni—nearly 200,000 are alive and recorded by Harvard—and this large group certainly has a long-term though less direct stake in the university in which they studied: the value of their degree is closely related to an institution's overall standing.[5] Furthermore, many alumni show a lifetime commitment by providing their institutions with financial and other types of support. Most of them, however, are very removed from the daily life of their universities. Harvard also has a faculty of some three thousand teachers, and about one-half are tenured. Non-tenured faculty, unless promoted, may stay eight to ten years, whereas a typical tenured career will last twenty-five years or more. We must also mention those serving on the governing boards, the lawful owners of the university-assigned fiduciary responsibilities. Theirs is a legal and moral trust that requires a few people to be oriented toward the present and future well-being of whatever has been entrusted to them. At Harvard, thirty-seven individuals—seven members of the Corporation (including the president and treasurer) and thirty elected Overseers—fall into this category. And then there are employees: senior career administrators, secretaries, technicians, plumbers, painters, and so on. Their number approximates 11,000.

What would be the effect of majority rule? One man, one vote would give those with the shortest time horizon the greatest influence. Influence would not be sufficiently weighted by the degree to which one has to live with the consequences of decisions and actions, and that is a bad

---

5. I am obviously referring to the extrinsic value of an academic degree: not what the student has accomplished or gained, but how the outside world evaluates universities and their individual programs. The intrinsic value of a Harvard MBA may not be significantly higher than the degrees offered by the competition. But that the Harvard Business School and Stanford dominate extrinsically—starting salaries, top positions in industry, etc.—cannot be doubted.

idea. My concerns can be illustrated by the recent widespread debates about South African divestiture. During the last few years, many universities and pension funds have sold all stockholdings in companies doing business in South Africa. The main purpose was to make a moral statement against *apartheid.* Those who urge divestiture also believe that it will force the government of South Africa to abandon this odious practice. I am not mentioning divestiture in order to discuss its merits. I am only raising the issue to show that appealing moral statements are unlikely to receive careful evaluation under university majority rule or with some American version of parity. In deciding on divestiture—as in most other decisions—one should carefully balance the pleasure of acting now versus the possible pain of long-range consequences. For example, not purchasing stock in businesses operating in South Africa *may* significantly reduce future earnings. Divesting may also be seen by some critics as the use of endowment funds for political purposes, and that could lead to greater politicization of donors and perhaps new government regulations. None of these fears may be realistic; they may only represent institutional timidity; but it is crucial that they be considered in detail and in a calm atmosphere. And that will not happen—experience tells us—when the consequences of the long term seem so unclear and even unimportant to most students, to many members of the faculty, and to many others. Will they really bring themselves to care about the possibility of a smaller income stream during the next generation? An affirmative answer is not plausible. Trustees who understand their responsibilities are the best hope for the careful consideration of the long run.

## The Fourth Principle

*In a university, those with knowledge are entitled to a greater say.*

I do not mean general knowledge. Student opinions concerning the desirability of a Democratic or Republican administration in Washington are as valid as those of their professors. An employee who works in the facilities and maintenance division should know more than professors about the upkeep of buildings. A university policeman may have a superior understanding of crime. And, of course, the large number of alumni embody a vast amount of knowledge about most everything, both general and specialized. What these constituencies lack—with the exception of some individual alumni—is expert knowledge about the primary mission of universities: teaching and research. Students in particular are associated with the university precisely *because* they lack knowledge and desire to acquire it. The individuals with expert knowledge are to be found almost entirely among the academic staff.

These are not arrogant statements or simple, unqualified absolutes. Students are consumers of teaching and usually have worthy notions about the quality of instruction; their opinions deserve consideration. Former students (alumni), especially of the professional schools, tend to be shrewd judges of their education and of the effectiveness of programs. These voices need to be taken into account. All of us also recognize that professional university administrators, and secretaries and technical personnel, store much wisdom in their heads. But reasonable opinions are not the same things as deep understanding and ultimate responsibility.

Final judgments on educational questions are best left in the hands of those with professional qualifications: academics who have experienced a lengthy period of apprenticeship and have given evidence of performing high-quality work, in teaching and research, as judged by their peers on the basis of broad evidence. This applies particularly to faculty control of curriculum. The chances of having courses taught well—with verve and imagination—are greatly diminished when content and structure are imposed by "outsiders" without debate and discussion. Anyone who has attended schools run by our armed forces will have little difficulty in appreciating this point.

Faculty members know the proper definition of subjects and standards, and are more likely to have a sense of intellectual frontiers. They are also more inclined to resist fads that happen regularly to capture the young and the general public. Does anybody still remember the "Princeton Plan"? In the early 1970s well-meaning students, quite a few outsiders, and some faculty members urged the adoption of a practice that originated at Princeton University: vacations during elections, and some campaign periods to allow students to participate more actively in the democratic process. This notion had about the same half-life as the hula hoop.

Let me stress again that the faculty does not wield unqualified power. Most educational decisions taken by a faculty are reviewed by academic deans, presidents, and trustees; academics are publicly judged by peers through rankings, surveys, and grant awards; and they are judged by the market in terms of the attractiveness of the institutions in which they find positions.

In justifying "a greater say for those with knowledge," one practice requires special discussion. American universities are unusual in that their administrations include a chief executive officer (CEO), almost always called a president. He or she is in charge in the sense in which a CEO directs a private company. The university president is responsible to a board of trustees that functions rather like a board of directors. He or she has the final say on new initiatives, the hiring and firing of most personnel, and many broad questions of policy.

Two notable differences between the CEO of a company and a university should be mentioned, however.

First, the university has no single "bottom line": standards of executive performance are therefore more difficult to establish. Secondly, a rough counterpart of middle and senior managements are tenured professors, who can be discharged only in exceptional circumstances. The university chief executive can be said to have one hand tied behind his or her back—but, as observed in chapter 10 on The Meaning of Tenure, for good and sufficient reasons.

The contrast with university systems based on the continental model is stark. In France and West Germany, in Japan, Israel, and nearly everywhere else, the chief administrator is likely to be a rector, in most cases a professor elected by an academic senate for a two or four year term. His fellow administrators, such as deans or chairmen of departments, are also elected for brief terms. The non-American procedures are both more political and more democratic—foreigners tend to describe our system as *unitary*—but the price in terms of efficiency and bringing about changes in direction is very high. In the American system, the buck stops—for all practical purposes—with the president. In the European system, the buck gets passed around until all are exhausted.

But how can American practice be reconciled with the fourth principle? In particular, what possible justification can there be for a presidential veto in *academic* matters? Should not the collective wisdom of faculty experts reign unquestioned and supreme? At Harvard, the president can stop promotions to tenure in any faculty even when expert professors are strongly in favor of a candidate. (Similar powers are given to many university presidents.) Obviously these powers cannot be rooted in any type of expertise: the chief executive's knowledge of chemistry, Romance languages, medicine, psychology, and dozens of other subjects will never be sufficiently embodied in one individual.

Presidential authority has little to do with individual expertise and therefore must be justified on different grounds. First and most obvious, the higher one's place in a hierarchy, the less emphasis can be placed on expertise. Everything looks pretty small from the top of a pyramid, but the field of vision becomes very much enlarged. A general need not understand all facets of an army's activities in detail; it would be an impossible and perhaps undesirable requirement. Yet the general is certainly given veto power over the opinions and actions of more expert colonels and captains. The same applies to all others whom we call general managers. They are users of expertise; specialists assist them in being better leaders.

Secondly, we may assume that conflicts of interest are less acute at higher levels of management, a topic more fully considered in discussing the fifth principle. Finally, presidential authority in the academic realm should be thought of as judicial rather than executive. The president is not given power in order to select who, in his opinion, is the best scholar of a certain subject. It is his task to monitor procedures, to adjudicate differences among experts—in brief, to develop a clear policy or to take a specific action based on the many voices of those with deep knowledge. The principle that those with knowledge should have a greater say is not, I believe, subverted by presidential authority.[6]

## The Fifth Principle

*In universities, the quality of decisions is improved by consciously preventing conflict of interest.*

When private advantage and public obligations clash, we are faced with a conflict of interest. Universities are complex structures: many of their citizens have communitywide (i.e., quasi-public) responsibilities, and we may reasonably assume that few of us are immune to the temptations of pursuing private interests.

Take a simple and obvious example: a department considering the award of tenure. Should non-tenured mem-

6. My friend Professor David Bloom of Columbia University asks an interesting question. Both the third and fourth principles put great emphasis on the positive relation between length of commitment and knowledge on the one hand and voice or rights on the other. Why, then, does our society place such heavy responsibilities in the hands of juries—on average, individuals with little knowledge and no long-term stake in the issues they consider?

Juries exist, I believe, in order to render a verdict concerning a very specific, static situation: has A murdered B or has Jones cheated on his income tax return, or have Firms C and D conspired to fix prices? None of these are issues of establishing or changing long-term policies. Those types of issues are left, perhaps indirectly, in the hands of judges. And judges in many ways resemble trustees, presidents, deans, and tenured professors.

bers of the department be given a vote? If one wishes to minimize conflict of interest, the answer is no because an affirmative vote could lower the junior professor's own chances of promotion since the number of places are limited. An affirmative vote could also—under certain circumstances—be cast for the wrong reasons. A non-tenured person might support someone merely in order to have a friend at court when his or her own case was to be considered. Of course, the desire for friends at court is not limited to any one group, but it is certainly more important to those whose fate still hangs in the balance.

Participating in the selection of non-tenured colleagues raises similar problems. Choosing the best candidates could reduce future opportunities for someone competing for a scarce tenured vacancy. (Whether or not students should participate in these procedures does not seem to me a question of conflict of interest. I would argue that they should be excluded on grounds of lack of competence. See the fourth principle.)

Faculty members and students can also experience group conflict of interest. Harvard rejoices in a large endowment, accumulated wealth donated by generations of alumni and other benefactors. It would be an easy matter, entirely within the law, to spend the proceeds at a more rapid rate, thereby diminishing the riches available to future generations while increasing the well-being of those currently in place.[7] Given Harvard's resources, the faculty might decide to triple its own salaries and benefits, and simultaneously to abolish all tuition charges. What an attractive, even virtuous idea! At the new salary levels no one could possibly decline an invitation to teach at Harvard and the quality of our faculty would attain new heights. For those already on the scene, tripled salaries might be said merely to recognize intrinsic worth, too long ignored by

7. This comes very close to the issue of length of commitment discussed under the third principle. The difference is that conflict of interest focuses on personal or group advantage, rather than on giving the most power to those who have the shortest time horizon.

impersonal market forces. As for abolishing tuition, that certainly helps the poor, the overburdened middle classes, and could conceivably raise student quality. And the money is available to do this and more for at least a few generations—after all, over $4 billion of endowment can last for quite a while.

These are fanciful examples, but they do make a point. Some authority is properly delegated to higher levels, thereby not placing individuals or groups in a position where the temptation to pursue private—or for that matter short-term—interests could prove irresistible. That is why we do not allow professors to determine their own salaries and benefits. These are set by deans, and—in broad fashion—reviewed by the president and trustees. The salaries of deans are set by the president, and the president's emoluments are determined by trustees. That is also why we do not permit students to grade themselves, to design their own graduation requirements, to set tuition, or to allocate portions of Harvard's endowment to the construction of low-income housing in Cambridge.

We assume, quite correctly I believe, that the degree of conflict of interest decreases as we ascend the pyramid of office. In setting salaries, a dean (or a chairman) can consider quality, performance, competition, and budget; none of these factors is effectively dealt with by individuals or groups that are direct beneficiaries of a particular decision. Similarly, faculty members are more able to judge students in a disinterested and professional manner than students themselves. Finally, the president and trustees, whose joint task it is to review all major policies, can do so with the least degree of conflict of interest: almost none of the common issues—salaries, academic standards and requirements, return on investments, etc.—affect them in a direct manner. I recognize that we are discussing shadings rather than entirely unambiguous differences. My point is that although absolute avoidance of conflict *may* be impossible, conscious and good faith minimization is crucial.

The logic of minimizing conflict of interest implies that

students, faculty members, and employees should only rarely serve as trustees of their own university. They would be the equivalent of "inside directors," and good business practice dictates, I believe, that this category should be a distinct minority on well-constituted boards, since the fundamental purpose of the boards or trustees is to evaluate management, not to join its ranks.[8]

## The Sixth Principle

*University governance should improve the capacity for teaching and research.*

Teaching and research are the main missions of universities and a suitable system of governance should, therefore, make these activities as efficient as possible. To an economist, a high degree of efficiency means maximum output per unit of input. That requires the careful use of scarce factors; one has to make certain that faculty time is used as productively as possible. Given the university's main mission, the entire enterprise has to be organized so as to allow members of the instructional staff maximum opportunity to do their work, and to minimize, insofar as possible, even officially encouraged diversions, primarily excessive administrative responsibilities. These priorities apply with equal validity to students: the structure of governance needs to reflect the premise that studying is the principal "right and responsibility" of students, and that other activities, while perhaps valuable life experiences, are secondary. (And that includes athletics!)

I insist on the consideration of this principle because it is

8. Inside directors normally are very senior executives who are asked to served because of their experience and wisdom. Perhaps some professors and employees could live up to this criterion. It is very hard for me to see a student usefully engaged in this role. I am not alone in this view. See "SUNY's Student Trustee: Discomfort on Both Sides," *The New York Times*, July 7, 1988. Donald M. Blinken, SUNY board chairman, said this about the student trustee: "I was very unhappy about his performance . . . when the time came to be counted, every time he caved in to student pressure. I am not totally happy with the idea of student trustees."

so often understood in theory and ignored in practice. The desire to participate is great, but self-governance comes only at a high price: it requires much time, knowledge, commitment, and lot of what the Germans call *Sitzfleisch*. In some university activities—examples might be promotions, chairing departments, curricular requirements—faculty participation is essential and well worth the cost. No other group can be an adequate substitute.

All too often, however, the benefits of such faculty participation are illusory. Faculty members typically complain of administrative burdens and of lack of time in libraries or laboratories. Yet they sit on innumerable committees without complaint, spending hours in fruitless and inconsequential debates. Perhaps the total number of hours used in this fashion is not all that large, but the cumulative effects are considerable. Any researcher knows that uninterrupted time is the most precious of all gifts, and that is what administration and governance all too casually destroys. Student behavior may be more rational. They are extremely anxious to gain seats on almost any committee, especially if the faculty is represented. It is, for them, a great symbol. When granted representation, students may discover the profound boredom associated with some of these assemblies, and their poor attendance reflects that newly gained wisdom. At other times I have found them to be faithful presences with valuable ideas. During our curriculum revision of the 1970s, undergraduates provided outstanding and mature service.

## The Seventh Principle

*To function well, a hierarchical system of governance requires explicit mechanism of consultation and accountability.*

I list the principle last, not because it is least important. It is just as important as all the others, and may actually be *the* most central because the efficiency and sincerity with which consultation and accountability are handled determine the overall quality of governance. From my perspective, there is considerable overlap between accountability and consultation; they operate like a chemical interaction.

Consultation encourages input into policy issues from the many constitutencies of a modern American university: students, white- and blue-collar employees, faculty, alumni, the community, and perhaps some others. This process generally moves from the bottom up—for example, from students to faculty or from secretaries to senior administrators—and obviously not everyone is entitled to input into every decision. Some test of relevance is reasonable. Some information that results from consultation or input is disinterested: visiting committees that review departments are, on the whole, neutral. Some information is very "interested," as when students discuss changes in academic requirements. Both kinds are valuable, and that we need to insist on a broad range of inputs is one of the most important lessons of the 1960s.

Accountability, operating from the top down, is the other side of this coin. It applies primarily to those with authority and describes how they should carry out their responsibilities. Neither accountability nor consultation imply a particular model of decision making. I noted earlier that not everything is improved by making it more democratic. That is not inconsistent with a recommendation for frequent and effective consultation.

A democracy uses elections to indicate the degree of satisfaction with those holding power. Universities in this country are not administered as participatory democracies, and there are few occasions to cast votes. Since universities are voluntary associations, it is easy enough to express dissatisfaction by not joining a particular community and choosing another (in the United States there is no shortage of substitutes); this applies to students, faculty, and employees. Yet this is much too glib an answer to a serious and difficult problem. Once individuals have made their choice as faculty members or students or in any other capacity, for the system to work requires the belief that it operates reasonably and justly, that it is not arbitrary. In other words, we require accountability in two accepted senses: first, the willingness to give full, honest explanations of all administrative actions; secondly, having everyone in the system accountable to some individual or group—but only for certain purposes.

Communication is a major form of accountability. Those in charge should regularly make information available concerning their views and policies. As dean, I started the practice of sending an annual budget letter to all faculty members—also available to anyone else in the community—which presented the current fiscal year in great detail.[9] Accountability is the willingness to explain decisions, backed by evidence, when questioned by students, a colleague, or anyone else. In the form of consultation, it also means making sure that the many voices of a community are heard. There is a need for organs through which opinions—supportive and dissenting—can be freely and efficiently expressed to all, and particularly to those at all levels of authority. The many consultative committees perform valuable service toward this end. Even the frequently provocative student press is a most valuable source of information.

Accountability also means that those entrusted with authority report to some individual or group. Thus, professors should be responsible to chairmen, most particularly when it comes to teaching responsibilities. Chairmen report to deans, who are appointed and if necessary discharged by provosts or presidents. And presidents report to boards of trustees. At Harvard, the president is directly responsible to the small (seven-person) "self-perpetuating" Corporation, and the Corporation is in important ways accountable to the Board of Overseers, requiring "ad-

9. It was an easy thing to do. The financial news was mostly bad and its full description increased faculty sympathy for a heavily burdened dean.

vice and consent" for many important decisions from that larger group elected by all alumni—except those working at Harvard. Most especially, it has become customary for the Board of Overseers to review and usually consent to major academic and administrative appointments.[10]

Accountability in the sense of reporting to a higher authority requires amplification when applied to universities. In performing their jobs, non-academic employees all have bosses, just as if they were working in any ordinary business. The same holds true for all administrators, academic and non-academic. Deans, chairmen, vice presidents, all serve at the pleasure of a higher-up, and that is well accepted. But the concept of accountability becomes more subtle when it is applied to the professoriate. As I pointed out in discussing the virtues of academic life, one way of defining a professorship is to say that it is a job without a boss. Faculty members are the beneficiaries of enormous freedom: their formal obligations are limited to a few hours in the classroom and are far less significant than the unspecified parts of the job—research, discussions and guidance of students and colleagues, university and professional service, and the like. In what sense are professors responsible to chairmen and deans, when it is almost impossible to discharge those with tenure? Do they serve entirely at their own pleasure?

Not at all, although accountability is more difficult to enforce. In nearly all universities, salaries will reflect the individual's research and teaching performance. Those who set salaries—primarily chairmen and deans—usually pay close attention to peer review and evaluation of teaching by students. (At Harvard, we should be more diligent in

10. The Harvard Corporation is self-perpetuating in the sense that when a member resigns or retires, the remaining members select a replacement who has to be approved by the Board of Overseers. This is an unusual, perhaps even anachronistic arrangement. Indeed, equally unusual are Harvard's *two* governing boards, with their delicately split responsibilities. Had my purpose been to concentrate on Harvard governance, I would have devoted far more space to these idiosyncratic arrangements. I have mentioned them mainly to underline that the selection of trustees undoubtedly affects the process of accountability. For example, elections are more likely to reflect populist concerns. Self-perpetuation will, with a considerable degree of certainty, produce a conservative bias.

this matter.) The extent to which these factors influence salaries and other benefits differs markedly from institution to institution, but a relationship always persists. In the university environment it is also understood—perhaps too vaguely—that "grave misconduct" and "neglect of duty" are failings for which professors can be held accountable by higher administrative authorities. If the transgressions that belong in these categories are widely known and clearly defined, accountability can be enforced.

During my years on the Harvard faculty I have known of a number of professors who resigned because they feared—and probably would have faced—charges of grave misconduct. If these had been formalized, alleged offenses would have ranged from financial improprieties to sexual harassment.

The most difficult case that occurred while I served as dean involved a political scientist of world stature. I have already given a description of an incident in chapter 3: students accused of being "inauthentic," walking out of class, and other forms of strange behavior. In many interviews, I could never get him to explain the meaning of inauthentic. I told him that we were an extremely tolerant society, that we could accommodate ourselves to almost anything except flagrant neglect of duty, and that walking out of a class is such an offense. It became increasingly obvious that I was confronting a case of mental illness, and under current laws there was no way to force this person to seek treatment. That was not his intention anyway. He probably believed that I was in need of medical attention, being totally incapable of understanding the concept of student inauthenticity. In the end, I was forced to place my colleague on involuntary medical leave, with pay and very much against his will. The poor, sick man resigned in protest, and some years later died abroad, alone and in poverty. It was an extremely painful episode. I mention it only to underscore our commitment to accountability. Nevertheless, I am ready to admit that in all our universities the rights of professors are far better understood and advertised than their responsibilities. That this situation is allowed to persist is a major administrative—dare I say managerial?—failure. This topic will arise again.

One last point concerning the need for explicit mechanisms of accountability. Neither optimal accountability nor consultation need mean open records, open meetings, or what the government calls sunshine laws. There is a very important distinction between matters that are not made public and are kept confidential for administrative reasons, and what some of our critics have called "the Hidden Rule." Private and secret are not the same thing, and the right to practice privacy—within limits—improves governance. Too much sunshine can cause sunburn by ruining searches for professors or administrators; students could be embarrassed by the release of unwanted information; and, most of all, the quality of open, candid collegiate discussion and debate would suffer all the way from the level of trustees to that of student groups. Operating within controlled and limited privacy is an asset not to be yielded lightly.[11] We all know the consequences of the so-called Buckley Amendment by which students and faculty have the right—unless waived—to inspect their reference letters. The result has been a tremendous degradation of the written word; now the "unwaived" letters are virtually without value and we resort to much more inexact and loose oral communication. Everyone is less well off.

### I Can Hear It Now

> *An exercise in Toryism.*
> *Too much authority given to administrators.*
> *Designed to preserve the status quo.*
> *Too much power in the hands of the old and established.*
> *No place for the creative insights and energies of the young.*
> *Just as bad as tenure.*

11. See Judith Block McLaughlin and David Riesman, "The Shady Side of Sunshine," *Teachers College Record,* vol. 87, no. 4 (Summer 1986).

During the last few years, I have presented my ideas concerning university governance to various audiences in the United States and elsewhere. A short piece in *The New Republic* led to several letters containing predictable accusations of elitism. A presentation to a group of German intellectuals produced a defensive reaction—was I criticizing continental universities? Yes!—followed by a wholly unsympathetic newspaper account of my thoughts. In Israel and especially at Hebrew University, where I have made suggestions for changes in governance at the request of the board of trustees, my name is mud. The professors at this perfect model of a nineteenth-century German university—*only* from the perspective of governance—consider me a traitor to my class, and what may even be worse, an Americanizer. Voices at Oxford University have recently joined the critics.[12]

The slogans at the opening of this section are just a few examples of reactions particularly common in this country. To some, these concerns will appear plausible—even logical. I do not believe that the facts lend support to this position. Remember that my intention has never been to discuss all of American higher education. I am deliberately confining myself to from fifty to one hundred top institutions. In considering their postwar history, can anyone seriously claim that the status quo has been preserved? Is it not true that most leading American universities are governed more or less in accordance with our principles? There should be no need to belabor the point; almost everything has changed. Student bodies are infinitely more diverse; to a lesser degree so are faculties. New departments, new fields within departments, new concentrations—all have flourished. Major curricular changes have also taken place. As usual, conservatives feel that there has been too much

12. J. R. Lucas, "Unamerican Activity: an alternative route to excellence," *Oxford Magazine*, no. 45 (Trinity Term 1989). For views closer to my own, see "Oxford's Fading Charms" and "Oxford University: poverty ringed with riches" in *The Economist*, July 8, 1989.

change—Great Books abandoned, grade inflation, trendy subjects—while those on the left believe that change has been insufficient. My inclination is to adopt a centrist position: to me, the rate of change seems an average, appropriate, but whatever one's view there can be little doubt that the status quo is a moving target.

From an intellectual point of view, American universities have changed more—and more creatively—than schools in other parts of the world. That fact is not unrecognized: abroad, proposals for reform of higher education usually begin with a consideration of the American model. I have argued that this is not accidental. Indeed, I strongly believe that the American philosophy of governance is a major factor in explaining the high quality of our universities. It permits leadership to be effective; it makes possible the implementation of new ideas; and the combination of competition and independence is a most effective pair of spurs urging us on toward ever higher levels of excellence.

The real element of contention is not lack of change. Rather, it is types and rates of change that concern our critics. Some are impatient with the pace of social transformation: why so few tenured women, black professors, or Hispanic role models? There are the usual answers, but they will not be taken as fully convincing. (Of course, some also believe that the pace of social transformation is moving too fast.) Some are intellectually impatient: a particular approach to a subject is not sufficiently represented, or perhaps the movement into new fields is too slow for enthusiasts. Some have a political agenda for which they would like to use the university: abolishing *apartheid,* universal disarmement, or preaching the virtues of free enterprise. And the fact is that our system of governance frustrates many critics for the right reasons.

By emphasizing length of commitment and knowledge, we discourage excessive consideration of short-term issues. There is no need to hurry because most of us will still be here in two or three years. At the same time, the "unitary structure" gives sufficient power to presidents, deans, and chairmen to implement big changes when they have broad collegial support. A great virtue of this system is that it permits, even encourages, action based on careful consideration of the long run. Unlike most American businesses, universities are not at the mercy of quarterly profit reports. Unlike government, there is no need to satisfy an electorate at regular and frequent intervals. Of course, these benefits that so powerfully strengthen our ability to perform do not come without costs. And that brings me back to the vexing matter of accountability, the seventh principle, and the weakest link in an otherwise solid chain. Without a doubt, the weak link is the tenured faculty.

As we have already shown, senior members of the faculty are subject to the strictures of "gross misconduct" and "neglect of duty," but these categories deal only with extreme situations. Difficulties related to accountability usually arise under much more mundane circumstances: how can we get Professor X conscientiously to meet her students during office hours? (She is usually at an international conference in Paris or Nepal.) Why is Professor Y so slow in providing thesis comments to graduate students? (He is rather busy running a private consulting firm.) Is it possible to convince Professor Z to make a greater contribution to his department by teaching a basic undergraduate course with large enrollments rather than confining himself—as has been his habit for many years—to a graduate seminar with two students in the classroom? (This could be interpreted as a demeaning suggestion to Z's sub-sub-sub-specialty.) These are real problems encountered by deans, chairmen, and students. They also occur with far greater frequency than grave misconduct or neglect of duty as interpreted by lawyers. To users of ordinary English, these labels might easily apply to this type of conduct.

One need not exaggerate; perspective has to be maintained. I have already provided the reader with a vigorous, and I hope wholly convincing, defense of tenure. I do not intend to withdraw one word of that defense. Great freedom—indeed, a certain unaccountability—is a necessary condition for productive and creative intellectual workers. I have also shown, in detail, that these privileges are not casually awarded. They are the by-product of what I believe to be the most vigorous selection procedures in existence for any profession. Furthermore, academic administrators are not totally defenseless; peer pressure most of all and salary adjustments are effective weapons in many cases.

Nevertheless, improvements in the effectiveness of accountability for senior faculty to students and perhaps employees should be a high-priority item for all academic administrators. I have nothing new or startling to suggest. But here are a few ideas that, in my experience, have had positive results.

1. Student evaluation—regularized and lightly supervised for fairness—is an excellent device both for identifying and rewarding excellent teaching (broadly defined) and for improving citizenship among all faculty members. No one, not even tenured barons, want their inadequate performance exposed to a wide public. Evaluation should apply to all aspects of student life: teaching, concentrations, curriculum, housing, etc.

2. Increasing the authority and dignity of department chairmen is another highly desirable step. Especially at our finest universities, these individuals are too frequently cast in the role of supplicants *vis-à-vis* their tenured colleagues. Within reasonable limits, they should be able to *assign* responsibility for courses, not just to beg for cooperation, and they should have a considerable say in the setting of salaries. Too frequently, departmental administrators stay in their jobs only for brief terms—three years is not untypical—impatiently waiting for the first opportunity to exit a demeaning (at the very least thankless) assignment. Making the post of chairman more attractive by increasing its authority and rewards would improve length of service and enforcement of accountability. Give chairmen the power to alter incentives; the rest will follow.

3. Despite my previously expressed skepticism about

committees—and especially student-faculty gatherings of this type—a good substitute unfortunately does not exist. They do more good than harm, especially when the topics considered are properly defined: curriculum, financial aid, social regulations, and similar matters. We should have an interest in hearing student voices and in interacting with them on many policy issues because they have some good ideas and also because the process itself is a valuable part of education. Few things are more beneficial to an authority figure than having to explain and justify his or her position (or the position of a predecessor) in front of a questioning audience. Beneficial change is frequently a result.

4. Throughout the university, everyone should be able to appeal any decision to a level one step above an immediate supervisor. A professor should be able to seek redress above the level of the dean of faculty; a student should be allowed to contest a professor's decision at the level of a departmental chairman; similar rights should be available to all employees. To be fully effective, these mechanisms of review and appeal have to be clear, simple to use, and highly publicized.

5. Lastly, an excellent suggestion from Jeffrey C. Alexander:

> The nonacademic and nonstudent nature of university governing boards often makes them too timid or too aggressive in deciding the relationship between university and society. Why? Because they themselves are not deeply in touch with value-rationality which the university must protect. Because of this, dangerous situations can arise, situations in which university interests are threatened in ways in which nonacademic boards could not have foreseen. . . . Formal and explicit advisory powers should be assigned to student bodies and faculty senates, according to which a vote by a certain percentage would require that an issue be discussed and eventually voted upon by the university governing board.[13]

13. "The University and Morality," *Journal of Higher Education,* vol. 57, no. 5 (September–October 1986), p. 472.

Alexander stresses formal procedures and votes, and that may not be necessary. Informally, all of these steps are already familiar to many trustees. Student and faculty opinions continually create new agenda items for governing boards, and they must be dealt with by votes or other means.

# 16

## Postscript:

### *Omissions and Conclusions*

Some readers may believe that many hard questions have been avoided in this manual. Could these sins of omission account for the rosy tint of the presentation? What about the difficult relations between government and the universities: research funding, overhead recovery, issues of secrecy, and similar matters? University relations with the private sector have also been slighted. There has been no in-depth discussion of the consequences of for-profit research financing and increasing faculty participation in technology transfer and private enterprise. And what about affirmative action, sexual harassment, minorities, community relations . . . the list could be much longer.

There are two reasons why I chose to give these questions less prominence. First, I deliberately confined myself to subjects with which I had personal and intimate contact. Given the nature of deaning, my job primarily related to the internal running of the university. External relations are the realm of presidents and similarly august personages. And many so-called difficult questions tend to have

289

the character of external constraints: intrusions from the real world. To be sure, these intrusions mattered enormously in faculty operations, but policy formulation and resolutions were handled by individuals who represented the whole university, and not just one sector.[1] When, for example, the government negotiated policies regarding overhead recovery—the indirect costs of government research activities—they dealt with vice presidents and not deans.

Furthermore, and this is my second reason, I am not convinced that these *are* the really hard questions. They are much on the mind of the public, and regularly featured in the pages of newspapers and magazines. Their manifest importance is frequently related to current struggles to improve American society—for example, to eliminate racism and sexism—or to immediate questions of public policy. These issues change; we can hope for improvement, even solutions. It seems to me that the verities I have discussed are more fundamental. How do we select professors? How do we govern ourselves? Whom do we admit? What do we teach? These are, for universities, the true, difficult, and timeless questions. They never go away.

I would, however, like to devote a few pages to a type of behavior—a temptation—that will probably never disappear from colleges and universities, not even when institutions reach a much higher level of social integration than is today imaginable. I refer to sexual harassment, unfortunately common in all societies at all times past and present, but all too rarely discussed or resisted. Without question it is a specially significant issue for higher education because of the invariant nature of our demography: young (adult) students, and faculty members of all ages exercising differing degrees of authority over these students. In the vast majority of cases, it is males that harass females, and it is only in recent years that women have begun to fight back. Circumstances required me not only to become very famil-

1. By the same token, I have had only little to say about faculties of medicine or law.

iar with the problem, but also to develop a philosophical approach and set of guidelines for action and control.[2]

Precisely, what is the "problem"? In the academic context, the term "sexual harassment" may be used to describe a wide range of behavior. The fundamental element is the inappropriate personal attention by an instructor or other officer who is in a position to determine a student's grade or otherwise affect the student's academic performance or professional future. Such behavior is unacceptable in a university because it is a form of unprofessionalism that seriously undermines the atmosphere of trust essential to the academic enterprise. The teaching environment and relations between individual faculty members and students are matters of particular concern.

In the last decade we have made considerable progress toward a genuinely co-educational environment. Overt discrimination against women seems to be quite rare. Most faculty members endeavor to treat all students fairly as individuals, and not as members of a category based on sex.

Nevertheless, we have not yet attained a state in which women never feel themselves in universities to be disadvantaged on account of their sex. Students continue to report behavior by members of teaching staffs that is discouraging or offensive to women. Alienating messages may be subtle and even unintentional. It may therefore be useful to offer specific examples illustrating a range of classroom conduct that tends to compromise the learning experience especially, but not only, of women.

Some teaching practices are overtly hostile to women. For example, to show slides of nude women humorously or whimsically during an otherwise serious lecture is not only

2. What follows largely reproduces my open letter of April 1983 to the Faculty of Arts and Sciences concerning sexual harassment. As a senior academic administrator, "I never wrote a letter that I signed, and never signed a letter that I wrote." This particular letter, and many other decanal pronouncements, were co-authored with Associate Dean Phyllis Keller. I notice with great pleasure that our thoughts were cited with approval in a recent legal journal. See Peter DeChiara, "The Need for Universities to Have Rules on Consensual Sexual Relationships Between Faculty Members and Students," *Columbia Journal of Law and Social Problems*, vol. 21, no. 137 (1988).

in poor taste but is also demeaning to women. (This is not an invented example!)

Other alienating teaching practices may be simply thoughtless, and may even be the result of special efforts to be helpful to women students. It is condescending to make a point of calling upon women in class on topics such as marriage and the family, imposing the assumption that only women have a "natural" interest in this area.

There is no specific term for the classroom practices just described. Their common effect is to focus attention on sex characteristics in a context in which sex would otherwise be irrelevant. For that reason, the general term "sexism" is often used to describe this category of unprofessional behavior.

Turning now to individual faculty members and students, I maintain that amorous relationships that might be appropriate in other circumstances are always wrong when they occur between any teacher and any student for whom he or she has a professional responsibility. Further, such relationships may have the effect of undermining the atmosphere of trust on which the educational process depends. Implicit in the idea of professionalism is the recognition by those in positions of authority that in their relationships with students there is always an element of power. It is incumbent upon those with authority not to abuse, nor seem to abuse, the power with which they are entrusted.

Members of the teaching staff should be aware that any romantic involvement with their students makes them liable for formal action against them if a complaint is initiated by a student. *Even when both parties have consented to the development of such a relationship, it is the officer or instructor who, by virtue of his or her special responsibility, will be held accountable for unprofessional behavior.* [3] Because graduate student teaching assistants may be less accustomed than faculty members to thinking of themselves as holding professional responsibilities, they would be wise to exercise special care in their

---

3. Many of my colleagues saw this as a new departure.

relationships with students whom they instruct or evaluate.

Other amorous relationships between professors and students, occurring outside the instructional context, may also lead to difficulties. In a personal relationship between an officer and a student for whom the officer has no current professional responsibility, the officer should be sensitive to the constant possibility that he or she may unexpectedly be placed in a position of responsibility for the student's instruction or evaluation. Relationships between officers and students are fundamentally asymmetric in nature.

In my opinion, these principles apply equally to relations between tenured and non-tenured faculty members.[4] Opportunities for the abuse of power are just as common, and for all of these transgressions, I urged clear procedures and stern punishment.

There is nothing funny about sexual harassment, but as is frequently the case, serious topics lend themselves to laughter. In preparation for my epistle to the faculty, we sponsored an extensive survey of female students, faculty, and employees concerning sexual harassment. The results were not at all pleasing: over one third of all respondents reported some form of unsuitable behavior by members of the opposite sex. One question, addressed to a woman professor, asked: have you ever been harassed by a person in authority over you? She replied: Henry Rosovsky is the only person in authority over me, and he is a perfect gentleman. An anonymous and treasured accolade.

A longer and more personal communication arrived from Professor *emeritus* J. K. Galbraith.

> Dear Henry:
> I was, as you will presently understand, both enchanted and distressed by your recent communication on behalf of the Faculty Council, entitled "Sexual Harassment, Related Matters." My pleasure had to do with the eloquence and delicacy of the language in which, in keeping with Harvard standards in such matters, your letter is couched. The reference to "amorous

---

4. And indeed to relations between supervisors and subordinates of all types.

relationships" in the "instructional context" is superb and reflects an acute sense of Harvard faculty and even New England sensibilities. For some years I have been an adviser to one of our well-known dictionaries—*The American Heritage Dictionary,* to be precise. I am today instructing its editors as to the usage to which henceforth they must conform if they are to have our approval here in Cambridge.

My distress is personal. Just over 45 years ago, already a well-fledged member of the Harvard faculty on a three-year appointment, I fell in love with a young female student. It was not in an instructional context; however, noninstructional amour is a "situation" against which you also warn. A not wholly unpredictable consequence of this lapse from faculty and professional decorum, as now required, was that we were married. So, and even happily, we have remained. But now my distress. As a senior member of this community, I am acutely conscious of my need to be an example for younger and possibly more ardent members of the faculty.

I must do everything possible to retrieve my error. My wife, needless to say, shares my concern. What would you advise?

I replied:

Dear Ken:

I am delighted that my letter on sexual harassment caused some enchantment in your life. However, I also deeply regret having caused distress. My warnings against noninstructional amour are not especially severe: mainly I urge the practice of "sensitivity." Knowing you, I am sure that was never a problem. But I do understand your *ex post* feelings of discomfort.

Two thoughts come to mind: one humane and the other decanal. The incident in question, by your own account, occurred over 45 years ago. I believe that the statute of limitations applies. As a dean and as someone who has recently been accused by a member of the faculty of behaving in the manner of a cardinal, I would be delighted to sell you an indulgence. How about a chair to celebrate your happy union and also a time when amour—instructional and noninstructional—was in fashion?

"As here shown," remarked Galbraith, "no Harvard dean ever answers a letter without giving some indication of need for financial support, such as the endowment of new academic chair.''[5] I am very tempted to conclude my book with this profound observation. But I will not do so because one final topic requires brief notice.

That I have written a positive book about universities and higher education is most unusual. More commonly, recent critics have labeled us as mind-closers, cultural illiterates, and protectors of professorial scams. We are said to cultivate overspecialization and obscurantism, and the chorus of critics has come from all corners of our diverse society: some students, parents, and alumni; the press and politicians; and from within our own professional ranks. Bloom, Hirsch, Bennett, Boyer have all aimed their heavy artillery at universities, with great popular success. Most recently, the report *Humanities in America* (1988),[6] issued by the chairwoman of the National Endowment for the Humanities, praised the interest of the general public in literature and art; had kind words for some television; lauded museums, libraries, and state humanities councils. Mrs. Cheney had almost nothing good to say about colleges and universities.

This avalanche of harsh judgments reminds me of a story. An American, a Frenchman, and a Japanese have been captured by a band of terrorists and face execution in the morning. A traditional last request is offered to each prisoner. The Frenchman asks that an elegant supper be flown in from his favorite Paris restaurant. The Japanese wants one final opportunity to give a lecture in which he can explain the real secret of his country's successful management techniques. The American asks to be shot *before* that lecture . . . the pain of one more sermon would be unbearable.

Two things are clear to me. My benign attitude will make some people mad; to be positive is never very popular in intellectual circles. But I also know that "shoot me first" is not a healthy attitude. Why am I an odd man out?

5. From *A View from the Stands* by John Kenneth Galbraith. Copyright © 1986 by John Kenneth Galbraith. Reprinted by Permission of Houghton Mifflin Company.
6. Reprinted in *The Chronicle of Higher Education,* September 21, 1988.

Many of the topics that so frequently agitate our critics have been discussed: for example, curriculum, teaching versus research, tenure, admissions and governance. But my conclusions have been rather different—on the whole, joyful instead of jeremiads. This cannot be because my focus has been on "Two Thirds of the Best." Those who find fault with us single out universities and university colleges as the leading sinners; as ideal-type illustrations of what, in their terms, is to be deplored in American higher education.

There are puzzling aspects here. At least for the moment, our most severe critics have a distinctly right-wing political flavor. Are conservative critics not made slightly uncomfortable by our obvious attractions in a free market? Is the market not their idea of a perfect referee? Private universities are accused of gouging students through high tuition charges, but there are any number of cheaper public alternatives of similar quality. It is said that universities concentrate too much on research and too little on teaching. But in our educational system, the majority of institutions do no research at all. Sometimes we are accused of caring only about graduate students. However, a prospective pupil can very easily choose among a whole range of colleges that hardly ever see a graduate student. Universities have no monopoly power. We operate in a highly competitive market, and survive only by being attractive to those who require our services. And the selective institutions have obviously done that very well.

Let me make clear that I agree with many specific criticisms directed at us. Incoherent curricula, uncaring professors, "gut courses"—wherever they occur—upset me at least as much as they do our inquisitors. We do differ, I am sure, about the presumed frequency of these occurrences. More significantly, I am troubled by an underlying set of attitudes and broader conclusions that are unwarranted.

I do not believe in overpromising the outcomes achievable through education.

I am not nostalgic.

I know that there will always be a difference between ideal and reality.

First, the exaggerated promise: that education is the answer to social ills. It is clear that current negative attitudes toward higher education are related to the student revolt of the 1960s, our defeat in Vietnam, the decline in U.S. competitiveness, and similar national sources of unhappiness. In short, it is a negativism that feeds on all the discontents in our society. Observers, critics, ordinary citizens look at the state of the Union, do not like what they see, and blame the schools. For example, blaming business schools instead of managers and workers for poor economic performance is easy and comfortable, and educators contribute to this inclination by overpromising. We imply that education assures good jobs, and when that does not happen—as in the 1970s—bitterness is the result. We sell education in dimensions of career or value added, instead of as an end in itself: leading a worthwhile, examined life, and not necessarily a financially more successful life. Too many of us tend to confuse good education with good character, and when the public reads that our famous schools graduate insider traders and other crooks, they draw a negative conclusion concerning the quality of higher education in America. Every faculty member should know, every administrator knows, every dean is eternally convinced that the relation between character and education is weak. Remember that many Nazis had read the right books. They were products of widely admired classical curricula. I am also certain that the Japanese pilots who bombed Pearl Harbor had—more accurately, would have had—high SAT scores. My point is simply that the positive and direct impact of education is limited. Better education should lead, on average, to a more elevated level of civic virtue; that is a basic assumption of our democracy—but there will always be many exceptions.

Much of recent carping is based on nostalgia, an emotion which I do not share. About forty years ago, when Messrs. Bloom, Bennett, Hirsch, and I were undergraduates, there allegedly existed a Golden Age, and as John Buchan said with irony, civilization has been in decline ever since. In those wonderful days, core was core (and the "gentleman's C" reigned supreme); adoring undergraduates sat at the feet of kindly mentors engaging in Socratic dialogue (the suggested image seems to be a 1930s Hollywood version of Oxford). These wonderful days were destroyed by the excesses of the 1960s: dope, sex, grade inflation, contempt for the classics, and rock music.

I like the university better today than forty years ago, and that may be the reason for my optimism. It is also my most important difference with the critics. Has common learning—so treasured by our critics—really disappeared in the last few generations? Only in the sense that the students and professors were far more homogeneous: need-blind admission was unknown; Jews, African-Americans, Asians, and women were often made scarce; there were few national universities and fewer national scholarships. Thus common learning was not so much the reflection of curricular or pedagogical virtue, but rather the consequence of narrow class privilege. It was a cheaper, easier kind of common learning, the privilege of the few, and I do not yearn for that time. Is it really true that forty years ago we—students—sat around our dormitories munching cookies and drinking milk while debating the merits of late Beethoven quartets? And now the only choices are Punk or acid rock, played at a volume that ensures deafness by age thirty? Not in my world.[7]

Although my attitude is positive, I know that the gap between ideal and reality is large in higher education. This is particularly apparent because there is far more posturing

7. In what has become a famous passage, Alan Bloom wrote: "Young people know that rock has the beat of sexual intercourse. That is why Ravel's Bolero is the one piece of classical music that is commonly known and liked by them." *Closing of the American Mind,* p. 73. In an attempt to do some casual empirical verification of this intriguing assertion (in my day the tango was endowed with similar powers), I asked a number of friends to show these sentences to their teenage children. I quote a particularly telling reply from Indianapolis: "I interviewed my teenage children who are both contemporary rock music lovers, and have found that they are only vaguely familiar with and do not like Ravel's Bolero. I hope this doesn't suggest some sexual dysfunction."

in colleges and universities than in primary and secondary schools, and that enlarges the gap. Professors like to wear the mantle of selflessness: underpaid servants of students and society, seekers of truth. And then the public sees us, from time to time in the press, as falsifiers of scientific evidence (cheaters!), money-hungry (a recent article about Harvard was cleverly entitled *In Pecunia Veritas*), and occasionally even as unpatriotic. I have compared us to judges and priests—attached to the dignity conferred by our robes—but academic behavior does not always conform to those ideal standards. That is a breeding ground for criticism.

None of this is surprising. Inevitably, universities will reflect their societies, pluses and minuses, ups and downs. That is one reason why, in modern times, repressive societies have never remained home to great centers of learning. However, by ourselves we cannot change society or lead it out of the wilderness. Our leadership has to be circumscribed. We can produce new knowledge, teach professional skills, and the liberal arts. We cannot alone eradicate racism, poverty, or the use of drugs. In a greedy society we will not be immune to temptation. We cannot be a paradise island in a sea of discontent.

But modesty and realism concerning the capacities of higher education do not in any sense imply that our role in determining the quality of society's life is small. We are leaders in the development of ideas and alternatives. We train students in the state of the art while attempting with all energy to change the frontiers of that state.

To our many critics I say: *honi soit qui mal y pense* (shame to him who thinks ill of it); what at first glance appears evil may be insignificant, innocent, or a reflection of wider social mores. To ourselves I say: do not risk self-satisfaction; strive for greater perfection; make the gap between ideal and reality as small as possible.

# Index